MEN IN THE SHADOWS

MEN IN THE SHADOWS

The RCMP Security Service

JOHN SAWATSKY

1980
Doubleday Canada Limited
Toronto, Ontario

Doubleday & Company, Inc.
Garden City, New York

ISBN: 0-385-14682-5
Library of Congress Catalog Card Number: 78-68374

Designed by Robert Burgess Garbutt
Printed and bound in Canada by the John Deyell Company

To Evan Evans-Atkinson
who taught me how to be a reporter

Acknowledgments

Many acknowledgments are due in the preparation of this book and my regret is that I cannot make most of them. The manuscript was compiled mostly from sources whose identities have to remain secret. It is unfortunate that I cannot give credit to the scores of people who deserve thanks because without them this book could not have been written.

Fortunately there are some debts that I can repay in public. I would like to thank Vancouver *Sun* Managing Editor Bruce Larsen for giving me a leave of absence and for generously extending the leave when my time expired. Marjorie Nichols and Patrick Nagle, my two former Bureau Chiefs in Ottawa, and Allan Fotheringham, who inspired me to become a journalist, made unsung but valuable contributions.

One RCMP employee can be officially thanked. The RCMP's single contribution to this book was granting me an interview with RCMP Historian Stan Horrall, who was professional and helpful throughout. His contributions made the chapter "In the Beginning" both more interesting and more factual.

I took full advantage of the facilities at the Parliamentary Library in Ottawa and the staff there was always helpful. I was particularly fortunate to have the services of the gifted Mary Lasovich as my principal researcher. I was also ably assisted in research by Judith Gibson and Christine Hearn, the latter being more than a researcher. Also, I was able to travel across the country on a shoestring budget because I had friends and family who put me up: Brian Kappler, Alex Shaw, Rod Mickleburgh, Jan O'Brien, Rick Morrison, John Twigg, Doug Riley and Adele Armin-Riley, J. and Marta Armin, Jock Ferguson, and, as always, my parents.

Nobody likes to have his book edited but my editor, Betty Corson of Doubleday Canada, was always reasonable and was similarly understanding when my research fell behind schedule. Stephen Williams planted the idea in my head while he was a senior editor at Clarke Irwin, which raised initial funding support from the Ontario Arts Council. Clarke Irwin's interest waned after Williams left.

I deliberately save the final thank-you for Larry Emrick, National Editor at the Vancouver *Sun,* who is truly an outstanding human being. Without his enthusiasm and unflagging support, I could not have started this book.

Preface

VERY LITTLE HAS been written about the RCMP's Security Service. As I write this introduction not a single book devoted exclusively to the Security Service has appeared. There are many books on the RCMP and some have included references to the Security Service. The press has discovered the Security Service as a news item since law violations have been exposed, but this flurry of reporting bursts forth in sporadic fashion and is confined to keyhole-peeping. The public still knows little more about the Security Service than before. My account seeks to probe into the institution itself. It is by no means intended to be a comprehensive account because such is impossible with the Security Service. While illegal activity is an important element that needs to be examined—and is covered in detail here—it constitutes only part of my objective.

I have studiously avoided the two official commissions that have been investigating the Security Service—Ottawa's McDonald Royal Commission and Quebec's Keable Commission. In conducting my research I purposely did not attend these hearings and, with one exception, did not consult their transcripts. Most of the headlines of the last few years originated from these two sources and it is my view that new and broader sources of information are needed. I hope I have contributed at least somewhat in this regard and urge my journalist colleagues to rely less on officially sanctioned sources and more on independent investigation.

I never expected my task to be easy. The Security Service is one of the most secret institutions in Canada. Since old newspaper clippings and other published sources have been only marginally useful, and both the RCMP and the federal government have denied me access to the documentation that exists, my research material has been acquired largely from personal sources involved in Canada's security and intelligence community. I traveled across Canada on more than one occasion interviewing active and retired members of the Security Service and other similar individuals. I was truly astonished at the response. In some ways the task was easier than anticipated. The amount of new information exceeded my most ambitious hopes. Old hands who had fascinating accounts to tell, but had never done so previously, told their stories. None of them told everything for they were still too inhibited after a long career of secrecy, but masses of hitherto suppressed information tumbled forth.

My research soon made me realize that understanding the Security Service required one to examine the origins of the organization and retrace the various events that over the years served to determine the size and direction of growth. Only by studying the crises and events that precipitated responses does one comprehend the Security Service's later actions. This study of Cold War history through the Security Service's eyes proved extraordinarily interesting.

In recounting the development of the Security Service I have tried to tell the story without overt comment so that the reader may arrive at his own conclusions. I do not pretend that my views and biases are not impregnated into the text, although many of these views also belong to the contributors of the information. In any case, I have attempted to be fair.

The book both praises and criticizes the Security Service. Unfortunately the criticism outdistances the praise. There are two reasons, one where the Security Service is the culprit and the other the victim. The first is that the RCMP, despite my pleas, refused to cooperate in the research. While a security service has legitimate secrets to protect, much can be told without compromising security. In fact much of the information the Security Service withholds is routine tradecraft information known by the Russians and every other country in the world. Consequently the loser is the Canadian public (which pays for the Security Service, although how much it pays is also a secret). The

RCMP, as already noted in the Acknowledgments, did grant me interviews with the RCMP historian, but ultimately it denied itself an opportunity to stress its merits and answer criticisms contained in the book.

The second reason involves the nature of the security and intelligence business which is best summarized by one of Allen Dulles' reported quips: "In this business only the failures are known. One of the great frustrations is that you cannot boast about your successes — or else they will no longer be successes." Dulles was a CIA intelligence officer but his observation applies equally well to counter-intelligence work. So circumstances conspire against the Security Service on this point and neither the RCMP nor a fair-minded journalist can untilt the balance, which is unfortunate.

Actually there is a third reason as well and it has to do with the inadequacies of journalism. This book and this author are no exception, or at least not strong exception. I have probably — but who knows for sure? — overstated the Security Service's weaknesses and understated its strengths. There is no mention of the fact that most Security Service members have qualities comprising of honesty and dedication, among others. These virtues are taken for granted. Fortunately we live in a society where one can assume such basic qualities and make reference to them only when they are missing. Nevertheless the Security Service excels in these and other qualities and by merely continuing to assume this I do the organization some injustice which I hope this reference will at least partly redress.

I have tried to stay away from stereotyping members of the Security Service, which is why no portrait is drawn of the average member. An average Security Service member exists no more than an average Canadian exists. Although most members have conservative political leanings — this is one of the few stereotyped characteristics that holds — one of my surprises was to learn that members have varying attributes. Some are truly gifted and possess talents that outstrip the professional demands upon them. Others are incompetent. It is thus in any organization.

I must make one important caveat at this point. This book is not about the Canadian security and intelligence establishment. It is about the RCMP Security Service, which constitutes one important element of this larger community. The Communications Branch, now operating within the Department of National Defence, receives only peripheral mention. The Department of National Defence as such gets virtually no mention despite its vast security and intelligence responsibilities. Although a chapter is devoted to the Department of External Affairs, almost nothing is said about its considerable security and intelligence capabilities. Likewise the Department of Communications and the Department of Supply and Services—few realize what a huge security operation the latter has—are accorded negligible or no attention. Another omission is the Police Security, Planning and Analysis Branch in the Solicitor General's office. It is limited to one footnote. All of these organizations need scrutiny and perhaps others will do the necessary research. It cannot be attempted here since the next 300 pages are not sufficient to cover fully the Security Service alone.

John Sawatsky
Parliamentary Press Gallery
Ottawa

Contents

1

The International Security Network

SERGIO PEREZ WAS watching the late movie on television in the early morning of April 4, 1972. The television set sat in one corner of the reception office on the top floor of the modern 12-story office building at 3737 Cremazie Boulevard in Montreal's north end. The entire floor was leased to the Cuban government and Perez was the night watchman. The consulate was to the left of the elevator, the trade commission to the right. Perez's wife and child slept in one of the rear apartments. Other apartments housed an assortment of Cuban personnel. Altogether, 21 people lived on the premises and one of the other residents was watching the movie with Perez.

At approximately 12:45 A.M. the doors of one of the elevators opened. This surprised Perez and he wondered who would come at this hour since all the residents were inside and accounted for. The 25-year-old guard got up and approached the open elevator but nobody was inside. Then, a split-second later, he was hurtled backward by a tremendous force, his body badly lacerated. A powerful bomb planted in the ceiling of the elevator had exploded and Perez stood in the path of the thrust. Perez's companion was out of the line of fire and suffered injuries, but survived.

A hole was blown clear through the roof of the building and the next elevator snapped its cable and plummeted to the sixth floor before emergency brakes halted it. The damage to the building extended down to the seventh floor.

1

Two Montreal city policemen arrived within minutes. Climbing the stairs, they left the stairwell on the twelfth floor to receive the shock of their lives: three Cubans with Belgian FN machine guns confronted them. The two city constables shouted: "Police, police." The Cubans responded by cocking their guns and the two policemen dove head first back down the stairs, one injuring his back so severely that he lay on the floor helpless and unable to move. The other constable heard Perez's groans and returned to the twelfth-floor reception area and administered superficial first aid as an armed Cuban poked him with the barrel of his weapon. The Cubans were so busy defending the premises they did nothing to aid their wounded comrade Perez, who died en route to hospital from multiple glass cuts.

With debris still falling and another explosion feared, the Cubans finally put down their weapons and evacuated the building. They were taken to Station 21 for questioning and released on orders from Ottawa. The group returned to the building, demanding to be let back in and, when refused, stormed the place, catching the police unprepared. The Cubans managed to barricade themselves inside, and six of them with pistols in their belts warded off the authorities while others attempted to destroy secret files, but without much success. The explosion had set off the sprinkler system and the wet material did not burn readily. The frantic Cubans loaded documents in bins and poured acid over them but the acid penetrated only the top layers. Finally the city police, wearing bullet-proof vests and armed with rifles and machine guns, overpowered the Cubans and took the six with pistols into custody.

The trade commission was Cuba's cover for its spy headquarters in North America and for hours afterward its secrets were left unprotected. Ironically, the Cubans' overzealousness in protecting the premises compromised security.

For the previous month the trade commission in Montreal had been harassed with several threats serious enough to have police provide extra patrols. This was the most sophisticated anti-Cuban bombing in Canada, but not the first. In 1967 a crude homemade bomb consisting of several sticks of dynamite rocked the same building. It was planted in another office on a lower floor but police believed the Cuban trade commission was the target. Then in 1971 an incendiary device was found in front of the same office and safely dismantled by Montreal police. The Cuban Embassy in Ottawa was successfully bombed in 1966 and an anti-Castro nationalist group based in Miami claimed responsibility.

Two curious incidents occurred in Ottawa the week preceding the blast that fatally injured Sergio Perez. Six days earlier, a 12-by-3-inch homemade bomb was left outside the residence of Cuban Ambassador Dr. José Fernandez de Cossio in the Ottawa suburb of Rockcliffe Village. It was discovered by a Rockcliffe municipal employee and defused. Then, less than 24 hours before the Montreal elevator explosion, a pair of small boys discovered in front of the Cuban Embassy a bomb similar to the one found in front of the ambassador's residence. The boys moved it to a snowbank in the laneway next door. The area was cordoned off by police and an army bomb disposal unit using shields and tongs removed it. Two pieces of paper with red markings bearing the words *Miami* and *Florida* were found at the scene. Was this clue a telltale piece of evidence or a "plant" to cause police investigators to think the master-minds behind the bombing in Montreal the next morning were Florida-based anti-Castro Cubans when in fact they were not?

More than three years later, in 1975, an aide to United States Congressman Ronald Dellums, a California Democrat and member of the House Intelligence Committee, issued a statement that the Montreal bombing may have been a diversion to allow the CIA and RCMP to gain access to the premises for the purpose of seizing documents. He claimed his statement was backed by supporting documents.[1] The RCMP rarely bothers to respond to such accusations but this time went to the trouble of making a formal reply: "The RCMP categorically denies any complicity in respect to the bombing of the Cuba Trade Mission April 4, 1972. Nor has a subsequent investigation by Canadian authorities to date produced any evidence the CIA were involved." There the matter rested.

The CIA, to put it mildly, was quite interested in Cuba's activity in Canada, and not without reason. Intelligence originating from both sides of the border made it clear that the Montreal trade

---

[1.] For the record, Dellums' office now claims it is classified information and will no longer discuss the matter.

commission was being used to run espionage operations against the United States. Countries usually use their embassy, consulate, or trade commission as espionage bases, but Cuba, having no diplomatic relations with the United States, lacked such facilities there. Consequently Canada became the easiest and most effective access point. The open border allowed Cuban officers to pass from one country to the other with relative ease and without serious risk of detection. Cubans enjoyed unrestricted travel privileges within Canada, unlike Soviet personnel whose movements 125 kilometers outside Ottawa were regulated.

The RCMP Security Service learned from the CIA that all messages coming into and going out of the trade commission were ciphered and that one of the Cubans living on the premises was a full-time cipher clerk. RCMP surveillance of the movements of personnel confirmed that a number of the individuals had duties having nothing to do with promoting the sale of Cuban goods in Canada. Observation of the premises itself pinpointed a room on the northeast corner with the windows blocked by sheets of white plywood. The other rooms had curtains that opened and closed regularly. The trade commission acted as a collection point for Cuban intelligence gathered in Washington and shipped across the Canadian border for transportation to Havana through diplomatic pouch. The corner room undoubtedly contained secrets and by gaining entry the RCMP and CIA were almost certain to uncover some of Cuba's intelligence operations in the United States.

The RCMP Security Service's Cuban Desk in Montreal worked closely with the CIA. During Expo 67 the CIA tipped off the Cuban Desk that anti-Castro Cuban nationalists were planning to blow up the Cuban pavilion. The Florida-based Cubans had smuggled into Canada a 4.5-inch rocket launcher capable of destroying a tank and from the south shore of the St. Lawrence River were planning to attack the Cuban premises. They were intercepted on the launching site.

However, the CIA also did things in Canada behind the back of the Cuban Desk. Members of the Security Service in Quebec frequently were convinced that certain individuals in Quebec labor and radical political movements were CIA infiltrators not known to the RCMP. Such operations violated existing agreements stipulating that the CIA would not conduct operations in Canada without the permission and cooperation of Canadian authorities. When such cases were exposed the RCMP usually did not get upset. One Quebec Security Service member interviewed during the research for this book said that he once tripped across a university professor in Quebec who admitted being a CIA agent. The professor, a credible figure, said he was "tasked" to associate with certain ethnic groups and report on their activities and on certain individuals. The Mountie passed on these disclosures to the RCMP hierarchy, which went through the formality of contacting the CIA, which in turn went through the formality of denying it.

"The whole thing was treated tongue in cheek, as if 'there they go again,'" he said. "I think that everybody just took it for granted. Nobody expected the CIA to admit it. It was just part of the game."[2]

The CIA confided in the Security Service when it needed to draw on RCMP resources, such as the time the agency sent a Cuban to McGill University in Montreal as part of a long-term procedure of building up pro-Castro cover for a future penetrator.

The extent of the RCMP's knowledge of the Cuban Trade Commission is still known only by a handful of members. The Mountie in charge of the Cuban Desk in Montreal was a corporal who lived in St. Theresse. It was a long ride from his home to the trade commission, yet he arrived on the scene soon after the blast—so soon that some Mounties later speculated on whether it was physically possible. During those precious hours when the building was vacant and unguarded the corporal entered the premises and went on a shopping spree. The sensitive documents the acid had failed to destroy were salvaged mostly intact. In fact the Cubans had done him the favor of piling them in one central spot. Negatives hanging to dry in the darkroom were plucked.

---

2. Without exception, all the current and former members of the Security Service interviewed in the preparation of this book say they believe the CIA, despite denials, operates clandestinely in Canada. The general attitude was that the CIA operates in all countries around the world and why should Canada be the exception. One current member said, "The CIA wouldn't be living up to its responsibility if it wasn't in Canada."

The Canadian government, unlike the RCMP, was concerned about CIA intrusion and every year or two protested vigorously when a case came to its attention. On at least one occasion a diplomatic note was sent. American authorities would inevitably apologize and explain that the operation occurred at a low level and did not represent CIA policy and would not be repeated.

But more valuable was the Cuban code book, which was found and taken. The Cubans promptly changed their code but all previous traffic was jeopardized. It was one of the Security Service's biggest intelligence windfalls since Igor Gouzenko defected from the Soviet Embassy in 1945 carrying 109 intelligence documents. There was at least one important difference. When Gouzenko defected, the RCMP studied his documents and conducted its own investigation. This time there was no RCMP investigation to speak of. Within hours the entire cache, code books and all, landed on a desk in CIA headquarters in Langley, Virginia. In this case the RCMP Cuban Desk served mainly as a messenger service.

The CIA did not have a natural entree to the Security Service and therefore had to jostle its way into RCMP graces. Foreign intelligence officers under diplomatic cover constantly pass through embassies and the host-country security service needs to know their background. Friendly security services around the world trade this information freely up to a point. This exchange provides intimacy among the security services belonging to this alliance. The CIA does not belong to this group because it is an intelligence-gathering agency, not a security organization. The RCMP's counterpart in the United States is the FBI.[3]

The CIA had to use two methods in order to get information from the RCMP: manipulation and barter. Bartering was mutually beneficial, in theory at least, since each organization coveted something the other had. The RCMP had jurisdiction over the Cuban Trade Commission in Montreal and the CIA desired to know what was going on there. On the other hand, the CIA possessed the most sophisticated bugging equipment in the world and the RCMP dearly wanted access to it. So the two organizations traded. The CIA received complete access to Security Service files on Cubans in Canada, including surveillance results—information that only a host government could effectively provide. In return, Canada got the

---

[3.]   One would expect the CIA to use the FBI to get such information from Canada, but the two American organizations have a history of noncooperation and even one-upmanship. FBI Director J. Edgar Hoover jealously guarded his jurisdiction and provided only minimal cooperation and in 1970 cut off all formal links with the CIA. Ties were not restored until after his death in 1972. Sometimes the CIA asked the RCMP for information held by the FBI since the RCMP had a better chance of getting it.

bugging hardware and CIA personnel (who were not really needed) to help install it. The Security Service received enough of these devices to have its own technicians install them in non-Cuban operations.

Bartering provided the CIA with information but it did not get operations conducted against Cubans in Canada. Cuba was a high-priority target to the CIA but not to Canada. How could the CIA convince the Security Service to put more emphasis on Cubans? Here manipulation was important. CIA officers came to Montreal for visits and their presence impressed the Security Service. CIA men were university-educated, sophisticated, and worldly; they operated around the globe. They stroked egos and offered information, advice, free drinks and lunches. They were specifically attentive to the Cuban Desk, a fact that made the handful of Mounties on that desk proud and others envious and somewhat resentful. The CIA even took the members of the Montreal Cuban Desk on a junket to Florida, put them up in a private house, and supplied liquor.

The relationship served the CIA well. The Cubans received a lot more attention from the Security Service and the results, naturally, were shared. The relationship also served the selfish interests of the Cuban Desk because it discovered things about the Cubans the Force had not known before. But it was detrimental to the Security Service as a whole because for everything discovered about Cuba—a nonpriority target for Canada—something went undiscovered about another target that *was* a Canadian priority. Like all organizations, the Security Service had a budget and it effectively put a ceiling on the number of "technical positions"—bugging installations—the Force could initiate because each position required significant expenses in back-up equipment and people. Each bug required a tape recorder to record the conversation, a translator to put it into English (or French), a stenographer to produce transcripts, a reader to analyze the material's importance, officers to make decisions, and ultimately investigators to follow up the leads. As well, technicians were needed for bug-planting, itself an extensive process requiring planning and coordination. Each desk received a quota for the number of technical positions and at budget time every year each would lobby to have its quota increased. Now the Cuban Desk received an allotment that was out of line relative to the need, especially since Cuba's Montreal operation worked primarily against the United States. That meant technical positions were diverted from targets working primarily against Canada.

The CIA intrusion was not entirely the RCMP's fault. RCMP management often accommodated the agency, but in many ways the Force was stuck with the CIA because Canada and the United States exchanged information at levels above the RCMP and this consti- tuted official policy. It started with the development of a continental defense policy in the years following World War Two. Planning a joint defense required both sides to share military information, and since the United States possessed the larger and more sophisticated military it naturally had more information and secrets to throw into the kitty. By 1953 the Canadian Department of National Defence sent Phillip Uren to Washington as liaison man with the full-time duty of acquiring information that Canada needed. Although the information was usually classified, the Americans were generous and fulfilled most of the Canadian requests.

The CIA, too, was generous with its intelligence but in a schizo- phrenic manner befitting its schizophrenic character. The CIA had two faces, or two organizations inside one. One organization was the clandestine division euphemistically known as the "Plans" Director- ate and it was deeply involved in cloak-and-dagger affairs and the manipulation of foreign events and governments. It was ultra-secret and intelligence from this directorate was never shared. The other organization consisted essentially of a group of academics who ana- lyzed data—much of it publicly available—and provided inter- national assessments. Ironically, this overt group was called the Intelligence Directorate. While Plans was exceedingly stingy, Intel- ligence was surprisingly generous. Many times Intelligence produced an assessment of the strength of the Societ economy or some other topic and a copy would land on a desk in Ottawa. The report might be sanitized to the extent that a few sentences relating to sources were deleted but the report itself was not otherwise altered.

Every month or so the CIA produced one of these reports—called a "national estimate"—on a subject of interest to the western world. The Department of External Affairs in Ottawa valued these estimates since it lacked the army of Ph.D.s needed to prepare assessments of its own. The commencement of regular U-2 reconnaissance flights over the Soviet Union in 1956 yielded a harvest of intelligence and Canada received a good selection of the resulting photographs. Information came not only from the CIA's Intelligence Directorate but from the State and Defense departments and other American agencies as well. By 1957 Uren's presence in Washington had become so valuable that he was transferred from National Defence to External Affairs and thus became attached to the department with responsibility for Canadian-American relations.

Since Canada had a liaison officer in Washington, the Americans wanted one in Ottawa. It was a reasonable request and the resulting exchange of liaison officers was straightforward in principle, but not in practice. The American liaison officer who arrived in Ottawa did not come from the State Department seeking information from External Affairs, which had little to offer that the Americans did not already know. He came from the CIA—and not from Intelligence but from Plans. Naturally enough, the Plans representative was interested primarily in the RCMP since it had most of Canada's clandestine information. The nature of the exchange became clear: Canada received a lot of finished analysis and supplied raw data that was more secret in nature.[4] The United State's finished material went to External Affairs and National Defence while the raw product it sought from Canada came from the RCMP. The Canadian beneficiaries were External Affairs and National Defence since they got much and gave little, whereas the Security Service gave a lot and got little. Since External Affairs had jurisdiction over Canadian-American relations, the RCMP had little input in the sharing arrangement. So the CIA had its foot in the door whether the RCMP liked it or not. But the Security Service by itself fell prey to the sales pitch.

---

4. There is one other component of intelligence exchange between Canada and the United States that must not be overlooked. It concerns communications intelligence—the interception of electronic signals—and is not included here because it involves a separate relationship between the U.S. National Security Agency (NSA) and Canada's Communications Branch. The United States, Britain, Canada, Australia, and New Zealand have carved up the world into spheres and pool their intelligence. Here, too, the volume of exchange is not equitable and Canada receives more from the United States than it gives. However, the Canadian contribution is of significant value since Canada, because of the real estate it occupies on the globe, has unique access to communications in the northern Soviet Union.

Communications Branch for years operated under the cover of the National Research Council. The cover was exposed in January, 1974, in a CBC television documentary produced by Bill Macadam and James Dubro. Since that time the Communications Branch has been transferred to the Department of National Defence.

Despite the Security Service's predicament, Canada and the United States both benefited from the over-all exchange, although it is debatable who gained more. The CIA represented the biggest and most expensive and in some ways the most sophisticated information-gathering agency in the world. Canada would have been stupid not to tap it, given the opportunity. Canada had no intelligence-gathering agency of its own and even if it had, it would have lacked the scale and resources of the Americans. The intelligence from the CIA and other American organizations provided External Affairs and National Defence with a better basis on which to make decisions. Canada was able to sit back and watch from a semi-insider's position the most powerful country in the world wrestle with developments.

The Security Service did gain some benefits. Canada received few defectors. Most of them went to the CIA, which had an aggressive defectors' program, and the CIA alerted the Security Service if debriefing disclosed information believed to be of interest to Canada. The Security Service would have preferred to have access to the complete debriefings of all defectors; nevertheless what it did receive was often priceless.

The policy of the Intelligence Directorate of the CIA to provide Canada with finished analyses costing millions of dollars—even though that got little or no information in return—was generous, but it was based on enlightened self-interest as much as anything. The theory was that if Canada had the same information as the United States, it would adopt similar policies. That's precisely what happened and Canada remained a firm ally, causing little trouble or concern for the United States. If American generosity with secret information played a role in this phenomenon, the policy was a bargain for the United States.

Occasionally Canada has been able to supply the United States with valuable intelligence since Canada has better access in certain quarters of the world. For example, Canada was a member of the International Control Commission in Vietnam and routinely briefed the United States about its workings and forwarded all reports.[5]

---

[5] This revelation was first made by CBC producers Bill Macadam and James Dubro in the television program noted in footnote 4 and has been independently confirmed by the author.

Canada is also a good hiding place for defectors or exposed CIA agents from Iron Curtain countries. While Canada worries about becoming a dumping ground for these burned-out agents, the agency has some leverage with External Affairs.[6] Canada also serves as insurance in the event the CIA is cut off from other established foreign sources, such as Britain. Although the CIA exchanges more information with Britain than does Canada, Canada's ties are nevertheless stronger and less likely to be severed. During the Suez Crisis intelligence traffic ground to a halt between Britain and the United States while the flow to Canada merely slowed down, although Canada and the United States adopted virtually identical positions against Britain in 1956. Washington requires an emergency link through Canada's Commonwealth connection, should Anglo-American relations cool down again.

There is one avenue of information exchange with the United States where the RCMP receives equality and that is with the FBI. The Force feels more comfortable with the FBI since as the national police force and security service its functions parallel the RCMP. Furthermore, G-men, unlike the liberal artists at the CIA, have tended to share with Mounties a policeman's good-guys-bad-guys outlook. Both the FBI and the RCMP historically have tended to view espionage and subversion as simple criminal acts and have failed to grasp the larger political context. Until 1955 FBI Director J. Edgar Hoover forbade his men to run double agents because they robbed the Bureau of prosecutions that generated publicity. The RCMP once lived by that philosophy and unofficially still sympathizes with it.

FBI-RCMP relations were reflected by Moss Innes, the FBI liaison officer in Ottawa for 15 years. Innes planned to retire in Ottawa. His daughter married a Canadian and he walked about

---

6. The process of resettling former agents into third countries is described in *The CIA and the Cult of Intelligence* by Victor Marchetti and John Marks, both former officers in the Washington intelligence community. The book says: "In the late 1950s, when espionage was still a big business in Germany, former agents and defectors were routinely resettled in Canada and Latin America. The constant flow of anti-communist refugees to those areas was too much for the agency's Clandestine Services to resist. From time to time, an active agent would be inserted into the resettlement process. But the entire operation almost collapsed when, within a matter of months, both the Canadian and the Brazilian government discovered that the CIA was using it as a means to plant operating agents in their societies."

RCMP headquarters as if he were a member of the Force. Occasionally he forgot and gave an order to a Mountie.

Yet even such intimate relations were disrupted occasionally. Hoover was a proud and inflexible man and cut off the flow of security information whenever he felt slighted, and his interpretation of an offense could be whimsical. When that happened, a Mountie would take an FBI man to lunch and say, "We've got a problem. I need some information." He invariably got it. When Hoover was cordial there was virtually no information in the entire Bureau too secret for the RCMP. As well, the RCMP and FBI needed each other more than the RCMP and CIA did. The exchange extended from criminal matters—stolen car rings, counterfeiting, and so forth—to counterespionage work involving the activities of foreign intelligence officers.

Since it has sole jurisdiction of internal security in the United States, the FBI is the most important source of this kind of information because the target countries have large diplomatic establishments in Washington and at the United Nations in New York. Foreign intelligence officers arriving in Canada under diplomatic cover often have spent time in the United States and as a result will likely have been the object of FBI scrutiny. As well, "diplomats" in Canada frequently use the United States as a location for "third-country meets" so as to frustrate Canadian surveillance attempts. These operations are monitored effectively only when the two countries coordinate their activities.

Cooperation is also essential in the investigation of "illegals." An illegal is a foreign agent operating inside the country under an assumed identity, usually that of a real person who died or disappeared without leaving a solid record. Sometimes the identities are manufactured. Intelligence officers attached to an embassy are "legals" since they are inside the country legally and generally use real identities. In deploying illegals, the Soviet Union—by far the largest supplier of illegals—takes advantage of an international boundary to help frustrate the checking of an individual's background.

At a training school for illegals in Moscow the Soviet Union provides its students with several years of intensive training in everything from spying techniques to speaking English with a North American accent and knowing who plays third base for the Yankees.

They are sneaked into the United States where they make friends, develop contacts, and generally maneuver their way into positions of trust. Many illegals heading for the United States arrive through Canada since they are harder to trace and the entry restrictions are less formidable and the freedom to roam is greater. (Canada has no alien registration.) Once in Canada it is easy for the individual to enter the United States, where he assumes yet another identity.

The most famous illegal was KGB Colonel Rudolph Abel who was captured in New York on June 21, 1957, and exchanged for American U-2 pilot Francis Gary Powers in February, 1962. Abel, whose American identity was sometimes Emil R. Goldfus and sometimes Martin Collins, landed in Quebec City in 1948 as Andrew Kayotis, a naturalized American of Lithuanian background who had died while visiting his parents in Lithuania the previous year and whose passport fell into the hands of Soviet officials. Abel shed Kayotis's identity after crossing the American border and mostly used the identity of Goldfus, who was born in New York on August 2, 1902, and died in infancy.

On December 17, 1958, a man posing as a Finnish American landed in Montreal from Russia under a false name. Upon clearing customs he destroyed his passport and assumed the fictitious identity of Robert White, a Chicago businessman, and took the transcontinental train to Vancouver for two days. The man was a Soviet illegal whose task was to settle down in New York and watch the movement of missiles, munitions, and troops through New York harbor. His real name was Kaarlo R. Tuomi[7] and he was born in the United States but was reared in communism by his Finnish stepfather. In 1933, at age 16, he emigrated to Russia along with his family. The father, despite his staunch communism, was killed in one of Stalin's purges and during World War Two his mother died of starvation. In late 1949 Tuomi was blackmailed into working for the KGB as an informer and after eight years of successful informing undertook intensive training as an illegal. He studied intelligence techniques including surveillance detection, the philosophy of intelligence, photography, cryptography, American studies, and

[7.] Details on Tuomi's background are taken from John Barron's authoritative book *KGB: The Secret Work of Soviet Secret Agents.*

English. As an illegal he left the KGB and joined its smaller espionage cousin in the military, the GRU.

Since Tuomi was born in the United States he used his real name. However, virtually everything else about his past was fictitious. According to his "legend," or cover story, he was born in Michigan and, abandoned by his stepfather, grew up with his mother on a farm in Minnesota. He married his childhood sweetheart, Helen Matson, and left the failing farm in 1941 and worked in a variety of places, including a job in a lumber camp on the Fraser River outside Vancouver and later at a lumber yard in Vancouver itself. His fictitious wife was unfaithful and deserted him.

The purpose of Tuomi's trip to Vancouver as Robert White was to allow him to view the lumber camp and lumber yard where he claimed to have worked so that he would be familiar with them if questioned. He also visited the Vancouver apartments he said he had lived in. Tuomi, still using the name of White, returned to Montreal and boarded a pullman for Chicago and once safely in New York City destroyed his passport and other documentation to become, finally, Kaarlo Tuomi.

However, Tuomi had been betrayed by a double agent before he left Moscow and fell under RCMP surveillance the minute he landed in Montreal and continued to be surveilled as he checked out his legend in Vancouver. As his pullman crossed the American border at Port Huron, Michigan, the surveillance passed over to the FBI. Thereafter the RCMP returned to Vancouver and through investigation punched holes in his cover story. This information, along with the FBI's own investigation of Tuomi's legend in American cities, was sufficiently strong for the FBI to confront Tuomi and successfully turn him into a double agent.[8]

Canada's intelligence liaison with Britain traditionally has been the most intimate of all and predates the United States connection by many years. The relationship is not only warm but free of the nagging suspicion that constantly clouds relations in the intelligence

---

[8.] Tuomi himself was later exposed, presumably by a double agent working for the Russians, but remained safely in the United States. He is now an American citizen living under still another false identity.

community, even among close allies such as the United States and Canada. This trust is possible only because the Canadian security and intelligence community grew out of the British system, along with parliamentary democracy, common law, and other institutions as Canada matured from colony to independent state. Ignorance is a breeding ground of suspicion and since the relationship was so close from colonial days, suspicion never had the opportunity to flourish. In former days Britain looked after Canada's internal security, whether American military threat, the Fenians, or Marxist ideology from abroad. After the Gouzenko revelations the RCMP sent a series of officers to Britain for training. The Force never used the CIA for training except for brief technical courses. One never knew whom the trainees would be working for once they got back. All through the 1950s Canada allowed the British to conduct sweeps for electronic eavesdropping devices in Canadian embassies abroad, a sign of implicit trust.

Canada and Britain share a similar cultural approach to handling security and intelligence functions in contrast to the Americans. The United States tradition features egalitarianism. Just as any American can grow up to become president, so can any kid become Director of the CIA. The American system tends to be aggressive since the leaders push their way to the top. American intelligence folklore features characters like "Wild Bill" Donovan, the intelligence chief during World War Two, and Allen Dulles, the Director of the CIA who loved gadgets and cloak-and-dagger work. Many of these men reached the top and, after they retired, wrote books about their exploits.

The British experience adopted by Canada featured the traditional practice of selecting top intelligence people from the upper crust of society who did their job quietly and retired in silence. Some of the prominent names in the history of Canadian security and intelligence include George Glazebrook, later history professor at the University of Toronto; Hamilton Southam of the Southam newspaper chain and later publisher of the Ottawa *Citizen;* and John Starnes, career diplomat and son of a wealthy Montreal grain broker. Britain and Canada had too few of everything—people, money, and equipment —and were constantly plotting ways to become effective despite these deficiencies. It was an experience not shared by the Americans, who had big staffs, ample money, and impressive mechanical aids. The American challenge lay in marshaling the resources that were available.

Canada after World War Two drifted away from British influence and into the American orbit. Geography and economics were powerful magnets but the postwar world was being polarized into two camps and Canada was inevitably attracted to the American camp. Although the British security and intelligence establishment remained one of the finest in the world, its influence over Canada waned. The Americans developed the U-2 aircraft, which at 80,000 feet—above Soviet anti-aircraft missile range—took photographs with new-technology cameras capable of discerning objects 12 inches in diameter. Britain could not produce such phenomenal intelligence. U-2 reconnaissance was canceled in 1960 following the crash of pilot Francis Gary Powers, but aerial surveillance resumed in 1961 with an even more effective satellite program from 90 miles above. The United States had larger diplomatic establishments abroad and hence picked up more information than Britain. The United States had more intelligence analysts too.

As Canada was pulled closer to the United States its security and intelligence establishment, of which the RCMP Security Service is one component, took on an increasingly American look. The British way of doing things diminished and American-style enthusiasm grew. This book examines the development of one institution, the Security Service of the RCMP, and follows this trend, which eventually brought disrepute to the entire organization because of acts that were ineffective and illegal.

The Men in
the Shadows

BY THE END of the 1960s the attitude of many Mounties toward the
Security Service began changing. Sentiment within the Criminal
Investigation Branch—one side of the RCMP—started turning
against the Security Service—the other side.[1] The Security Service
differed from the rest of the RCMP and had always demanded
special treatment. Spy chasers were different from policemen and
many of them wanted to separate and form an independent civilian
security service like MI5 in Britain. CIB savored the presence of the
Security Service since it gave the RCMP class and status. In England
a policeman was a policeman. He gave out traffic tickets and conducted criminal investigations. But in Canada a Mountie also chased
spies and matched wits with the KGB. The Security Service satisfied
the RCMP's desire to be the one organization protecting Canada
from all threats, whether criminal, subversive, or espionage. Most
Mounties started in CIB and finished there. Nevertheless, anyone might
find himself suddenly transferred to the cloak-and-dagger world,
since about one in five Mounties belong to the Security Service side.

[1.] The Criminal Investigation Branch no longer exists as the only non-Security Service
organization within the RCMP. It is now called the Criminal Investigation Directorate and it
consists of eight non-Security Service directorates: Criminal Investigations, Protective Policing, Organization and Personnel, Services and Supply, "Air" Services, Records Services,
Laboratories and Identification, and Canadian Police Information Centre. However, the term
CIB has come to identify the non-Security Service side of the Force and, in keeping with this
popular usage, is used in that context.

With the advent of the 1970s, the Security Service became increasingly less desirable to many CIB Mounties. They were more interested in policing than in security work. They saw the Security Service as a parasite, for while CIB did the recruiting and training, the Security Service siphoned off the best talent. There was also the arrogance. The Security Service never hid its elitism. In the old days CIB's awe of the Security Service overpowered its resentment. Now the awe was diminishing and the resentment rising.

Members of the two sides saw little of each other. Contact came mainly in the mess, where CIB members discussed their cases while the Mounties from the Security Service would say: "Sorry, I can't talk. National security." This kind of put-down prompted many Mounties to wonder why they had to tolerate the security side. They felt their work was every bit as important and sophisticated.

A lot of CIB's silent resentment became vocal in 1977 when the Security Service was being discredited in public for having conducted illegal activities. The Security Service had operated not only illegally but badly. It had done some stupid things and regular Mounties began to wonder what klutzes these supersleuths were anyway. They believed they could have done better and stayed within the law. The Mounties posing for tourists on Parliament Hill occasionally were asked for more familiar poses, such as a furtive crouch beneath a window. Others giving out speeding tickets in northern British Columbia were asked: "How come you get away with your illegal acts and I can't get away with mine?" CIB was shouldering the backlash on behalf of the Security Service, which did not meet the public and indeed avoided it. More importantly, the century-old reputation CIB had built was being challenged by the unenviable legacy of the Security Service. Even the officer corps began to wonder, for the first time, whether keeping the Security Service was worth it.

The public reaction more than ever emphasized that the RCMP is not one organization but two. Each side has its own values and priorities with little in common with the other. They have much in conflict. CIB is by far the bigger. They are the cops who staff the detachments across the country.

When recruits join the RCMP they pledge to "faithfully, diligently and impartially execute and perform the duties required of me ... without fear, favour, or affection of or towards any person." It is a solemn occasion. Six intensive months of training at Regina pounds into them the concept that they are the servants of the law and not the government and that the role of the police in a democratic society is to uphold the law and nobody, regardless who the transgressor is, can interfere. If the Prime Minister makes an illegal U-turn he must receive a ticket. After graduating, they are full-fledged Mounties and spend the rest of their careers putting theory into practice. Although some of the idealism fades, they still adhere to the principle that everyone is equal before the law.

Any Mountie who moves into the Security Service must unlearn those very principles to become a good counterintelligence officer. No longer is he the servant of the law. He now works for the political benefit of the country, and his objectives are now set by the political masters. No longer can he take action when observing illegal acts, for he no longer is a law-enforcement officer and lacks the police powers of search, seizure, and arrest. Even if he could take legal action, the country's foremost interest might be best served if he did nothing and allowed the illegality to continue. The concept of justice goes out the window. The aim is no longer rightness but effectiveness. Thoroughly despicable scoundrels and traitors not only go free but are rewarded and decent, innocent people are sacrificed. Some are unable to adapt and return to police work, where it is easier to know good from bad. Others accommodate themselves to the new environment. Occasionally Mounties who have succeeded in the Security Service ask for a transfer back to police duties. They used to be scorned when they left; now that is diminishing.

Security Service uniforms were banished in 1970 by John Starnes when he became the first civilian head. Before then a Security Service member had to possess uniforms conforming to RCMP dress regulations but obviously could not wear them for security reasons. Every year the individual toted his uniform to the office in a bag and put it on for the annual inspection, once in red serge and again in brown serge. Some Mounties whose physical dimensions were changing got new uniforms every year for this one event. They could not get married in uniform. They could wear them at formal

RCMP functions but, again, could not wear them on the way to the event and would have to change after arriving. Ironically, the Security Service's strict policy against uniforms compromised security as much as protected it. When a CIB Mountie suddenly stopped wearing a uniform everybody knew he had joined the Security Service.

The Security Service, not surprisingly, has a passion for secrecy. (One Security Service member could not play on the RCMP hockey team because spectators might identify him. He protested and was finally permitted to play in out-of-town games.) Most Security Service Mounties don't tell their wives about their cases and some won't even disclose the nature of their work. Several wives were shocked when the federal Royal Commission into RCMP wrong-doing heard testimony from their husbands. They had no idea their spouses did such things. Retired Commissioner Charles Rivett-Carnac provides a glimpse of the stress such secrecy can cause in his book *Pursuit in the Wilderness*. Rivett-Carnac at the time (1945-46) was in charge of the Gouzenko investigation:

> ... my wife began to have serious doubts about my behaviour. I could of course tell her nothing and, after working at the office until very late at night would pace the floor of the bedroom through the early hours of the morning, smoking innumerable cigarettes and trying to decide where a certain course of action might lead or whether some other course would be best. The seal was finally put on her doubts when, on one occasion, I left the house and went to the office at three o'clock in the morning to check on some matter I was worried about and felt needed attention. When I returned an hour or so before dawn she was much concerned; nothing she could visualize could warrant my doing this and yet I could not explain.

The Security Service is highly centralized. Everything is controlled from headquarters in Ottawa. In CIB each division—each province is a division except for Ontario—has a life of its own with its separate chain of command. A member of the Security Service is in the same division whether he works in Montreal, Ottawa, or Victoria. What counts is his section since that dictates his function, whether counter-espionage or countersubversion or whatever. There are 10 sections and each is designated by a letter.

A SECTION (Security Screening)

A new recruit to the Security Service almost invariably starts in A Section because the work is not popular, being dull and usually unrewarding. The screening department, as it is called, is responsible for checking into the backgrounds of the thousands of people who have access to confidential government information. Should a civil servant be promoted into such a position, he is automatically subjected to a security check. Or if the federal government gives a private company a munitions contract involving official secrets, the employees with access to that information will be screened.

A Section checks into the individual's background to determine first of all if he is who he says he is — i.e., he is not an "illegal" — and, once that's established, checks to determine whether anything in the individual's past precludes him from knowing official secrets. The Security Service is specifically interested to know whether the person has extremist political associations that might throw doubt on his loyalty to the existing political structure, or if he has any "character weaknesses" that make him vulnerable to blackmail. These weaknesses include alcoholism, gambling, indebtedness, or overspending (thus making the person susceptible to selling information for quick gain), extramarital romance, or merely a loose lip. A Section had an abnormal interest in homosexuals and created a subsection called A-3 to hunt down homosexuals in the civil service since secret homosexuals were targets for KGB blackmail. The Security Service continued to pursue homosexual investigations after Pierre Trudeau as Justice Minister legalized homosexuality between consenting adults because, while it was no longer illegal, it could constitute a possible security threat for homosexuals still in the closet. The Security Service's paranoia over homosexuality is examined in some detail in later chapters.

Every month a member of A Section is given the files of 12 individuals who are to be screened. He first checks the RCMP criminal files and then the Security Service's subversive index and then does a routine credit check. After that he talks to former neighbors to check out background and to determine whether the information on the application form is generally accurate. "We just want to make sure he actually lived here for two years," the investigator tells the neighbor.

After that, in an offhand way—as if it's not too important—he asks: "What was he like?" This is the most critical part of the investigation since it is former neighbors who usually produce detrimental information. Character references are not likely to do so since they are picked by the subject. If the neighbor makes an accusation or somehow sets off an alarm, a more thorough investigation is conducted and former work associates are interviewed. The Security Service collects the information and writes a report; it does not decide whether a security clearance is given. That decision is made by the concerned department and is based largely on the information provided by the Security Service.

B SECTION (Counterespionage)

B Section is the elite of the Security Service. Its purpose is to counteract the intelligence-gathering activities of foreign powers in Canada, and much of the effort is directed against the Soviet Union. It is the largest section in the Security Service and, in a sense, the coordinator of other sections. It is responsible for scrutinizing the foreign embassies in Canada. It checks over the names of immigrants coming to Canada for a possible espionage role. In some cases it conducts investigations into targets who have not satisfactorily passed the security screening of A Section. It carries out investigations of people who are friendly with Soviet Embassy personnel to see whether they are agents and, often, to co-opt them into working for the Security Service as informers against the Soviets.

The technical name for embassy-watching is Residency Analysis and it is the biggest single function of B Section. A foreign country must notify the Department of External Affairs every time it changes diplomatic staff, and supply the name of the new individual and apply for a visa. When an unfriendly country is involved, the names of these visa applicants are passed to friendly foreign security agencies, such as the FBI in the United States and MI5 in Britain, for the background information. B Section then decides whether to scrutinize the individual through various forms of surveillance.

B Section is divided into regional desks with members specializing in one country or group of countries. If a particular city has many Poles the local B Section will have a Polish Desk. Otherwise Poles and Czechs might be combined in one desk. If the Security Service outlet is very small in the region Poland might be part of the Satellite Desk.

Russian Desk.   This is the biggest desk by far, not only in numbers, but in scope of action. It is an initiating desk since it does more than respond to situations. The Soviet Desk plants double agents, recruits agents, and works to frustrate the Soviets even without evidence that they are dealing in espionage since they usually are. Residency Analysis is a science on the Russian Desk because nearly half the "diplomats" in the Soviet Embassy do intelligence work at some level.

The Russian Desk identifies the functions of many embassy people within a year of arrival. Sometimes the chauffeur is a ranking intelligence officer and the passenger a flunky decoy. When caught, the Soviets are never charged since most of them have diplomatic status and are immune from prosecution. Often the operation is let run to learn more about Soviet methods and targets. When the action gets too warm the operation is rolled up and the key Soviet participants are expelled (often quietly). The USSR invariably replaces one intelligence officer with another and the game of trying to identify the individual starts over, which is why it is often better to leave him in place since that way you know who your opponent is.

Czech Desk.   Since the STB, the Czechoslovakian intelligence agency, is one of the most aggressive in the Communist Bloc, Czechoslovakia usually gets a desk to itself. The Czech service tends to be insular and interested mainly in the Czech community in Canada, which makes it easier to defend against. If activity deviates from this pattern, chances are good the Czechs are fronting for the Soviets, which is not too unusual.

Hungarian Desk.   Hungary also has tried to recruit agents in Canada but not always successfully and with the Russians sometimes stage-managing the affair. Although Hungary is less troublesome than

Czechoslovakia, it is not positively determined whether agents were slipped into the immigration stream following the aborted revolution of 1956 who have since disappeared into Canadian society. Hungary also runs operations from its embassy.

Satellite Desk.   This usually includes Romania, East Germany, Bulgaria, and possibly Poland, although any one of these countries, particularly Poland, can have its own desk. The size of the Satellite Desk depends mostly on the concentration of immigrants from those countries in a given locality.

Cuban Desk.   The Cuban Desk is a constant reminder of Canada's junior status in international security and intelligence. As noted in Chapter 1, since Cuba has no embassy in the United States it uses its diplomatic establishments in Canada as a base of operations against the Americans. Cuba also uses Canada to further its military adventures in third-world countries—such as recruiting mercenaries—a new form of diplomatic abuse that disturbs the Department of External Affairs.

C SECTION (Administration)

C Section has no operational capacity and does what its designation suggests: handle personnel matters, transfers, cash advances, expense accounts, and the like. Although technically a section it is not well defined and some members do not realize it exists.

D SECTION (Countersubversion)

D Section is responsible for "individuals and organizations of subversive interest" and is the second largest. While B Section (Counterespionage) investigates operations emanating from outside Canada, D Section monitors anti-state activity originating within the country. Maoists, Trotskyites, Quebec separatists fall under D Section's jurisdiction as well, naturally, as the Communist Party of Canada.

This section is aggressive in recruiting informers and offering money for information. One of its most effective feats was the undermining of the Communist Party of Canada in the 1950s through penetration and disruptive tactics. Some small branches of the Communist Party were kept alive only because of the participation of the Security Service's informer or informers. D Section's greatest failing was its inability to comprehend the 1960s political dissension of the youth. It assumed they were subversive and treated them as such and as a result the Security Service was often clumsy, heavy-handed, and illegal.

E SECTION (Electronic Surveillance)

The functions of E Section proper are routine enough. It has responsibility for transcribing wiretapped and bugged conversations for investigators and analysts to study. Many of the targets are foreigners and often the conversations need translation, so E Section is filled with translators and stenographers.

There is, however, another side to E Section that many Mounties don't know about. Buried within the organization is the most secret and sensitive section of all—E Special. In most localities E Special consists of a windowless office inside another room with a sophisticated lock and alarm on the door. Inside are locked filing cabinets encased in heavy safes containing the most explosive secrets the Security Service has to offer. Even senior officers are denied access to the rooms, let alone to the files, unless they have direct chain-of-command authority.

E Special is a "service" section and the services it provides are clandestine operations or, more simply, break-and-enter jobs. If the Security Service wants to rummage through the home of a radical leader or a foreign operative, or take computer tapes belonging to the Parti Québécois, E Special is responsible for planning and conducting the operation and ensuring it comes off smoothly and safely.

E Special first watches the targeted premises for several weeks and, aided by a wiretap, determines when it will be vacant and ripe for a clandestine entry. One of its locksmiths opens the door while others surveil key individuals to ensure they don't drop in while the operation is in progress. Just in case, lookouts are posted to warn against the unexpected arrival of unsurveilled individuals or passers-by. E Special always has a "disaster plan" designed to get the operatives out of danger in case something goes wrong. No E Special operation proceeds without headquarters authorization. The plan is submitted and scrutinized by E Special personnel in Ottawa and approved once they are convinced the risks have been minimized. The various E Special units across the country have done hundreds of operations and have never been caught. E Special is described in greater detail later.

F SECTION (Files)

Nowhere is the highly centralized structure of the Security Service more evident than in F Section, where thousands of files on individuals and groups are stored away at headquarters in Ottawa. A copy of every Security Service report is dispatched to this central storage location where it is indexed, cross-referenced, and filed away. The files are truly massive. (The file on the late Communist Party leader Tim Buck exceeded 20 volumes.) F Section represents the central repository of all Security Service information with the exception of E Special's clandestine activities and L Section's informer's files. Since F Section possesses the combined files of all the regions, only headquarters has complete information on any suspected group and therefore only headquarters is in a position to make policy decisions regarding the monitoring of these groups.

G SECTION (Counterterrorism)

This ill-fated branch was established in 1971 and existed only in Quebec and Ottawa. It kept track of radical Francophones in Quebec including, notably, separatists, while D Section (Countersubversion) maintained jurisdiction over radical elements in Anglophone Quebec. G Section lasted only a few years but its brief lifetime will be remembered; it represents a low in the history of the Security Service because of its eagerness to engage in acts that were illegal, ill considered, and often counterproductive. Although not the only section to engage in illegal activities and dirty tricks, it was G Section's clumsiness and aggressiveness that eventually exposed the Security Service. The group has since been reamalgamated with D Section and is now a subsection called D-5.

H SECTION (Chinese)

H Section was established in 1969 when Canada and China started negotiating diplomatic recognition since it was clear that China would be establishing an embassy in Ottawa which would need watching. Before that, China had been virtually ignored. Nobody in the Security Service spoke the language and China did not even rate a desk. It was a subdesk of the Russian Desk in B Section. With the advent of diplomatic relations and an embassy from which China could conduct intelligence operations, the Security Service overreacted and decided nothing less than a brand-new section was needed. The lids went off budgets across the Security Service and everything—surveillance, bugging etc.—was increased. However, since recognition, China has kept quiet, either doing little spying or doing it so well it was not getting caught, and H Section has shrunk from lack of work.

I SECTION (Physical Surveillance)

I Section, which is known as the Watcher Service, is responsible for following the movements and observing the actions of targeted individuals. Physical surveillance is one of the few functions in which the Security Service excels. Ironically, the Watcher Service is comprised mainly of civilians who never underwent training at Regina. They are so good it is virtually impossible to tell whether you're being followed even if you are looking for it. The Watcher Service is described in detail in Chapter 3.

J SECTION (Bugging)

J Section plants bugs (but not wiretaps, which is done by the telephone company on behalf of the Security Service). It works hand in hand with E Special. While E Special plans and conducts the actual clandestine entry, J Section accompanies it and drills the holes and inserts the listening devices. Because the task is technical in nature the section is made up of a combination of civilian technicians and Mounties with special skills. J Section relies considerably on foreign agencies like the CIA and MI6 in Britain for equipment.

K SECTION

As far as is known, there is no K Section. For some reason the letters jump from J to L. One Security Service member theorized that K Section may exist but plays such a minor role that nobody knows about it. "Either that," he joked, "or it exists and is *very* important."

L SECTION (Informers)

L Section is the repository of information on thousands of Security Service informers spread across the country. It is also the resident authority on the delicate process of recruiting informers and is consulted on the process. Once an informer is recruited, L Section evaluates the worth of the information and decides the amount of payment and other matters such as when to pay bonuses and what form payment should take: retainer, piecemeal, or both.

The Security Service protects—usually—the identity of its informers with the same zealousness that journalists protect theirs. L Section has its own filing system containing informers' identities and it is guarded in a Chubb safe to which only members of the section have access. The information produced is distributed throughout the general filing system (F Section) with the source listed as a code number.

The Watcher Service

ON SATURDAY AFTERNOON, October 8, 1960, Soviet Cultural Attaché Lev Burdiukov left the Russian Embassy compound on Charlotte Street in Ottawa and headed into the country. Although Burdiukov was officially a diplomat, his car that day did not carry the red diplomatic license plates that stand out like beacons in the Ottawa traffic. The car bore white-and-blue Ontario-style plates specially issued by the Department of External Affairs to help foreign embassy officials blend into the Canadian scenery when not on official business.

Three minutes later another Soviet with diplomatic status driving a car with similar plates drove through the iron gates of the embassy and kept near Burdiukov until he left the city. His task was to determine whether Burdiukov was under RCMP surveillance and, if so, attempt to lure the Mounties into following him—or, at the very least, to split the RCMP's available surveillance resources into two.

Burdiukov, accompanied in his car by embassy colleague Rem Krassilnikov, motored to the town of Brockville about 110 kilometers south of Ottawa and for four hours conducted a series of military-like maneuvers. He drove fast and slow, made U-turns, then doublebacked and traveled over seldom-used back roads where nobody could see them. When convinced nobody was shadowing them, the two Russians returned to Ottawa and parked the car in the outlying suburb of Bell's Corner and walked across the street to a second-rate motel. There they met an elderly man who was later identified as George Victor Spencer, a postal clerk from Vancouver who was feeding information to the Soviets.

The Spencer case is well known. Although Spencer's usefulness was limited because he lacked access to confidential information, his case was debated in the House of Commons and a Royal Commission was struck to determine whether the federal government acted properly in denying him a pension. What is only vaguely known is the role played by the RCMP's efficient surveillance team in exposing Spencer. From an observation post opposite the Soviet Embassy, the RCMP watched Burdiukov start the journey for his eventual meet, not knowing that there was anything significant about this trip. A few blocks away, a team of disguised Security Service cars one by one started picking up the trail and maintaining it without the knowledge of Burdiukov or his colleague conducting countersurveillance in the second car. Even on country roads the surveillance squad remained hidden.

The surveillance branch, officially designated I Section but commonly known as the Watcher Service, is by far the most effective arm of the Security Service. Virtually every RCMP success in counter-espionage originated with the Watcher Service. Each time a foreign diplomat has been expelled from Canada, the Watcher Service has been responsible for exposing the real activity or at least has played a crucial role in cementing the case. And the few Canadian spies the Security Service has caught have been largely the result of the Watcher Service's work.

The vulnerable link in espionage activity is communication. A Soviet spy in the Department of External Affairs can carry away Canadian secrets in his head without fear of detection. But sooner or later he must communicate the information to his Soviet masters. He can avoid wiretaps and bugs by using telephones and premises not covered by these devices, such as pay phones and hotel rooms. He can even stay clear of possible informers. But sooner or later a physical meeting becomes necessary and it is here that the Watchers play their role. Only knowledgeable informers inside the embassy of unfriendly foreign powers are more valuable than physical or technical surveillance, and since the Security Service has been relatively ineffective in recruiting informers or planting bugs in such sensitive places, but has been successful in discreetly following people, the Watcher Service ranks as the most effective aid in counterespionage cases (but not in cases of subversion which require different investigative techniques).

The Watchers are normally almost impossible to detect; even trained intelligence officers, who always suspect they are being followed, rarely confirm their suspicions. "The first time I went out with them I was in the target car," says one Security Service officer. "We had a radio and were monitoring their broadcasts, knowing everything they were doing. They followed us around the city of Ottawa for three hours and I never saw one Watcher's car. Not once. I looked around. I did everything to try and identify them. Not one car."

The Watcher Service does not rely entirely on its mobile crew. It has throughout the city an infrastructure of informers such as hotel employees, taxi drivers, barmen, waiters, newsstand operators, and city policemen who can act as observers with virtually no risk of being detected. Major hotels are routinely covered. Thus it is possible to trace an individual's movements through a city's downtown core with little moving surveillance.

The RCMP's Drug Squad has a surveillance team and so does the RCMP's National Crime Intelligence Unit, which fights organized crime. However, their techniques are different and they lack the skills of the Watchers, who are the tops of their specialty. The Drug Squad once used 22 cars in a surveillance stretching 87 kilometers. "They had to use 22 vehicles," said one of the Mountie participants. "We busted them two hours later. The guys had no idea how it happened. And that's only the criminal surveillance team. The Security Service is better. They'd follow you to the bathroom and tell you how many sheets of toilet paper you used." The Watcher Service never needs 22 cars. It never needs more than six cars, and even then six cars are used only for trained intelligence officers like Burdiukov.

For his meet with Burdiukov, Spencer was registered at the motel under the name of MacNiel, his mother's maiden name. To the RCMP he was at first merely a UM—unidentified male. Naturally Spencer himself was put under immediate surveillance and followed to the Ottawa airport and when his plane touched down in Vancouver a new Watchers team was on hand to follow him home and to work at the post office the next day. For more than four years Spencer was subjected to regular surveillance. Somebody at the post office kept an eye on him and alerted the Security Service about suspicious activity or unusual movements. When he took a vacation in the British Columbia Interior in the summer of 1961 he was followed every mile by Watchers who snapped the same pictures he took. When Spencer wandered through graveyards recording the names of dead people so that Soviet spies could assume their identities, the Watchers were discreetly behind him jotting down the same names. In two and a half years Spencer flew to Ottawa for a total of seven meets and each time he was met at the airport by the Watchers. On at least one occasion his motel room was bugged.

The Spencer case, more than anything else, exposed the Soviets technique of running Canadian spies from the embassy in Ottawa. The Soviets would drive into the countryside for three or four hours and "clean" themselves and return to Ottawa for the meet. In 1966 the Force had reason to believe the Russians thought the Watcher Service did not operate regularly on weekends and until 1965 that was substantially correct. A Soviet attaché, Evgeni Kourianov, left the embassy at 4 A.M. on February 13, 1966, a Sunday morning, on the assumption that no Watcher would be available to follow him at that hour. A full Watcher team was on duty and followed Kourianov to the edge of town and let him go into the country unsurveilled. The RCMP had adopted a new policy. While Kourianov was undergoing his countersurveillance motions, the Watchers were marking off entrance points on the key routes back to Ottawa. Observation posts were established so that surveillance could resume the minute he returned to the city, which he did almost on schedule, from the west along Highway 15. He parked his car outside the apartment building of a Canadian friend in the Bayshore area of West End Ottawa. Since Kourianov was a known KGB agent, the Canadian, a drugstore owner, had already been investigated by the Security Service and quickly uncovered as a homosexual. The Canadian's apartment was bugged in the hope of discovering a homosexual relationship between the Canadian and Kourianov so the Security Service could blackmail Kourianov into becoming a double agent for Canada. But the Force soon learned that the relationship was innocent and involved neither espionage nor homosexuality. Kourianov did not visit his Canadian friend that Sunday morning and later it became clear that he parked his car there only to help make his trip appear casual.

Kourianov boarded several city buses that eventually took him to the Billings Bridge Shopping Centre in south Ottawa. After walking for an hour and a half he boarded another bus to the Elmvale Shopping Centre in Ottawa's East End and met an unidentified young man for about 40 minutes. The man was Bower Edward Featherstone, a printer in the mapping section of the Department of Mines and Technical Surveys who was later convicted and imprisoned for selling classified maps to the Soviets.

The Featherstone case was a laurel for the Watchers, but their reputation was really made with the capture of Lucien Rivard. The Security Service had no interest in a common crook like Rivard. Since he was a drug peddler, he was the responsibility of CIB, which possessed a surveillance team of its own. After Rivard escaped Bordeaux Jail in 1965 while awaiting extradition proceedings for drug-smuggling charges in Texas, CIB made repeated attempts to follow his acquaintances in the hope they would lead the RCMP to Rivard. But somehow Rivard's friends always detected the unmarked RCMP cars and would throw them off or avoid making a meet with Rivard. Both the RCMP and the federal government were desperate. The Rivard affair was a national scandal that was causing the minority Liberal government of Lester Pearson serious embarrassment because Rivard had attempted to avoid extradition through influence-peddling and then escaped from jail after getting permission to water the prison ice rink in 40-degree (F) weather. In an action that was unusual, the Commissioner of the RCMP assigned the Watchers the task of surveilling Rivard's friends. CIB's four-door posts with blackwalls were replaced by the Watcher Service's two-door hardtops with white-walls. The Watchers pinpointed Rivard's location at a summer cottage only a half-hour drive from Montreal. Rivard was arrested and the government relieved.[1]

Until the 1950s surveillance and investigation were regarded as the same thing. At that time there was no surveillance section in the

---

[1.] CIB's surveillance units have in subsequent years become more proficient and are not nearly so likely to require assistance from the Watcher Service.

RCMP. The hard-pressed investigator would put his target to bed at 2 A.M. and be back waiting at 7A.M. When the target made a contact the Mountie scribbled down a license plate number and chased down that lead next week—if there was time. Later, as surveillance became recognized as important, the investigator would be loaned a few Mounties from other sections from time to time. Most surveillance occurred in B Section (Counterespionage) and most members of the Security Service were striving for a transfer into that section and so were eager to help out. Although they were a group, they were hardly a team for they lacked radio equipment with which to communicate among cars. They were lucky to have binoculars!

Although other cities lagged behind, Ottawa began forming an actual surveillance unit in the early 1950s when Sergeant Phil Keeler was transferred from Alberta. Keeler's style was not conducive to surveillance for he had a habit of making himself conspicuous to the targets he was following. A robust individual, he had close-cropped hair, a military mustache, and wore a cloth-checked cap and a military overcoat with extra pockets and brass rings. He loved cars and drove a long black Packard while on surveillance.

He did everything but display the RCMP crest on his door. Later the Packard was replaced by a used Austin, which was also inappropriate since it was underpowered and mechanically unreliable.

The modern Watcher Service started to emerge in 1955 when Sergeant Henry Tadeson replaced Keeler and was immediately sent to Britain for training. By this time the unit already had several civilians but Tadeson increased the number while developing their expertise and molding them into a team. Civilians were not only cheaper but better since surveillance was their only profession and they quickly acquired not only the technique but a detailed knowledge of the city, including every alley and short cut. By the time Tadeson was transferred to other duties in 1960 the Watcher Service had become an effective organization and was being expanded to other major cities.

The reputation of the Watcher Service spread within the closely knit western intelligence community and countries like Britain, Australia, and Holland came to Canada to observe it in action. The foreign observers were interested in the Watchers' technique, certainly, but they were especially curious about the Canadian concept of employing teams of civilians for surveillance duties. Even the FBI in 1969 was studying the Watchers with a view to implementing the civilian concept. The FBI's surveillance section was suffering since it was comprised of castoffs from other departments or young officers who aspired to more fulfilling duties and never stayed long enough to develop the needed skills. At the request of the Americans the RCMP prepared a detailed paper on the Watcher Service and the FBI was ready to adopt it until J. Edgar Hoover personally vetoed the proposal. For Hoover it was a matter of pride not to imitate the RCMP.

The individual Watchers are "special constables"; they receive a six-week instruction course at the local level on the methodology and practice of shadowing people. In training they are taken to shopping plazas and other congested urban areas for exercises equivalent to the military's war games; only in this case nobody but the participants know what is going on. They start by learning to follow someone on foot without arousing suspicion. They are shown how to act as a team and anticipate the target's movements. If the subject enters a theater, chances are that a member of the team is up ahead in the line-up. Later they graduate to cars, where they learn to remain out of sight while keeping track of the target. Watchers are taught it is no disgrace to lose the target. Losing the target is preferable to exposure. When the target is lost the entire team spreads out for a search. Most times the target is found and the team resumes formation.

One of the most difficult elements in being a Watcher is learning to observe critically and to remember every detail. The target's every action, no matter how innocent, must be noted even if it is as routine as removing a jacket or stepping off a curb. The details may seem inconsequential at the time but six months later may form part of a pattern for an analyst at headquarters. If the target encounters anyone, even for a brief hello, the stranger's face must be remembered. Often the person will be placed under immediate surveillance, depending on the judgment of the Watchers. Never are Watchers permitted to relax or lower their level of concentration. It is strenuous work.

Watchers must be relatively innocuous in appearance, which is another reason why they are civilians and not Mounties. They are neither too tall nor too short, too fat nor too thin, too beautiful nor too homely. They possess no unusual physical characteristics, such as flaming red hair, that attract attention. They dress in dull colors and nondescript styles so that they melt into crowds. The clandestine nature of their work even carries over into their personal lives as they lie to their best friends about their careers. In case somebody asks them about their jobs, they have a cover story.

Virtually every Watcher has either a family or social connection with the RCMP or the military. Since the Watcher Service is not supposed to exist, the RCMP cannot advertise for jobs in the usual manner. Recruiting is carried out through individual contact by members of the RCMP or the military. Nepotism is not only permitted, it is encouraged. The likelihood of penetration decreases remarkably when the job seeks the individual rather than the other way around. The RCMP once did attempt to recruit through advertisements in the newspaper under a cover story but found the results disappointing and reverted to the grapevine technique.

Watchers work 10-hour shifts. The first shift begins as early as six or seven in the morning at a stakeout in front of the target's home and is relieved in the afternoon by the second shift responsible for putting the subject to bed. Sometimes a third shift stands watch all night. The day begins at a briefing at the Watchers' secret base of operations, a location so carefully hidden that few people in the Security Service know its whereabouts. That information is shared on a need-to-know basis only. At the briefing the Watchers are told whom they will be following that day and are given sketchy information about the individual, such as name, nationality, a few notes on personal habits, and a picture, which they study with care since it often is the sole means of identification. Sometimes the photo is old or inaccurate. The target may be 50 pounds heavier, may have started wearing glasses or grown a beard. The target's place of residence will have been checked out the previous day by the supervisor, for back entrances or any unusual features. An observation post will have been established, often in the form of a van parked across the street which looks empty but contains a Watcher concealed inside the panel section. The target's personal habits will already have been well studied for daily routine so that the RCMP usually knows what time his day begins. As soon as the observation post spots the target leaving home, the Watchers swing into action and begin picking him up several blocks away.

The Watchers avoid the street the target uses whenever it's feasible to do so. When they use the same street they keep well back and out of sight. In case they lose the target by dropping too far behind, other cars that keep abreast on parallel streets take control. At other times the Watchers keep tab by crisscrossing behind the target at each intersection. Or they will post a "99"—a passenger in the car—on the sidewalk to observe the subject drive by. By the time the target is out of sight, another 99 will have picked him up. The moment the first 99 yields control she is picked up by her driver, who leapfrogs her to the next checkpoint, if necessary by breaking speed limits and disobeying red lights. The drivers know every short cut and the cadence of every traffic light and will do what is necessary to beat the target to a destination. If the subject changes direction the whole team shifts over.

The Watchers' biggest challenge arises in the country since there are few buildings to hide behind, little traffic to fade into, and hardly any parallel roads to exploit. Being particularly vulnerable in the countryside, they employ tactics such as changing license plates on the run. However, such petty tricks are only marginally effective since intelligence officers pay little attention to license numbers, which they know are phony. For countryside surveillance the Watchers use techniques that do not resemble those used in a city. The Security Service guards these techniques most closely of all.

The size of the surveillance team varies with the sophistication of the subject and the number of cars the RCMP has available that day. A top-flight Soviet intelligence officer commands up to six cars, whereas an unschooled local subversive may get only two. The average crew has four cars and 10 people: two people in each vehicle, one person in the observation post at the residence, and another in the observation post at the office. A city the size of Ottawa, with its concentration of embassies and diplomats, has about 10 Watchers teams.

Allocating the Watchers' resources is itself a political game within the Security Service. Surveillance is so valuable an investigative tool that every day the Watchers are besieged with requests they cannot accommodate. As one Mountie put it, the Watchers would have to put a person on every street corner in Ottawa, not to mention the

Ottawa Valley, to handle all the surveillance requests. The requests always come from B Section (Counterespionage) and D Section (Countersubversion) and priorities between the two—and sometimes within the two—are worked out by the inspector in charge of the Watchers. He acts as an arbitrator. If his mediation fails, the dispute goes to the chief superintendent, whose rulings usually stick since his command includes both B and D Sections.

The Watchers are good but the targets who are trained intelligence officers are equally good at thwarting surveillance, particularly the Soviets, who train their officers in the art of countersurveillance. They take all the normal precautions to determine whether they are being followed, even to the point of driving down one-way streets the wrong way or stopping at green lights, thus forcing the surveillance car to pass. On foot they double back, duck into alleys, cross back yards, and go into theaters. One of the oldest but most effective tricks is getting into a subway train and jumping out a second before the doors close. If the Watcher jumps out also he exposes himself. If he remains inside the train he loses his target. Either way the target wins. A Soviet intelligence officer may also have colleagues providing countersurveillance to assist in determining whether he is being followed. One intelligence officer got on and off 22 buses and took a few cab rides in between without the Watchers detecting anything. He may have slipped something to one of his seat mates on the fourth bus and then taken another 18 buses. Or the whole exercise might have been a charade. Or the Soviet might have been trying to smoke out the Watchers so that a colleague could identify and follow them back to their secret headquarters.

The drug traffickers being followed by CIB Mounties take precautions only when they are doing something illegal. That in itself betrays them. The trained intelligence officer takes precautions all the time so that his behavior won't give him away when he really is making a meet.

For years Soviet Embassy personnel were not permitted to travel more than 42 kilometers outside of Ottawa without supplying the Department of External Affairs with a detailed itinerary 48 hours in advance. This assisted the Watcher Service immensely because the Soviets were required not only to list the destination, place of lodging, and length of stay but also to submit the method of travel and hour of arrival. If transportation was by car they had to disclose the selected route and the places they would stop for lunch. The Soviets always adhered to their itineraries. The rules were liberalized by Howard Green when he was Minister of External Affairs in the Diefenbaker government and the travel limit raised to 125 kilometers. The new limit was exceedingly burdensome to the Watcher Service since Soviets had the freedom to dodge around the Rideau Lakes area where surveillance was most difficult. Howard Green became a dirty name in the Security Service.

When the Watchers change shifts the switch-over is gradual—one car at a time. And before heading back to the base, each car cleans itself. It would be a catastrophe for the Security Service if a Watcher were ever followed back to the office because the entire surveillance network would be exposed.

Linda Lane worked as a Watcher for one and a half years. She was a passenger in the surveillance cars driven by men. (Women at that time were not permitted to drive.) When the target parked and went on foot, Lane got out and followed. Or she would be stationed on a street corner with a two-way radio in her purse waiting for the target to pass her checkpoint. Lane, a small blonde, left her native Newfoundland at 18 for a more exciting life in Montreal, but ended up in a secretarial pool for a large company of chartered accountants. She lived with three other young women, one of whom was a Watcher who recruited her. "Our roomates were never told what we were doing," she says. "We'd come home sometimes at unbelievable hours and we'd start really early. We'd have exciting things to talk about. But we couldn't talk."

"Robert Lemieux used to give us the runaround quite a bit. He was a radical lawyer but he dealt with subversives. I think they wanted his contacts. We had to be careful when we were following him. I think he probably knew he was being followed. I used to like working on him. He was a mover; he kept us moving. Some guys sit in one place for hours and hours. Lemieux would keep us busy."

Lane, who worked for the Watchers in Montreal on a two-year contract, one day received a phone call from a friend in Ottawa saying the RCMP had been around inquiring about her. Then the apartment of a friend in the Watchers was raided by the RCMP and both women decided to quit.

Lane's background as a Watcher became known only because her name was mentioned in the documents the RCMP submitted to Federal Court in 1974 concerning the dismissal of Mounties Don McCleery and Gilles Brunet, which is described in Chapter 16. And Lane agreed to talk about her past only because the Force bad-mouthed her in the documents by alleging she was fired for pot-smoking when she possesses a letter signed by a deputy commissioner confirming she was given a free discharge. It took her several years to talk about her old job and even then she emphasized that she would not discuss any Watchers' secrets. Every Watcher personally fears the time he or she may be exposed. Being burned is the disaster that outranks all others for it not only ruins the day's work but may jeopardize forever the usefulness of the individual Watcher. Targets have on occasion finessed a Watcher into a dead-end street and defiantly displayed an upright thumb. Linda Lane and her partner were once exposed by a Soviet in a hotel restaurant in downtown Montreal. "The guy we were following finished his breakfast and we left after a couple of minutes," she said. "I thought it was too fast. I said, 'Wait, it's too soon.' But he decided we had to go. We paid our bill and went into the lobby looking because we had lost him for a second. There he was standing at the entrance waiting to see who would come out. I wanted to burst out laughing in his face." Lane was finished for the day and would never again be assigned to that Russian.

A Watcher who is burned returns to the office immediately for debriefing. The Security Service wants to know every detail. If a car is involved, it gets repainted or traded. A badly burned Watcher is removed to an inside job. An Ottawa Watcher was approached by his Soviet target at the train station and asked if he was having a good day. The incident went unreported because the Watcher feared losing his position. However, he told colleagues and he was yanked when the story reached the office.

"I was paranoid for three years after I left the Force," says Lane. "Everywhere I'd go I'd look to see if anyone was following me. Even now I still feel it. If I go out shopping and see the same face more than twice, I follow him. It's in my blood."

A Seamy Business

Now, obviously when you are dealing with informants, whether it involves criminal matters or security matters, they do not get their information by going to Sunday school. They have to be pretty close to the operation and they have to be right in the know and frequently they are very close to the centre of those operations. If they choose to speak to us about their knowledge, believe me, we will accept...

—*Commissioner Robert H. Simmonds appearing before the House of Commons' Standing Committee on Justice and Legal Affairs, November 24, 1977.*

THE SECURITY SERVICE rarely discusses its involvement with informers. Commissioner Simmonds was denying the charge that the Force used *agents provocateurs* when the words inadvertently tumbled from his lips. Informing is a seamy business on both sides. It requires the RCMP to wade knee-deep into the world of crime, espionage, subversion, or whatever and barter with the wrongdoer. No organization likes to admit to such associations.

When the McDonald Royal Commission into RCMP wrongdoing in March, 1978, started investigating techniques for recruiting informers, the Force objected vigorously to the disclosure of a document outlining Security Service policy on informers. The practice was so close to the heart of a security service's operation that one lawyer arguing the RCMP case said he found it incredible the subject should be even discussed. The RCMP view prevailed and the McDonald Commission agreed not to release the document.

Reliable informers with deep roots in a targeted organization are the most valuable assets a security service can have. One good informer displaces the need for a dozen bugs and wiretaps and scores of surveillance agents. One appropriately placed individual compromises the effectiveness of an entire organization and without the need for breaking and entering, wiretapping, blackmailing, or other forms of illegal or questionable activities. When the Security Service gets interested in an organization its first move is (or should be) to secure an informer. "... we regard them [informers] as essential to an effective security posture," concluded the 1968 Royal Commission on Security. "We would go further, and suggest that it is impossible fully to comprehend or contain the current threat to security — especially in the field of espionage — without active operations devoted to the acquisition of human sources."

There are several kinds of informers. The supersleuths described in novels are usually penetrators. They are a special kind of informer. They infest one organization on behalf of another. Some of the most famous real-life spies were penetrators like Kim Philby, who became an ideological recruit to Soviet communism at Cambridge University during the Depression and joined British Intelligence as an active Soviet agent. His two colleagues, Guy Burgess and Donald Maclean, were also penetrators. On the other hand George Blake, now a friend of Philby's in Moscow, was not. According to his confession he joined British Intelligence as a loyal officer and was recruited during his three-year internment in the Korean War. The role of a penetrator is risky and often exciting, which is why novelists write about them. The first known Canadian penetrator of significance was Thomas Miller Beach, who in 1867 started successfully penetrating the Fenians under the name of Henri Le Caron on behalf of Britain, which was then protecting the interests of colonial Canada.[1]

The RCMP's predecessor, the North-West Mounted Police, never bothered recruiting informers among the natives and paid the price in the second Louis Riel Rebellion. The Mounties, caught by surprise, suffered defeat by armed Métis at Duck Lake, Saskatchewan,

---

[1.]   Beach later wrote a book about his experience called *25 Years in the Secret Service*.

in March, 1885, because no insider tipped them off. A good informer would have provided not only plenty of warning—the revolt had been brewing for more than a year—but also the exact time, place, and strategy along with a detailed assessment of the Métis' human and equipment resources. The mistake was not repeated in the Winnipeg general strike of 1919, when Frank Zaneth under the name of Harry Blask successfully infiltrated radical labor and later in court helped the authorities secure convictions against the leaders.

Mounties who go undercover as penetrators are known as "green light" cases. They take on a new identity and acquire a false background, or legend, to cover their past and help them withstand investigation from the targeted organization. Once they are in the organization, their objective is to work their way into a position of trust and access.

The most renowned Canadian penetrator was Johnny Leopold, the Mountie who went undercover in 1921 as a local Communist in Regina and rose as a party official. Following his exposure and expulsion in 1928, the RCMP hid him in Whitehorse as a police officer but three years later, dressed in red serge, he appeared in a Toronto courtroom to testify against his former comrades in the famous Communist Party trial.

Not all of the Security Service's penetrators are Mounties or even Canadians. Warren Hart[2] is a black American who became an informer for the FBI in 1968. He penetrated the Black Panthers and rose to the rank of captain but was later reduced to the rank of lieutenant for his political moderation and lost much of his effectiveness to the FBI. As an FBI informer he went to Toronto for nearly a week in April, 1970, to attend a conference of black militants. At the same time the Security Service was experiencing great difficulty recruiting an informer in the black community of Canada.

A year after his Toronto visit Hart was transferred to the RCMP and went to work for the Security Service at $900 a month plus expenses. His assignment was to get close to black radical Rosie Douglas. The black community in Canada was fractured and Douglas was one of the few common elements. Douglas at that time was in

[2.] The Warren Hart story received widespread publicity. The best account came from CTV and its Sunday night news magazine program W5 (then called Prime Time) on February 26, 1978. I want to thank co-host Jim Reed for his valuable assistance.

prison for his part in the 1969 computer riot at Sir George Williams University in Montreal, so Hart concentrated temporarily on Douglas's assistant, Horace Campbell.

To build up cover, Hart was arrested and deported from Canada as an undesirable and in the process spent five days in Toronto's Don Jail. The Security Service soon sneaked him back into the country. The Department of Immigration took no action over his illegal return because of his association with the Security Service. Hart became a successful penetrator and, as an aide to Douglas, a valuable asset. He quit briefly in 1973 and returned to Baltimore but soon received visitors from Canada and an offer of a $400-a-month raise to return.

Hart was even more effective upon his return to Canada. As driver to Rosie Douglas he accompanied the black leader everywhere and taped conversations with his body-pack tape recorder. One of the meetings he taped was with the RCMP's boss, Solicitor General Warren Allmand, when Douglas met him in Montreal to discuss prison reform. Hart also taped Member of Parliament John Rodriguez (NDP—Nickel Belt), once at a meeting in Sudbury and once in Hart's car, which was specially equipped with a hidden tape recorder. On several occasions Hart visited the Caribbean Islands and spied on local militant black groups although that intelligence was of interest mainly to the CIA and MI6.

In 1975 Hart received the golden handshake and $6,000 in cash and was told his services as an informer were no longer needed. Since he was in Canada illegally and no longer associated with the Security Service he was sent back to the United States.[3]

Hart was at the height of his effectiveness when Joe Burton started a series of trips to Canada from his home in Tampa, Florida. As an FBI informer, Burton received $400 a month plus another $400 a month in expenses. The FBI had formed a phony Maoist group called the Red Star Cadre and recruited Burton to join it. On the FBI's instructions Burton used the organization as a pretext to visit

---

[3.] Hart's case became known only because he had a grievance over his treatment from the Security Service. Hart says that when he returned to work in 1973 he was promised a civilian position in the RCMP when his effectiveness as a penetrator was over. Living in poverty near Baltimore and trying to support his Canadian wife and two children, Hart in 1977 wrote member of Parliament Elmer MacKay (Conservative—Central Nova) who made his plight public.

other Maoist groups for the purpose of spying on them and, by happenstance, these groups included Canadian Maoist groups. Burton claimed to have infiltrated the Communist Party of Canada (Marxist-Leninist) and become close to leader Hardial Bains, and also infiltrated the Communist Party of Quebec (Marxist-Leninist). While still an FBI informer, Burton worked in conjunction with the Security Service when he was in Canada. For his trips to Canada he received extra expense money and posed as a businessman when passing through customs. He claimed to have visited Toronto, Montreal, London, and Windsor.

The Burton case became public in 1975 when he became upset after the FBI pressured him into withdrawing from the race for city council in Tampa. Solicitor General Allmand confirmed that Burton had come to Canada with the approval of the RCMP—the FBI agreed to pass on the information collected in Canada—but Allmand said the RCMP knew of only four trips. Burton said he came to Canada on 10 or 12 occasions from 1972 to 1974.

Around the time Burton was informing on the CPCML in Toronto, Corporal Tom Kennedy under the alias as Kenny penetrated the CPCML and also got close to Hardial Bains. In 1971 Constable Rick Bennett, using the name Richard Benning, successfully penetrated the Partisan Party in Vancouver for nine months. (The Bennett case is examined in detail in Chapter 20.) The Leopolds, Harts, Burtons, Kennedys, and Bennetts are the exceptions: most informers are not penetrators but are recruited in place and bear little resemblance to the informers in some of the spy novels. In fact their life is often dull.

Some informers are walk-ins—people who have access to secret or sensitive information and for their own reasons voluntarily offer to cooperate on a one-time or continuing basis. These people may be ideological defectors or losers in an internal struggle or sometimes seek simple revenge against an individual for personal reasons. One can never be certain of motive or reliability and that is why walk-ins are treated with initial suspicion. They may be double agents.

Most informers are recruited and it is here that Simmonds' Sunday school metaphor is most appropriate. The Security Service recruits members of radical groups in a completely systematic and amoral way. It will already have a list of the organization's members by monitoring either public demonstrations or meeting places, or through the planting of bugs and wiretaps or, sometimes, by stealthily entering the office and stealing a membership list.

Once the members are identified, the Security Service starts to target individuals who for a variety of reasons are potential informers. It compiles a psychological profile to determine the individual's susceptibility to a direct approach. The first step in this profile preparation is a check into family background to see if the subject's political orientation is deep-rooted. The person may have a genuine ideological grievance against society or may be merely engaging in adventurism. Family members, neighbors, friends, co-workers, and employers may be interviewed. The checking is so low-key and careful that the interviewees, let alone the subject, do not realize it is happening. The investigator may claim to be doing a credit check, or strike up an idle conversation with a stranger and turn the discussion. Even the interviewees are sometimes investigated to ensure safety. The process can last months but the results, if successful, are so valuable that the time is a good investment.

After several months the investigator starts to assess the chances of a successful direct approach. He looks for a weakness to exploit. The individual may be psychologically weak and be susceptible to bullying, or greedy and amenable to bribery, or just disenchanted. He may also have a skeleton in his closet and be vulnerable to blackmail. The individual may become the object of wiretapping, bugging, or physical surveillance. His home may be entered surreptitiously. Nothing is taken or moved but the investigator examines the household to get a better insight into the individual. It is often at this stage, when bank statements and personal letters have been examined, that blackmailable evidence is discovered.

By this time the chances of failure in a direct approach have been reduced, but the target may still refuse. Something can be salvaged from outright rejection. The Security Service may continue the campaign and keep approaching him so openly that his colleagues cannot help but notice and start wondering about their comrade. The individual may become discredited among his own peers and while the Security Service may not have recruited an informer, it may have neutralized a radical.

Like any bureaucracy the Security Service follows established procedures in dealing with informers. The rules emanate from L Section, which deals exclusively with informers. Mounties are instructed how frequently and when to meet their contacts and generally how to handle them. They are told to be firm and develop a one-way relationship. The Security Service must always have control and impress the informer that it gives the orders and he takes them. Social relationships are prohibited. It is the practice more than the exception for the Security Service to change handlers from time to time. Frequently one Mountie recruits an informer and control is then assigned to somebody else.

L Section is precise and somewhat stingy with money. It approves every payment, no matter how small. A taxi fare can cause bureaucratic indigestion if not properly documented. In order to receive money from the Security Service the informer signs a receipt and it becomes a permanent entry in his file. That procedure is used as a safeguard against Mounties pocketing money earmarked for informers.

Members complain continually about the rigidity of the L Section's receipting requirements. "I've had guys tell me there was no way they'd sign a receipt," says one former Mountie. "And I'd wind up with a great big fight to get the money. One guy said, 'Look, the Russians don't ask me for a receipt. And yet you guys want a receipt. They're giving me thousands. You want a receipt for a $15 cab fare. Maybe I'm not dealing with the right guys.' They demanded I get a receipt from this guy. I eventually forged the guy's name to save a big hassle."

How much to pay informers is a matter of judgment and constitutes another of L Section's duties. Some of the best informers work for nothing. Generally countersubversion informers are paid, while counterespionage informers receive expenses only. The former generally have a conspiratorial interest and have to be enticed to turn traitor and money is often the persuader. The latter usually are innocent Canadians who through a set of circumstances happen to know a Soviet Embassy person or are otherwise innocently connected, such as commercial suppliers to the embassy. They usually have no conspiratorial interest and cooperate for the good of the country. The exceptions are the counterespionage targets themselves, primarily members of the Soviet Embassy who are sometimes enticed with huge amounts of money.

The form of payment varies. Some informers receive commission-type payments according to the perceived value of the information. The flaw in this arrangement is that it provides an incentive for the informer to manufacture information to boost earnings. To reduce this risk some informers receive a monthly retainer but are also provided periodic bonuses to forestall slothfulness. Another system provides for minimum and maximum payments, depending on the amount of activity in the informer's area. Since it takes considerable effort to recruit an informer, the Security Service hesitates to divest itself of one, but sometimes it is necessary when particular groups or movements fold. Occasionally attempts are made to move redundant informers into a new atmosphere. If that fails, the Security Service pays a bonus and says good-bye, like it did to Warren Hart.

Each time an informer is debriefed the Mountie handler writes up a report that goes into the general filing system. For the informer's protection, a code number instead of his name is used on each report. It is necessary to be able to identify an informer so that if he turns out to be unreliable or a double agent his contributions can be removed from the filing system. Only the handler and the people in L Section know both the code number and the informer's name. Alongside the number is an assessment rating such as "reliable," "unknown reliability," or "believed to be reliable." As the informer establishes a track record, his rating is progressively upgraded.

Once the report goes into the general filing system (F Section) it is distributed with paramilitary efficiency. If, for example, the Security Service in Winnipeg is running an informer in a local Marxist group, the report is filed in Winnipeg, with copies going to headquarters in Ottawa where, after photocopying, it is cross-referenced into several files. The first copy of the report is filed under the name of the organization, with subsequent copies filed under the names of each individual listed in the report, assuming a file on that person exists. If one doesn't it soon will, once the person's name crops up in two or three reports. To open a new file, Winnipeg advises F Section in Ottawa which assigns a file number. If the Winnipeg informer is prominent within the organization a dummy file is opened on him for his own protection, for it soon would become apparent he was an informer if he had no general-circulation file. If the group he is informing on holds a national meeting in Winnipeg his report will list the individuals attending from outside centers like Toronto, Edmonton, and Vancouver. A copy is sent to the Security Service in each of those cities so it knows who of its targets were at the Winnipeg convention. Chances are one of the visitors is also an informer, in which case more than one set of reports on the meeting will circulate.

The nerve center of this mammoth filing system resides on the fourth and fifth floors of RCMP headquarters in Ottawa. When the RCMP first moved into the gray stone building the filing system was put in the basement. The building was erected as a Catholic seminary and could not withstand the weight of the files. Later the files were moved upstairs when G and H wings were added.

The files, in keeping with the government's classification system, have three levels of classification: Confidential, Secret, and Top Secret. The Confidential files resemble ordinary business files except that the tabs contain a sequence of multicolored stripes for easy identification. A glance at the color scheme tells the file sorter what section the file belongs to. The files are so numerous and the file number so long, the sorter would otherwise go bug-eyed. Files are listed by number first and name (of individual or organization) second.

Files classified Secret use the same kind of folder with the multi-colored tab but the reports inside have a half-inch green stripe down the right-hand side from top to bottom. Most files on alleged subversive organizations and individuals are classified Secret.

Top Secret files are distinguished more prominently. A black border surrounds the folder itself and the subject's name is missing from the tab. Only a code number is listed. The reports inside have red stripes down the right-hand side. Top-Secret reports are filed in a separate area and only sergeants or above can sign them out. Corporals and constables can read them only if they have their sergeant's signature. This rule leads to anomolies. One constable wrote a report that he was barred from receiving because it was classified Top Secret. As a result he needed his sergeant's permission to read his own report.

Some successful informers have been journalists, including members of the Parliamentary Press Gallery in Ottawa. Journalists usually are paid off not in money but in kind. In effect the two sides trade information to mutual but not always equitable advantage. Journalists are valuable to the Security Service because their cover is almost perfect. They can snoop around and ask questions without arousing suspicion. One of the Press Gallery informers was the late Peter Dempson, who represented the Toronto *Telegram* in Ottawa from 1949 to 1965. Dempson in June, 1958, collaborated to induce Polish Chargé d'Affaires Mieczyslaw Sieradzki to defect to Canada. Dempson tackled his assignment with gusto and had the support of the *Telegram*. He cultivated Sieradzki for two months with lunches and visits to his home in order to build up a friendship. Despite the planning and Dempson's enthusiasm the attempt failed.

A less controllable but nevertheless valuable journalist was Tom Hazlitt, who worked for the Toronto *Star* and, like Dempson, was recruited while a member of the Press Gallery in Ottawa. Hazlitt was one of the most prolific suppliers of information and in return received more exclusive information than anybody else. His biggest spy-related story concerned Cuban defector Orlando Castro Hidalgo. It was published on June 28, 1972, and filled part of the front page and an entire inside page of the *Star*. To get the story Hazlitt flew to an unspecified American city, took a bus and cab to another unidentified American city, and met the Cuban in a room opening into a busy courtyard.

Dempson and Hazlitt were not the only journalists passing information to the Security Service. As one Mountie put it, some journalists who are very prominent today were at one time cooperating. Journalists undoubtedly refused Security Service advances but not a single approach became public until April, 1977, when Constable Jeff Hemming attempted to enlist columnist Kitty McKinsey, then of the Ottawa *Citizen*, to cultivate and inform on Soviet members of the Press Gallery. The usual procedure for recruiting a journalist is to initiate an acquaintance and, once trust is established, trade information subtly so that at the beginning neither party acknowledges the process.

"Subtle is not the word I would use with him," says McKinsey about Hemming.

Hemming tried to recruit her at the first meeting, one stranger to another. His opening words were: "We want information about the Soviet journalists in the Parliamentary Press Gallery." Furthermore,

Hemming volunteered, he had a list of journalists he wanted to approach, and then proceeded to mention one of those names, which did not inspire much confidence in his discretion. As the meeting progressed, it became obvious to McKinsey he knew very little about her. He was aware she had visited the Soviet Union the previous year but did not know about her first visit four years earlier—a fact he could have picked up from newspaper files since she had written about it extensively. Also, Hemming did not know whether to expect cooperation or antagonism.

"As a journalist I wouldn't interview people knowing so little about them," says McKinsey.

The Ottawa *Citizen* published the story and created a debate within the journalistic community over the proper relationship with the Security Service. The publicity precipitated disclosure of another crude recruitment attempt by Hemming a few months earlier, this time Peter Myers, a free-lance member of the Press Gallery. Hemming used the same approach on Myers as he later did on McKinsey: a cold telephone call followed by a visit in which he wasted no time coming to the point.

Myers, as it happened, was on friendly terms with Alexander Palladin, a Soviet member of the Press Gallery ostensibly representing the Novosti News Agency but almost certainly an intelligence officer since few legitimate Soviet journalists are so urbane and intelligent and drive a big car with power windows. Hemming said he was prepared to offer big money as an inducement for Palladin to defect and Myers supposedly was to use his friendship to facilitate the operation. Myers, in summing up the encounter, says Hemming made a tactical error in alleging that some of Myers' American friends were CIA operatives.

"I think he made a very serious tactical error in raising the subject of money," he says. "He hadn't sized me up enough."

Myers' opinion of Hemming's competence fell lower when it later became clear he did not have a membership list of the Press Gallery. The lists are printed for public distribution and even the Soviet Embassy has a copy.

"I couldn't believe it," says Myers. "I thought they were amateurs but that was just too much to believe." Myers promised to get Hemming a list.

The Keystone Cops bungling can be explained by several factors. First, the press over the years has grown more independent and more insistent on an arm's-length relationship with other organizations including, in post-Watergate North America, the Security Service. Recruitment attempts were undoubtedly bungled in the days of Dempson and Hazlitt but they were not exposed. Modern journalism sanctions such exposure. Second, the Security Service does not excel in the recruitment of informers despite its carefully honed procedures. Mounties function in a paramilitary structure based on order and discipline and are isolated from civilian life in many important ways. They are accustomed to receiving orders and obeying them; giving them and expecting compliance. They do not sufficiently appreciate tolerance of modern society and view life as "us against them" after most Canadians have adopted a different outlook. So it is not surprising that when they approach a target who is not philosophically hostile (i.e., not a member of a subversive group) they fail to undertake sufficient background checking. Third, Hemming was the wrong individual for such a delicate assignment. He was young and impatient—precisely the wrong qualities for recruiting informers.

These factors may explain the shortcomings of 1977 but fall short in accounting for the bizarre abandonment of accepted recruiting practices in Quebec during the early '70s in the aftermath of the FLQ Crisis of 1970. For about three years established techniques were replaced by thuggery and physical intimidation. These circumstances are examined separately in Chapter 19.

In the Beginning

ON THE MORNING of June 18, 1921, a lone workman, trowel in hand, climbed to the roof of Fred Farley's barn off a little-traveled road outside of Guelph, Ontario. He pretended to patch the chimney. In fact he was keeping lookout for the police, for in the hayloft of the barn 22 delegates were plotting to establish Canada's own Communist Party. The workman was Bill Moriarity, later to become General Secretary of the Communist Party of Canada, and his vigil was only part of the deep conspiracy that marked the birth of the underground party.

Over a 48-hour period delegates from Communist groups in central Canada had assembled surreptitiously at the five-acre farm. Arriving singly by round-about routes, using different modes of transportation, and traveling under pseudonyms, the delegates attracted no overt police attention that weekend. Some had deliberatedly planned their arrival for after midnight. Traffic between the cottage and the barn was kept to a minimum.

"We were not just a group of youngsters coming together in an adverturous spirit because we wanted to do something conspiratorial," said Tim Buck, who later led the party for more than three decades. "It was a very serious undertaking." Earlier experiences had taught them the value of employing strict security measures. In 1919 a small confidential gathering of activists, meeting to discuss the formation of a Communist Party, was interrupted by the appearance of the Royal North-West Mounted Police, which conducted similar raids on various other radical groups under the provisions of the War Measures Act. They were arrested before the organization could be launched.

Communism was relatively new to Canada. Previously the threats to the status quo were different in nature and had always been directed from outside the country. Through most of the 19th century the United States was interested in annexing Canada and sent north a series of agents to collect intelligence and stir up sentiment for secession. In those colonial times counterespionage operations were run by Britain on Canada's behalf. And Canada wasn't always the target; sometimes it was—through Britain—the perpetrator. For example, prior to the War of 1812 Sir James Craig, the ex-governor of Canada, hired—with London's knowledge—a man named James Henry to spy in New England and determine the possibilities for a Northeastern secession. His promised reward was a patronage position in Canada worth £1,000 a year. But the British reneged on the commitment and Henry took his story to the American Secretary of State and the Henry documents played a role in securing approval for the War of 1812 from a previously apathetic Congress and disinterested public.

By the 1860s the Fenians' romantic obsession with the idea of invading Canada from American bases to help Ireland win independence from Britain posed an irritating threat to Canada. To counter this menace a string of Canadian undercover investigators was established along the American border and was known as the Frontier Police, which became the first Canadian organization able to claim the description of Secret Service. It was headed by Gilbert McMicken, ostensibly a police magistrate in Windsor who himself would sometimes embark on undercover operations. In addition to watching the Fenians, the Frontier Police sought to prevent the work of "scalpers," Americans who encouraged soldiers to desert Her Majesty's service for the United States Army.

Secrecy was the watchword of McMicken's network: each member was issued a numbered card identifying his employment and only "in cases that admit of no delay" was he to reveal himself to the most active magistrate in the area. "You will use your utmost diligence with discretion and judgement to find out any attempt to disturb the public peace, the existence of any plot, conspiracy or organization, whereby peace would be endangered, the Queen's Majesty insulted or her proclamation of neutrality infringed," read McMicken's "General Order No. 1" on April 9, 1865.

McMicken's secret network comprised 11 men, all stationed along the American border—in Sarnia, Windsor, and the Niagara Peninsula; and in the American cities of Chicago, Detroit, and Buffalo. The American government naturally was not told about the intrusion into its territory. Boundaries and concepts of political sovereignty meant little to operatives on both sides of the border. The men were paid $1-1.50 a day plus expenses and records indicate that delays in recovery of expenses were a source of grievance. They submitted written reports to McMicken every Wednesday and Saturday.

McMicken proved highly successful in infiltrating the Fenians and got to know just about everything about the Brotherhood. One of his informers was Thomas Miller Beach, a penetrator from British Intelligence who joined the Fenian camp in 1867 under the name of Major Henri Le Caron. He promptly organized a Fenian post at Lockport, Illinois, and had access to all official reports and documents. Le Caron rose through Fenian ranks, starting as Military Organizer for the Irish Republican Army and reaching the rank of Inspector-General. In this capacity he traveled to Canada to locate arms and ammunition dumps and he used these sojourns to make contact with McMicken.

The Dominion Police was established in 1868. McMicken became Commissioner and the Frontier Police was absorbed as an arm in the new police force. The Fenians planned a raid in Manitoba a few years later and McMicken personally went there to counter it and remained in the province. When the Fenian threat died out, McMicken was elected to the Manitoba legislature and for a brief time was the Speaker.

The Dominion Police reported directly to Sir John A. Macdonald, who throughout the Fenian period was both Prime Minister and the Minister of Justice. Evidence suggests that McMicken discussed operational details with the Prime Minister although it does not appear Macdonald generally shared this intelligence with his cabinet colleagues, at least in a formal way. The Macdonald papers suggest that mail and telegraph interception formed part of the intelligence-gathering process. Secret service funds were deposited into an account in the Bank of Montreal with Macdonald possessing signing authority. He continued handling the account after he lost power in 1873, and irregularities later became a subject of debate in the Commons.

The security threat to Canada around the turn of the century was minimal since United States' designs on Canada were diminishing and because the terrorists of the day, the anarchists, were not active in Canada. There was an alleged attempt to blow up the Welland Canal and, in 1901-02, a group of Americans in Alaska called the Order of the Midnight Sun were reportedly planning to seize the Yukon. The Mounted Police sent undercover investigators to Alaska, San Francisco, and Seattle but the report was never verified in a substantial way.

During this lull the entire Dominion Police force consisted of about 150 men and almost all were security guards in front of public buildings in Ottawa. A handful had secret service duties but lacked staff and operated in a low-key liaison role. If a foreign dignitary visited Toronto, the secret service contacted the Toronto City Police to ensure protection was provided. The Toronto Police forwarded the results of the work along with a bill for the expenses. When other police forces were not available, the work was contracted out to private security firms such as Pinkertons. The practice created some dissatisfaction because the firms used were American.

The Mounted Police was formed in 1873 as the North-West Mounted Police but its role in security lay a number of decades in the future since it was confined to the west and lacked jurisdiction over espionage. In those years its contributions to maintaining Canada's security from outside sources was limited to carrying out the Dominion Police's requests in the same way that other local police forces did. Plans were devised in 1887 to hire four men as clandestine detectives who would be "ever secret and watchful" but were abandoned because of cost. A similar scheme was approved in 1904 and this became the forerunner of the Criminal Investigation Branch. It was the closest the Mounted Police came to creating a secret service in its pre-RCMP days.

When Canada went to war in 1914 security operations were made the responsibility of a number of agencies and departments by regulations passed under the War Measures Act. Postal regulations covering the opening of mail came under the Postmaster General; censorship was the duty of the Secretary of State. Military Intelligence fell under the militia. The Dominion Police was supervised by the Minister of Justice, and the NWMP came under the jurisdiction of the Privy Council. Everything was decentralized and uncoordinated.

When the hastily conceived War Measures Act was passed in August, 1914, hundreds of thousands of immigrants from countries such as Germany, Austria-Hungary, Poland, and Czechoslovakia became enemy aliens overnight and some were interned. The Dominion Police had responsibility for the investigations and internment. During this time the Mounted Police were policing Alberta, Saskatchewan, northern Manitoba, and the Territories and, as well, had become agents for the Dominion Police in these jurisdictions. The circumstances changed quickly after the British intercepted and decoded a telegram from Germany's Foreign Secretary, Arthur Zimmermann, to his Ambassador in Washington ordering German agents to begin subversive action against Canada from inside the United States.

> JANUARY 3, 1916. (SECRET).—GENERAL STAFF DESIRES ENERGETIC ACTION IN REGARD TO PROPOSED DESTRUCTION OF CANADIAN PACIFIC RAILWAY AT SEVERAL POINTS WITH A VIEW TO COMPLETE AND PROTRACTED INTERRUPTION OF TRAFFIC. CAPTAIN BOEHM, WHO IS ON YOUR SIDE AND IS SHORTLY RETURNING, HAS BEEN GIVEN INSTRUCTIONS. INFORM THE MILITARY ATTACHE AND PROVIDE THE NECESSARY FUNDS.
>
> ZIMMERMANN

The telegram was cause for alarm since Canada was virtually defenseless against this kind of attack. The United States was not in the war at that time and so little scrutiny was being placed on German descendants living in that country, thus allowing German Americans to cross the border at will for acts of sabotage. The Canadian government concluded that an efficient border patrol was needed to stop such forays, and consequently the Mounted Police dropped its provincial contracts and re-formed into a border unit. Soon thereafter the British intercepted and decoded another

Zimmermann telegram, this one ultimately intended for the German Ambassador in Mexico City, offering sections of southwestern United States to Mexico if it supported Germany in the war. The telegram was given to the Americans and brought them into the war, thereby dissipating the need for a Mounted Police border force because Americans started scrutinizing German descendants and nationals inside their border. There never was any German sabotage in western Canada.

Radical left-wing activity within Canada mushroomed toward the end of the war, inspired to some degree by the Bolshevik Revolution in Russia, although there were other stimulating factors as well. Growing labor militancy also frightened the government. The Wobblies, the Industrial Workers of the World, were founded by American socialists impatient with the conservative approach of established trade unionism and made inroads into western Canada with their call for workers' control of industry, mines, and transport, and for direct union action that circumvented the traditional democratic process. Alarmed employers began pressuring the federal government to curb such activity. The government was more concerned about these groups' opposition to the war, seeing it in the context of treason. Systematic surveillance of radical organizations began in the fall of 1918. The Dominion Police, the Mounted Police, Military Intelligence, Immigration, and the Press Censor compiled dossiers on several hundred known radicals and Prime Minister Robert Borden's security analysts began urging a hard line to shut down radical organizations.

In May, 1918, the Prime Minister commissioned Charles Cahan, a Montreal lawyer who worked with the British Secret Service against German espionage in the United States, to study radicalism across Canada. Cahan was an alarmist and submitted a report in mid-September identifying Bolshevism as the root cause of radical militancy and implicating the Wobblies in the perceived Bolshevik conspiracy. (Sir Percy Sherwood, the Commissioner of the Dominion Police, disagreed with Cahan's view of the Wobblies.) He recommended that the list of enemy aliens in Canada be extended to include Russians, Ukrainians, and Finns. In addition, Cahan called for centralization of security operations, suppression of radical organizations, prohibition of "foreign" language propaganda, and a "widely extended" right of search. He also proposed establishment of a Public Safety Branch of the Department of Justice to coordinate security operations. Within two weeks the government had banned 14 radical organizations and outlawed meetings held in the languages of countries with which Canada was at war, as well as Russian, Ukrainian, and Finnish. Cahan was appointed Director of the newly created Public Safety Branch. Howver, Cahan's hard-line approach soon proved too extreme for the government and he resigned early in 1919 and was not replaced.

The return to Canada of thousands of demobilized soldiers, facing high unemployment and rising prices, set off a new round of fears in Ottawa. Labor militancy culminated in Winnipeg on May 15, 1919, when building and metal trades workers put down their tools and refused to work until employers both recognized their collective status and raised their wages. Within weeks the traditional economy of the entire city was stopped as other workers struck in sympathy. Even the city police force became sympathetic and was dismissed and replaced by special constables to maintain order. As well, supporting strikes erupted in other cities. The Red Scare had reached its peak and the government viewed the events as a seditious conspiracy directed by Bolsheviks from Russia. The strike broke into fatal violence when demonstrators persisted in holding an illegal march on June 21 and the Mounted Police, after the riot act was read, moved to break it up. Two men were killed and more than 30 injured. Four days later the strike ended.

After it was over the shaken Borden government introduced two pieces of legislation to ensure that such an event would never happen again. First, on July 7, 1919, the notorious Section 98 of the Criminal Code was enacted (virtually without discussion in the House of Commons) making it an offense punishable by up to 20 years in jail to belong to "an unlawful association"—defined as one the professed purpose of which was "to bring about any governmental, industrial, or economic change in Canada by use of force, violence, or injury to persons or property" or by threats of such methods. The onus was on the accused to disprove membership in an illegal organization once a statutory minimum of evidence had been produced.

The Borden government's second piece of legislation followed quickly and disbanded the Dominion Police and upgraded the Royal

North-West Mounted Police into a national force called the Royal Canadian Mounted Police. For the first time security was carried out by one organization and the RCMP would have detachments in each province and sufficient staff to do the work without resorting to local police forces or private detective agencies.

The forming of the RCMP brought secret service work into the public spotlight for the first time. Prior to 1920, few people realized that Canada had a security organization and those who did rarely discussed it. After 1920 the RCMP's work of surveilling and infiltrating radical groups became identified and the subject of controversy. J. S. Woodsworth, for example, almost every year in the House of Commons called for the dissolution of the RCMP's Intelligence Branch. There was also a significant change in circumstances. Previously the threat to Canada's security always originated outside the country, whether from the Americans, the Fenians, the Germans, or the international Marxists. But in the last few years local Communists in Canada had flourished in number so much that the new RCMP perceived the threat as originating almost entirely from inside the country (although with assistance from external sources).

So it was in this unfriendly atmosphere of political militancy and official prosecution that the Communist Party of Canada was formed in 1921. The party was illegal the minute it was born because the lingering War Measures Act remained in force, not to mention the outlawing effect of Section 98 of the Criminal Code. The party's heavy emphasis on security and secrecy is understandable, for one of the 22 delegates in the Guelph barn was an RCMP agent who had been originally recruited for the Dominion Police by a private detective agency.

The Communist Party existed under the leadership of General Secretary Bill Moriarity but because of its secrecy nobody knew about it. The leaders soon realized that little could be accomplished without publicity and an established base from which to operate. The decision was made to go public and the Communists circumvented the legal ban by forming two parties: the "A" party, called the Workers' Party of Canada, which constituted the public wing and its legal base; and the "Z" party, the Communist Party itself, which remained underground and illegal. With the Workers' Party of Canada acting as a front for the banned Communist Party organizing got underway. When the War Measures Act finally lapsed in 1924 the overt Workers' Party and the clandestine Communist Party were merged into a single unit as the Communist Party of Canada. From then on the party adopted a high profile although it remained effectively illegal under Section 98 which could be invoked at the government's pleasure.

From the moment it was founded, the Communist Party of Canada became an unquestioning disciple of the Soviet Union. A Comintern envoy from the United States named Caleb Harrison— assuming the alias "Atwood" while in Canada—was in the barn at Guelph that June weekend in 1921 and provided $3,000 from Moscow and generally supervised the convention. The new party, after pledging its loyalty and allegiance to the Soviet Union and recognizing Moscow's primacy in world communism, adopted a resolution applying for affiliation with the Comintern. The application was accepted and the acceptance, Tim Buck said later, "made us feel proud no end." The Canadian stalwarts were mesmerized by Russia and Moscow could not impose policies or duties unpalatable enough for the Canadian party to reject or rebel. When new recruits applied for membership they signed a form pledging allegiance to the Comintern and the Communist Party of Canada—in that order— and agreed to abide by party discipline. Once accepted, they were expected to be Communists first and Canadians second. Their commitment to party discipline was no empty pledge. Once the party took a position it was gospel and had to be supported with enthusiasm. Failure to do so was grounds for expulsion. Every year the party sent delegates to Moscow and they returned with instructions on Moscow's new party line which was inevitably accepted.

Reverend A. E. Smith, in his book *All My Life*[1] about his experiences in the Communist Party, illustrates the hero worship for all things Russian, especially regarding his visit to the Soviet Union in 1932:

> Finally, the moment came. The guard shouted: "Crossing the Soviet border." Tears of joy, which I could not repress, streamed down my face. I said to Fred: "It overwhelms me to realize that I have lived to the day when my old eyes shall see the Land of Socialism." I will never forget that moment. It was at that moment I had a new sense of the purpose of my life. I

[1.] *All My Life* (Toronto: Progress Books, 1949).

had a new comprehension of the purpose of the universe. The Soviet Union, in abolishing, once and for all, the exploitation of man by man, has advanced the well-being of modern human society to a greater degree than any other single event in history.

Smith visited a prison. "What a contrast to our Canadian prison system!" he wrote. "The principal object in the Soviet in dealing with crime and criminals is to seek a remedy without punishment, if possible. This is the very reverse of capitalist practice where we have punishment without remedy." According to Smith, the Russians were tearing down prisons because they were empty and soon all prisons in Russia would be torn down. (He also concluded the Soviets would soon cure alcoholism.)

The Maurice Spector incident shows how Communists were punished within the party if they ever questioned or contradicted the official party line as dictated by Moscow. Spector was the party's theoretician, a brilliant individual, and the only original member with an academic orientation. He was one of the 22 original delegates at Guelph and was only 23 years old when he was made chairman of the Communist Party's early overt wing, the Workers' Party of Canada. He was barely 30 when he became the only Canadian ever elected to the Executive Committee of the Comintern, the Comintern's highest body, where he sat with individuals like Stalin, Molotov, and Bukharin. When Spector returned from the Comintern's Sixth World Congress in Moscow in 1928 he admitted his support for Trotsky after keeping quiet several years. Leon Trotsky by this time had been denounced and was living in exile in Central Asia. As soon as Spector expressed his feelings the Canadian party's Central Committee convened an emergency meeting to investigate the "political position of Comrade Spector." Spector was summarily dismissed.

The man who convened the emergency meeting and pressed the charge against Spector was Jack MacDonald, who as General Secretary was the party's leader. Within months he, too, was in trouble for being too right-wing. MacDonald had expressed support for "American Exceptionalism," which claimed that North America was an exception to the Marxist theory of revolution and therefore would have to be overthrown in a different economic cycle. This contradicted the Moscow line that Marxism applied equally to all capitalist countries and MacDonald was given a leave of absence and later expelled when he refused to submit to a Comintern directive ordering him to recant and lead the fight against American Exceptionalism. MacDonald was succeeded as General Secretary by Tim Buck, who unwaveringly supported Moscow throughout his 33-year rule and approved initiatives such as the 1956 invasion of Hungary.

The Canadian party adopted a position on Canadian independence until Moscow rebuked it and insisted that Canada was an imperialist country despite the fact Canada had no army to speak of and no colonies. Party stalwart Stewart Smith, who spent two years at the Lenin School in Moscow, wrote an article in the Canadian party's official organ, *The Worker,* confessing the error of his ways. And to show it was not merely going through the motions of recanting, the party set out on an investigative hunt to unearth evidence proving that Canada indeed was imperialistic.

The Communist Party denounced the CCF (Co-operative Commonwealth Federation) when it was founded in 1933 and said the new party represented a retrogressive step in the path to socialism. This stance was taken because Moscow decreed that moderate left-wing organizations represented the biggest enemy of communism. J. S. Woodsworth was personally branded a "yellow dog" and "traitor to the working class." However, soon after Hitler took over Germany the Soviet Union started worrying about his designs on Eastern Europe and the official line laid down at the Seventh Congress of the Comintern in August, 1935, was that fascism represented the biggest enemy and that henceforth Communists around the world were to forge alliances with moderates and socialists. The Communist Party of Canada obediently offered to form a People's Front with the CCF to fight the growing menace of fascism in Canada but was decisively spurned. That did not stop the party from withdrawing half a dozen nominated candidates in the 1935 federal election to avoid splitting the working-class vote. At one point, at the initiative of Moscow, the Canadian party even proposed an alliance with William Aberhart's Social Credit regime in Alberta.

The anti-fascist policy shifted somewhat a few years later when Hitler and Stalin signed a non-aggression and friendship pact. Again the party dutifully accepted the change. Hitler soon thereafter invaded Poland in what was to become the start of World War Two and General Secretary Tim Buck's first action was to send Prime Minister Mackenzie King a telegram declaring his "full support of the Polish people." Buck's concern was that British Prime Minister Neville Chamberlain would again compromise with Hitler and leave poor Poland abandoned. It was after Buck sent the telegram that Stalin joined the attack and, by agreement, divided up Poland with Hitler. This latest turn of events proved extremely unpalatable but the Canadian Communists again swallowed principle and reversed their position. Thus an "anti-fascist war" became an "imperialist war." The Communists mounted an all-out anti-war campaign and did everything possible to retard and subvert Canada's war effort. The Canadian government responded by banning the Communist Party and arresting key leaders although a number of them, including Tim Buck, escaped arrest and went underground where they continued their fight. The Toronto *Clarion,* one of several Communist underground newspapers, declared: "Canadian capitalism, not German capitalism, is our main enemy."

The ultimate flip-flop happened in 1941 after Hitler invaded Russia. The Canadian party again followed its Soviet masters and the "imperialist war" became a "just war." Six days after Hitler's action the Communist Party issued a statement that included the following: "For the party and the working class movement, the question is simple. The Soviet Union is attacked and everything must be done to ensure the decisive defeat of the fascist aggressor." The underground Communist leaders surfaced and, after short stays in jail, became the hardest-working and most dedicated leaders in support of Canada's war effort. The Communists did not limit their attacks to the war's opponents. Supporters whose efforts were only lukewarm also came under fire. Ironically, the bourgeois capitalists producing armaments became virtuous while working-class militants who insisted on immediate reform were dishonorable for refusing to surrender the right to strike during the war.

The Communist Party, which after 1943 became the Labour Progressive Party, partly to circumvent the illegality of the old party, sacrificed popular support by adhering to the strict dicta of the Moscow line. The disclosures of Igor Gouzenko in 1946, the Czechoslovakia take-over in 1948, the Berlin blockade in 1948, the Hungarian Revolution in 1956, the Czechoslovakian invasion in

1968—with each event a segment of members could take it no longer and left the party until it was reduced to a shell in the late 1950s and 1960s.

Given the compliance of the party, it is not surprising that members started gathering intelligence on behalf of the Soviet Union. According to the Royal Commission into the Gouzenko disclosures, espionage activities dated back as early as 1924:

> It became manifest at an early stage of this Inquiry, and has been overwhelmingly established by the evidence throughout, that the Communist movement was the principal base within which the espionage network was recruited; and that it not only supplied personnel with adequately "developed" motivation, but provided the organizational framework wherein recruiting could be and was carried out safely and efficiently. In every instance but one, Zabotin's Canadian espionage agents were shown to be members of or sympathisers with the Communist Party.

The Communist Party also became involved in a successful passport operation that saw Communist espionage officers around the world traveling under false identities with Canadian passports.

The party attracted close scrutiny from the RCMP but none of these espionage activities was discovered until Igor Gouzenko defected from the Russian Embassy. The RCMP viewed the Communist Party in a criminal context in terms of stopping the activities and arresting the perpetrators and gaining legal redress and not in a subversive or espionage one (in terms of neutralizing or undermining the activities) though through much of the '20s the Force, under Commissioner Cortlandt Starnes, generally opposed laying criminal charges against the Communist Party. However, the Conservatives under R. B. Bennett were elected in 1930 and the new Prime Minister was obsessed with communism and appointed as Starnes' successor Major-General James MacBrien, who was an even greater anti-Communist fanatic. On August 11, 1931, 11 days after Mac-Brien's appointment took effect, plainclothes RCMP officers and municipal police in Toronto raided the party's headquarters and arrested General Secretary Tim Buck and seven other leaders at their homes. They were charged under Section 98 with being members of an "unlawful association."

At the trial disbelief greeted John Leopold when, clad in an RCMP uniform complete with red tunic and big hat, he strode to the witness stand and snapped to attention. Leopold, an RCMP non-commissioned officer, was known to the defendants as Jack Esselwein, one of the first recruits to the party after the Guelph convention in 1921. He had held the positions of President of the Painters' Union in Regina and Secretary of the Trades and Labour Council. Leopold had been taken into the Force specifically to infiltrate the Bolshevik left. Born in Czechoslovakia, he fell four inches short of minimum RCMP height requirements and possessed a pair of sad eyes and a nervous demeanor that fitted perfectly his eventual role as a hunted and harassed Communist. Leopold successfully maintained his cover for eight years—from March, 1920, to April, 1928—which represents an impressive run in such circumstances. M. J. Coldwell at one point described him in the Commons as the most rabid Communist agitator in Regina. Leopold was an organizer in Regina and was transferred to Winnipeg and Toronto for party work and had suffered arrest for taking part in a Communist demonstration and become good friends with many of the leading personalities, including Tim Buck and Comintern representative Charles E. Scott.

The eight Communists were convicted on one charge of being officers of the Communist Party of Canada and on another one of being members of the party but went free (on appeal) on the charge of being involved in a seditious conspiracy. They were sent to the penitentiary at Kingston. It was a case of winning the battle but losing the war. Section 98, which put the onus of proof on the accused, was such an unjust and sweeping piece of legislation— it restricted the rights of association, freedom of discussion, and publishing of literature and carried a maximum penalty of 20 years in prison; one man in Montreal was charged for wearing a badge—that the convictions made martyrs out of them. A campaign was launched for Tim Buck's release and the repeal of Section 98, led by the Canadian Labour Defence League whose membership rose from 25,000 to 43,000. During the latter part of 1933 nearly half a million Canadians, most of whom had no sympathy for communism, signed resolutions and petitions demanding Section 98's repeal. Opposition Leader Mackenzie King promised to do so once he regained power. Even Prime Minister R. B. Bennett was sufficiently pressured to free the jailed men years ahead of schedule in November, 1934. Buck's release was supposed to be quiet but by the time his train arrived in Toronto 4,000 people jammed Union Station, immobilizing street traffic outside, not to mention the railway station. Mackenzie King returned to power the following year and, as promised, repealed the legislation in short order. The laying of charges against the Communist leaders succeeded in nothing except winning sympathy for a party that deserved none.

With the rise of Hitler, vigilance on Fascists in Canada was resumed. Fascism won some support across the country but particularly heavily in Quebec, where journalist Adrien Arcand founded the National Social Christian Party based on Hitler's nazism and Mussolini's fascism, and the prairies where vast numbers of German immigrants had settled. Some of these groups imitated their European counterparts so closely that they wore regulation blue, black, or brown shirts and used stiff-armed salutes. In 1938 various Fascist groups across Canada combined into the National Unity Party under Arcand's leadership. The party, ordered to disband by the government under the War Measures Act soon after World War Two started, went underground. Raids were conducted on the party offices in the spring of 1940 and so much material was confiscated that six trucks were required to cart it away. Arcand was captured in his mountain hideout along with his chief lieutenant, a dentist named Dr. Noël Lecarie, who had $7,000 stuffed in his pockets. Arcand and some of his key aides were placed in internment camps until the end of the war.

During the war the RCMP had much more success in scrutinizing the underground Nazis—although not the Italians—than it ever had with Communists because here the Force's operations more closely resembled a security agency than a police force. This change in tactics was uncharacteristic and may have been inspired by the RCMP's German translator, who had been a Communist working as a sabotage officer for the Russians before defecting and joining British Intelligence. Then when he was exposed as a British agent, he was given a civilian job in the RCMP. He was one of the few employees on the Force who had legitimate intelligence training and experience and he worked on anti-Nazi duties for the Force. The RCMP controlled and manipulated the underground ring of Nazi conspirators in Quebec during World War Two. The effort was aided by ingenuity and luck on the part of the RCMP and incompetence on the part of German Intelligence. Germany had a habit of recruiting agents through pressure and force and this proved to be an over-whelming weakness, for lacking the motivation and dedication, the agents tended to be either ineffective, not loyal, or vulnerable to reverse pressure.

During the war the RCMP took into custody at least three German agents slipped into Canada for the purpose of gathering intelligence. The first agent was captured in southern Ontario and the circum-stances surrounding the capture are still not public.

German spy number two was dropped off by submarine in Chaleur Bay off Quebec's Gaspé Peninsula on November 10, 1942. The man buried his German uniform on the beach and, wearing civilian clothes and carrying two suitcases, walked to the nearby town of New Carlisle and booked a day room in the local hotel, intending to board the afternoon train for Montreal, which would be his base of operations. As it happened, the hotel owner was an amateur Sherlock Holmes and was aware that the Gaspé area was a convenient place to drop off German agents. So when the stranger showed up at his hotel out of the tourist season he was naturally curious. The owner casually asked if he had arrived by bus. The agent said he had. That reply aroused suspicion since no bus had arrived. The owner also detected a strong odor, which he could not identify but which was the odor people get from traveling in a submarine. While the agent was in the dining room having lunch the owner entered his room but could not open the luggage. However, he found a discarded package of Belgian safety matches that had been out of circulation since before the war. His suspicions were confirmed when the stranger, before leaving for the train station, paid for his lunch with outdated, oversized Canadian bills. The hotel owner called the Quebec police who, after boarding the train and sitting beside the man, searched his baggage and found $5,000 in Canadian bills, another $1,000 in gold coins, a radio receiver and transmitter, and a revolver. By the time the RCMP arrived the man had confessed to being a German naval officer. He had risen to the rank of captain in the German Navy and had been decorated with the Iron Cross, but when the Gestapo discovered he had an association with a woman who was part Jewish, he was sent to a concentration camp and forced to become an espionage agent.

With this kind of background, the German agreed to become a double agent. The RCMP set him up in Montreal, where he made two broadcasts a day to his masters in Hamburg. Whether the double-agent operation was successful is not known positively. It did not seem to be, for despite the RCMP's efforts communication went only one way. Hamburg asked the questions and Montreal supplied "information," but it was never possible to draw any clues out of Germany. Furthermore, Hamburg refused to acknowledge the agent's requests for more money. Evidence suggests the RCMP erred in transmitting directly to Hamburg. In order to transmit over such a distance the Force boosted the power of the agent's radio since his equipment was incapable of reaching Hamburg. The Germans undoubtedly were aware of the broadcasting range of their agent's radio and must have become suspicious when his dispatches reached Germany directly. It is likely that German Intelligence had planned on picking them up through submarines in the Atlantic. The agent never would have been told this. After nearly a year of unsuccessful effort, by which time the agent's money would have ordinarily run out, the RCMP terminated the double-agent attempt. His usefulness finished, the agent was put into the custody of British Intelligence. At this point the case normally would have been finished as far as the RCMP was concerned, but the Force adeptly got extra mileage out of the spy's existence. The RCMP German translator took on the agent's identity and, with the help of a low-level infiltrator, made contact with underground Quebec Nazis. The translator pretended to be a ranking German intelligence officer sent to Canada to oversee the Quebec party's activity in performing espionage on behalf of Germany. The Quebec Nazis fell for the scheme, with the result that their duties were dictated by an RCMP employee. The translator was regimental and domineering in his relations with the Quebeckers and scorned their amateurishness. He put them to work collecting intelligence concerning the locations of armaments factories and checking freighter traffic along the St. Lawrence River. "Some of their reports were most interesting and would have been of value to the enemy," wrote Cliff Harvison, the Mountie in charge of the case who later became RCMP Commissioner.[2]

[2.] This case is outlined in detail by Harvison in his book *The Horsemen* (Toronto: McClelland and Stewart, 1967). Most of the information used here is taken from his account.

By early 1944 the Quebec Nazis were getting restless and yearned for larger operations, such as carrying out acts of sabotage. In fact they were getting so aggressive that the RCMP translator feared losing control. To hold them in check, German agent number one, captured in Ontario, was brought to Quebec for one meeting with three leading Quebec Nazis. He was billed as the chief German intelligence officer in North America and was even more arrogant and demanding.

"I am told that you and your associates are eager to get on with the business of sabotage," the supposed spy master said after keeping them waiting nearly an hour. "This is nonsense. We are not playing a game of fireworks. We are fighting a war, and you will follow orders just as soldiers in the field must follow orders. I want no more of your idiotic talk of sabotage. When the time comes, you will get your orders. Until then there must be no nonsense."[3] The German "officer" ordered everybody to remain in the room for half an hour after he left and departed in a hail of heel-clicking and "Heil Hitlers." That performance intimidated the group and kept the Canadian Nazis in line for the rest of the war.

German agent number three landed by submarine on a sandy beach about 20 miles northeast of Saint John, New Brunswick, in the late summer of 1943. The German had immigrated to Canada before the war and worked in Flin Flon, Manitoba. He had enjoyed Canadian life and had returned to Germany to visit his parents when the war broke out. He was conscripted into the German Army and earmarked for espionage duties in Canada. After receiving training in shortwave transmission he was given a National Registration card removed from the body of a Canadian soldier killed at Dieppe as well as a wad of American currency and other supplies, and shipped across the Atlantic. The agent wanted nothing to do with espionage and upon landing in New Brunswick buried his equipment on the beach and took the train to Montreal to spend his money and live the good life. He wanted to turn himself in but believed the authorities would confiscate his money and send him to a prisoner-of-war camp. In Montreal he was picked up by the RCMP as a found-in in a brothel but avoided exposure by playing the role of a worried husband.

[3.] Quote taken from Harvison's *The Horsemen*.

He moved to Ottawa and buried half his money in a park and continued a life of leisure and spent hours listening to the debate in the House of Commons. After almost a year, in need of more money, he went to retrieve the other half of his hidden supply but forgot precisely where he buried it. Out of money, he turned himself in to the RCMP in the fall of 1944. By this time he was useless as a potential double agent and was interned in a prisoner-of-war camp until the end of the war and then became an interpreter in refugee camps.

All these operations, whether against the Communists or the Nazis, were carried out by regular members of the Force. Although an Intelligence Branch had been established when the RCMP was formed in 1920, it performed only a liaison function and had virtually no staff. Colonel Charles Hamilton, officially called the Liaison-Intelligence Officer, headed the branch for most of the period between the two world wars, starting with its formation and continuing until his death late in 1933. Before joining the old Royal North-West Mounted Police in 1914, he was a journalist, former member of the Parliamentary Press Gallery in Ottawa, and reporter for several newspapers, including the Toronto *Globe* and the Montreal *Gazette*. In covering the Boer War he got the world scoop on the Battle of Paardeburg for the Toronto *Globe*. The Intelligence Branch for the most of the rest of the between-war period was headed up by Charles Rivett-Carnac, later RCMP Commissioner, who in 1935 was appointed Intelligence Officer and Editor of the *RCMP Quarterly*.

Canada seemed safe from systematic espionage. Canadians never appreciated the fact that Communist espionage included Canada in its objectives and the RCMP had uncovered little evidence of intelligence-gathering. But shortly after World War Two ended cipher clerk Igor Gouzenko defected from the Soviet Embassy in Ottawa and brought with him secrets revealing that Canadian institutions were penetrated by Soviet spies. The disclosures prodded the Canadian government into adopting measures for the security screening of civil servants and slowly made the RCMP realize it had to change the structure of the Intelligence Branch and revise its strategy.

The Gouzenko Defection

IT WAS HOT that evening of September 5, 1945, and cipher clerk Igor Gouzenko tagged along with a group of colleagues walking from the Soviet Embassy on Charlotte Street in Ottawa en route to a nearby movie theater. As they neared the theater Gouzenko feigned disappointment.

"Damn it, I've seen that show," he said. "You fellows go ahead because it's a good picture. I'll take a streetcar and go to another show downtown."[1]

With that, Gouzenko headed toward the nearest streetcar stop, but as his friends disappeared into the theater he turned around and retraced his steps to Charlotte Street and the Soviet Embassy. His actions there would make history.

Officially, Gouzenko was secretary and interpreter to Colonel Nicolai Zabotin, the military attaché in the embassy. In fact Zabotin was the head of Military Intelligence for Canada and Gouzenko his cipher clerk. Gouzenko was short, heavy-set, blond, and only 26 years old. He had come to Canada two years earlier with his wife Anna and infant son Andrei, and in that short time both he and Anna had become alienated from Soviet life and enamored with prosperous and free Canada. But Gouzenko was being recalled to Moscow and

---

[1]. This quotation and details of Gouzenko's movements on September 5-6 are taken from his autobiography, *This Was My Choice* (London: Eyre and Spottiswoode, 1948).

he and his wife, dreading the thought of returning, after much discussion and soul-searching decided to defect. But they felt they needed collateral and the embassy's espionage secrets to which Gouzenko had access would be that collateral. Gouzenko returned to the embassy that night for the last time to get the documents that would make him a hero in Canada and guarantee his acceptance and protection by the Canadian government.

Zabotin, his boss, was out of the way for the evening, attending a function at the National Film Board. Gouzenko nodded to the security guard at the entrance as he signed in for some supposed night work. A second later he almost froze as he spotted Vitali Pavlov sitting in the reception room. Pavlov was officially Second Secretary but was in reality the dreaded chief of the NKVD [the secret police later renamed the KGB] in Canada. Gouzenko worked for Military Intelligence, which was independent of the NKVD; nonetheless, he was terrified of Pavlov. He managed to act naturally and, paying no heed to the eagle-eyed Pavlov, walked to the staircase leading to the top-secret cipher room on the second floor, and pressed the secret bell underneath the bannister to signal his arrival. Once on the second floor, as usual, he pulled open the heavy velvet curtains hiding the steel door leading to the secret operation center and put his face in front of the door's small opening so the guard inside could identify him. Even the ambassador was denied access to this secluded area. After that an even larger and more formidable steel door had to be opened for him. Inside was a carpeted corridor with offices opening off it. Each office had a steel safe and windows painted solid and protected by iron bars and steel shutters. Gouzenko was the only member of Zabotin's staff who worked permanently behind this steel fortress.

"Working late again?" inquired his friend Ryazanov, the cipher clerk for the commercial attaché.

"No," replied Gouzenko. "There are just a couple of telegrams to do and then I'll catch an 8:30 show."

He disappeared into his office, Room 12, on the right side of the corridor and scooped out of his desk a pile of documents revealing that Soviet Military Intelligence operated several spy rings in Canada and had acquired vital nuclear secrets from Canada's project at Chalk River. For a month, ever since Gouzenko was told of his recall, he had scoured the files and memorized material, turning up the corners on the most important documents so that he could retrieve them quickly on the day of his defection. Earlier, Gouzenko had removed two telegrams and a report and replaced them with duplicates in the event his plan failed. The three documents were in his apartment on a pantry shelf next to a box of matches in case they had to be destroyed quickly. If Gouzenko was discovered, Anna was to flee with their son Andrei and use those documents to buy protection and asylum in Canada. The two telegrams were requests from Moscow for information on the atom bomb, and the report was from the embassy to Moscow giving details on the re-election of a key Soviet spy, Member of Parliament Fred Rose, a senior member of the Communist Party of Canada who acted as a talent spotter for the Soviet Union.

Today was the day. The documents, a collection of 109 pink, blue, and white pieces of paper, had been carefully culled from the files earlier in the day and placed in his desk. Now he opened his shirt and carefully arranged them around his body. He looked sloppy with the documents bulging underneath his clothes but he thought the evening was so warm he would attract no interest.

"It's too hot to stick around here," Gouzenko called out to Ryazanov as he left. "Why don't you skip out with me to the show?"

"Fat chance of getting away with anything around here," grumbled Ryazanov. "Besides, Pavlov is downstairs. Thanks just the same, I'd better stick around."

The mention of the NKVD chief's name once again made Gouzenko shudder. He descended the staircase carefully lest the hidden documents shift and make his shirt bulge too obviously or one of the smaller papers slip past his waist and down a pant leg. Although he was sweating at this point he did not dare reach into his pocket for a handkerchief in case he disturbed the documents. Fortunately Pavlov had gone by the time he signed out.

Gouzenko boarded a streetcar for the Ottawa *Journal* on Queen Street where he planned to turn over the documents and tell his story. Once the *Journal* exposed Soviet spying in Canada he would be safe. When Gouzenko reached the sixth floor where the editor had his office he panicked and fled. Running and walking, he returned to his apartment on Somerset Street and pulled the perspiration-soaked papers out of his shirt. His cool and courageous fair-haired wife counseled him calmly as she tried to dry the papers by fanning them through the air. His composure regained, Gouzenko set out for the *Journal* again.

The editor had gone for the night but Gouzenko produced the documents for Night City Editor Chester Frowde and explained that they proved that the Soviets were stealing atomic secrets from Canada. Kooks were always coming into the office with fantastic claims. Frowde, a short, thin man with a pinched face and a perpetual worried look on his face, was busy putting out the Northern Ontario edition. Besides, the documents were in Russian. He hardly glanced at them from beneath his green eyeshade before dismissing the scoop of the decade.

"I'm sorry," he said. "This is out of our field. I would suggest you go to the Royal Canadian Mounted Police or come back in the morning to see the editor."

Gouzenko protested that by that time the Russian secret police would be after him.

"Sorry, I'm busy," said Frowde as he stood up and walked away, leaving a dejected Gouzenko by himself.

Gouzenko walked the few blocks to the Justice Building, which housed RCMP headquarters as well as Justice Minister Louis St. Laurent's office. He was stopped at the door and sent away by a Mountie who told him to come back in the morning.

"But it is desperately necessary that I reach the minister right away—by telephone at least," the Russian pleaded.

"It can't be done," replied the Mountie.

Dejected and at wits' end, Gouzenko returned home. He and Anna agreed to try again in the morning. They figured they were safe until midday since he did not have to report to work until noon and the documents were not likely to be discovered missing before that. The next day Gouzenko and Anna, six months pregnant, set out with two-year-old Andrei for the Justice Building in hopes of giving the documents to Mr. St. Laurent. The papers were stuffed in Anna's purse and in the event that the NKVD spotted them she would flee with the papers while Gouzenko created a diversion.

Gouzenko's explanation for urgently needing to see St. Laurent produced no results. "I am very sorry, the minister is unable to see you," said the secretary after the Gouzenko family had sat in the office for two hours and been shuffled from his departmental office to his parliamentary office.

The Gouzenkos decided to try the Ottawa *Journal* one more time and were interviewed by a kindly woman reporter who listened carefully and studied the documents before showing them to the editor. She returned and handed them back.

"I am terribly sorry," she said. "Your story just doesn't seem to register here. Nobody wants to say anything but nice things about Stalin these days."[2]

Why didn't they see the RCMP and take out naturalization papers, the woman asked. So they went back to the Justice Building, only to be told the RCMP had nothing to do with naturalization. They were advised to go to the Crown Attorney's office, which happened to be in the direction of the Soviet Embassy. By that time it was one o'clock and too late for the Gouzenkos to reconsider their destiny.

At the Crown Attorney's office they were told to return the following day for photographs. When informed that the naturalization process takes months Anna burst into tears and Gouzenko poured out his story to one of the women in the office. The woman was sympathetic and phoned another newspaper saying she had a story of "world importance" and a reporter should be dispatched immediately. She, too, was rebuffed but called a reporter she personally knew. He appeared half an hour later and examined the documents.

"It's too big for us to handle—much too big," he concluded. "It is a matter for the police or the government. I suggest you take it to them."

The Gouzenkos were so discouraged that despite all the dangers they returned to their apartment on Somerset Street. They weren't there long before a fist banged on the door.

"Gouzenko. Gouzenko. Gouzenko," the voice boomed out. It was Under-Lieutenant Lavrentiev, the chauffeur and contact man to

---

2. It was the second time the *Journal* had turned down Gouzenko but the newspaper's involvement in the story did not end there. Later when Gouzenko was finally taken into protective custody from his apartment reporters from both the Ottawa *Journal* and Ottawa *Citizen* were on the scene but did not write stories. This piece of information became known to *Journal* management five months later when the case became public and the *Journal* reporter was fired, even though his editor and night editor turned away Gouzenko a day or two earlier.

Gouzenko's boss, Colonel Zabotin. The Gouzenkos did not answer and Lavrentiev left, but the folly of staying in their apartment much longer was all too apparent. Living next door was Sergeant Harold Main of the Royal Canadian Air Force. Main and his wife were sitting on the balcony escaping the heat when Gouzenko climbed over the railing and told his story yet another time.

"I'm going to get the police," said Main, who set out on his bicycle.

Gouzenko until this point had avoided the police because his Soviet experience had taught him they were the enemy. He believed the police, including the RCMP, were in league with the NKVD and would promptly hand him back to the embassy.

"The idea of consulting the police no longer alarmed me," Gouzenko wrote in *This Was My Choice*. "I was between the devil and the deep blue sea and the capable, assured manner of my Air Force friend carried a confident impression that everything would soon be all right."

Meanwhile arrangements had been made to put up the Gouzenko family in the apartment of a neighbor across the hall. Two Ottawa City constables arrived and promised to keep the premises under surveillance. Shortly before midnight the dreaded Pavlov and three of his henchmen arrived and broke into Gouzenko's apartment as he watched through the keyhole from across the hall. The Ottawa police were called and the same two constables appeared just in time to catch the four Soviets rifling the drawers of Gouzenko's desk and bureau.

"This apartment belongs to a fellow member of the Soviet Embassy, a man named Gouzenko, who happens to be in Toronto tonight," explained Pavlov in an official voice. "He left some documents here and we have his permission to look for them."

"Did he also give you permission to break his lock or was this done with your bare hands?" retorted Constable Thomas Walsh.

"How dare you talk to me like that?" snorted Pavlov. "We had a key for this apartment but lost it. Anyway, this lock is Soviet property and we can do what we like with it. I order you to leave this apartment."

Pavlov, claiming his diplomatic immunity had been violated, soon disappeared with his three underlings.

The following morning an inspector from the Ottawa City Police arrived to take Gouzenko for questioning to RCMP headquarters in the Justice Building that had twice refused him in the previous two days.

Shortly after ten on the morning of September 6, Louis St. Laurent was told by his secretary that waiting in his office in the Justice Building was a nervous Russian who claimed he had urgent business to convey about Soviet spying in Canada which could only be told to the minister. St. Laurent was in his parliamentary office several hundred yards away. The claim about Russian spies stealing atomic secrets sounded dramatic, as did the description of the scene with the man, his pregnant wife, and their two-year-old son conversing in Russian. St. Laurent thought about it for some time and even moved the Gouzenkos to his parliamentary office. But in the end he decided not to see them. With that rejection Gouzenko announced to St. Laurent's secretary he had no alternative but to commit suicide since his life was worthless back in Russia.

From St. Laurent's office, word of the Gouzenko visit was passed on to Norman Robertson, the distinguished Undersecretary of State for External Affairs, who grasped immediately the implications of the events. When Prime Minister Mackenzie King arrived in his office at 10:45 A.M. for an 11 o'clock sitting of Parliament, Robertson and his assistant, Hume Wrong, were waiting. They sketched for the Prime Minister the news of Gouzenko's visit to St. Laurent's office along with some of the information the Russian had blurted out, including the fact the Soviets had a spy as assistant to the United States Assistant Secretary of State Edward Stettinius and also one in Canada's research laboratories where atomic experiments were going on. Since Gouzenko represented a volatile political issue and would affect diplomatic relations with the Soviet Union, the two External Affairs officials wanted King's consent to have Gouzenko picked up by the RCMP and questioned. King refused. The Prime Minister said Gouzenko posed only snarls in the relations between two friendly allies and should be returned to the Soviet Embassy. Despite the pleas of Robertson and Wrong, Gouzenko was a "hot potato." The Prime Minister later that day recorded the meeting in his diary:

I said to both Robertson and Wrong that I thought we should be extremely careful in becoming a party to any course of action which would link the Government of Canada up with this matter in a manner which might cause Russia to feel that we had performed an unfriendly act. That to seek to gather information in any underhand way would make clear that we did not trust the Embassy. The man might be only a crank trying to preserve his own life. If he had information of the kind in his possession during the war, he should have given it to us at that time, if he had wanted to help the Government. It looked as though he was trying to make out a case which would cause our Government to protect him which, of course, he admitted was what he wanted.

Robertson seemed to feel that the information might be so important both to the States and to ourselves and to Britain that it would be in their interests for us to seize it no matter how it was obtained. He did not say this but asked my opinion. I was strongly against any step of the kind as certain to create an issue between Russia and Canada, this leading to severance of diplomatic relations ...[3]

After the meeting King attended the session of Parliament. As the proceedings concluded that afternoon St. Laurent remained behind in the Commons chamber to tell the Prime Minister what had transpired in his office that morning.

Both St. Laurent and I felt that no matter what happened we should not let it be assumed that the Government of Canada had itself sought to spy on the Embassy or to take advantage of a situation of the kind to find out something against a trusted ally. As Robertson says, however, it makes the whole question of suspicion of Russia greater than ever ...

My own feeling is that the individual has incurred the displeasure of the Embassy and is really seeking to shield himself. I do not believe his story about their having avowed treachery. There is no doubt that most countries have their secret spies, but that is another matter. For us to come into possession of a secret code book—of a Russian secret code book—would be a source of major complications.[4]

[3.] J. W. Pickersgill and O. F. Forster, eds., *The Mackenzie King Record* (Toronto: University of Toronto Press, 1970), Volume III.
[4.] *Ibid.*

Robertson met the Prime Minister a second time that day to brief him further on the Gouzenko story and to persuade him of the need to act upon this godsent opportunity. The best he could do was convince King to assign a secret service man in plainclothes to watch the Gouzenko apartment—and this only because Gouzenko had threatened to commit suicide which, if carried out, would create political complications in itself. King thought Robertson was acting irrationally in pushing the matter.

"Robertson obviously is greatly fatigued," King wrote in his diary that day.

King was returning from a diplomatic garden party late the next afternoon when Robertson briefed him on what the RCMP's preliminary interrogation of Gouzenko had uncovered. Gouzenko's fantastic claims were true. Not only was Stettinius employing a spy (later identified as Alger Hiss) but Canada was penetrated too. Dr. Allan Nunn May, the quiet British scientist working in Canada on the top-secret heavy-water pile project, was passing information to the Soviets. It was the first disclosure of an atomic spy. As well, a Soviet agent in the cipher room at External Affairs was turning over to the Russians not only messages but the actual ciphers. Similarly, the ingoing dispatches at the British High Commission were being read by a Soviet agent in the registry department. And, of course, two well-known Canadians active in the Communist Party of Canada before it was banned were implicated as active recruiters for Soviet Intelligence. They were Sam Carr, imprisoned during the Communist Party trial of 1931 and interned briefly during World War Two, and Fred Rose, a sitting Member of Parliament who had been re-elected in Montreal in the general election earlier in the year. And there was more. The size of the espionage effort surprised even Robertson.

King possessed a pathological fear that his government would provoke a world war. In 1939 he had made sure Britain and France declared war on Germany first. He had always held that Prime Minister Arthur Meighen's initiative in getting the Japanese alliance denounced at the Imperial Conference in London in 1921 played a central role in Japan's decision to enter World War Two. In 1941, under King's government, Canada had declared war on Japan before the British and before even the Americans. King had wanted to show leadership but not two hours had passed when he started regretting it. "The Japanese in the long run are going to hold this against Canada," he had told an aide.[5]

Upsetting the international apple cart preyed on King's mind. Once it became obvious that the Gouzenko complication would not disappear, he consulted the British and Americans. King undertook a seven-week trip to the United States and Britain and discussed the matter personally with President Truman and Prime Minister Attlee. If Russia's wrath could not be avoided, at least it could be distributed among the three countries. The Canadian Ambassador in Washington at the time was Lester Pearson, who sensed King's real feelings and described them in Volume III of his memoirs:

> Mr. King wanted me to get an expression of opinion from the United States government on whether we should go ahead with the prosecution of the Soviet spies. I had the feeling he was rather hoping they might say something like: "Kill it in the interests of peace and the organization of the post-war world" or "you had better forget about this for the time being, or hold it in the background." Mr. Byrnes [U.S. Secretary of State] was not having any of that. I remember he was full of praise for the manner in which we had handled the matter; this was our responsibility, our business, and we could be trusted to deal with it. We should go ahead on our own and do what we thought was best.

Five months passed after Gouzenko's defection and still nothing public happened. The world had yet to be informed of the event. No arrests had been made, although the RCMP was investigating actively. The Americans grew impatient with Canada's procrastination and leaked the story to the famous newspaper columnist Drew Pearson, who broke the story on a February 3, 1946, radio broadcast. Now King could delay no longer. Until that point the secret had been so closely guarded that even his Cabinet knew nothing about it. Jack Pickersgill, his Principal Secretary, also was not told.

[5.] Arnold Heeney, who was Secretary to the Cabinet at the time, recalled in his book *The Things That Are Caesar's,* that Gouzenko's defection cast King and Canada "in a role he considered unsuitable and uncalled for. What had we to do with espionage, cyphers, secret agents, and all the sordid paraphenalia of intrigue associated with older more sophisticated and less fastidious states? He struggled to escape, but there was no avoiding the necessity for action."

"I knew something was going on because these meetings were being held in Norman Robertson's office," Pickersgill says. "It was obviously some cloak-and-dagger business but I wasn't told what it was."

King two days later appointed a Royal Commission made up of two Supreme Court judges, Mr. Justice Robert Tascherau and Mr. Justice R. L. Kellock. It happened so quickly that a potential conflict of interest was overlooked. The findings of the Royal Commission were likely to result in the laying of charges that could easily be appealed to the Supreme Court, where the two commissioners happened to be sitting judges.

The commission began taking evidence from Gouzenko on February 13, 1946, and early on the morning of February 15 the RCMP arrested 13 persons who, according to Gouzenko's testimony and documentation, were passing classified information to the Russians. At the last minute Robertson discovered that the RCMP raids were set for 3 A.M. and since both he and King abhorred the police-state atmosphere of middle-of-the-night arrests, the RCMP was ordered to hold off until at least 7 A.M.

King read the first evidence (Gouzenko's testimony) from the Royal Commission the morning of February 17 and noted in his diary that it was "an astounding revelation" and would provide "a terrible shock to the free nations of the world." In the same entry he wrote:

> It can be honestly said that few more courageous acts have ever been performed by leaders of the government than my own in the Russian intrigue against the Christian world and the manner in which I have fearlessly taken up and have begun to expose the whole of it. I see the full significance.... I have come to the conclusion that a break between Russia's and Canada's diplomatic relations is wholly inevitable.[6]

Complaints soon arose over the treatment of the detainees held at the RCMP training center in the Ottawa suburb of Rockcliffe. Those arrested were stripped of their rights by Order in Council and denied visits from their families and lawyers. They were held

[6.] From *The Mackenzie King Record,* Volume III.

incommunicado and King became disturbed by reports that husbands were taken from their wives and not heard from for weeks. It violated King's humanitarian instincts as well as his political sense. He was particularly bothered by a report—although it is not established that it was true—that lights were kept on all night in the cells.

Canadians seemed to be dividing into two camps over the arrests. There were those so shocked at the espionage disclosures they felt that lack of due process was a secondary issue since the detainees were coldblooded traitors. But there were others who could not believe the allegations, particularly since Russia had been such a good wartime ally, and felt the RCMP's tactics were repressive. King, not knowing which way to turn, started pressuring the Royal Commission to produce its report quickly.

"You know," King told the commission, "this is the worst political fix I've been in in my career. You must get out a report."

The commission was not prepared to produce a report so quickly but, under the Prime Minister's urging, put out three interim reports to accommodate him.

Gouzenko turned out to be a perfect witness. He was articulate and had amazing recall and was always precise and forceful in his many hours of testimony, before both the Royal Commission and the criminal trials that followed. He was the main witness without whose contribution the trials could not have proceeded. He never contradicted himself. Some of the most clever lawyers attempted to ambush him and failed. The 733-page Royal Commission report said it was "impressed with the sincerity of the man, and with the manner in which he gave his evidence, which we have no hesitation in accepting ..." The Commission also said: "In our opinion Gouzenko, by what he has done, has rendered a great public service to the people of this country, and thereby has placed Canada in his debt." It was a movie-script ending. All that remained was for Gouzenko to fade modestly into Canadian society and enjoy his new freedoms. But it would not happen that way.

One of the Mounties assigned to the Gouzenko investigation in 1945 was Cliff Harvison, who later wrote a book. According to Harvison, Gouzenko was not overly modest:

Gouzenko was not a humble man given to underestimating his own ability. In fact, one got the impression that his considerable talent was somewhat outstripped by his estimation of that talent. Undoubtedly, the reasons for his defection were as given in his statement to the Royal Commission, but I believe that his vanity provided additional motivation. The Soviets had failed to recognize him as a borderline genius, or to promote him to a rank more in keeping with his intellectual powers. Resentment of that slight might well have been blended with his other reasons for defecting.[7]

That opinion was echoed in less diplomatic tones by another retired senior Mountie who observed him over many years and was interviewed for this book.

"Gouzenko was not a true lover of liberty," the officer says. "He was a thoroughly ignorant Russian peasant who had no connection with the Russian Intelligence Service except as a cipher clerk. I have known him for quite some time and feel he is an unsavory character. In Intelligence it doesn't matter whether you are a saint or a devil. What matters is whether you have information. Gouzenko had information and he also had a good memory. He had almost total recall. He was absolutely invaluable. Fred Rose and the others would have gotten away scot-free without him."

Gouzenko achieved celebrity status and enjoyed it. He met Prime Minister King, and, wearing a dark hood that would become his public trademark, he was interviewed by Drew Pearson, the American newspaper columnist. He received offers to write a book. When he dealt with the RCMP, he preferred senior officers.

The threat of Soviet reprisal against Gouzenko was real in the early years and the government took elaborate steps to provide a new identity, including a birth certificate and cover stories. The Gouzenkos were relocated in southern Ontario. The address was need-to-know information and withheld even from the Prime Minister. The RCMP, continually horrified at Gouzenko's tendency to violate security precautions, urged him to be more careful but without much success. On one occasion Gouzenko's identity was exposed by a group of curious women who met over coffee. The Gouzenkos had

---

[7.] From *The Horsemen*.

to be moved after that incident. Despite his intrepidity Gouzenko had recurring fears that the Soviet secret police would hunt him down and kill him. He wanted his RCMP bodyguard and yet he did not. Sometimes he was indiscreet, other times his caution bordered on paranoia.

With his fame came riches—instant riches. The Canadian government at first paid him little, but Gouzenko wrote well and his first piece appeared in the February, 1947, edition of *Cosmopolitan* Magazine. He was well paid for the article, and it secured his immediate future financially. This money was augmented by an Ottawa businessman who set up a trust fund providing monthly payments for life. Then his autobiography, *This Was My Choice,* published in 1948, netted him a windfall. With that it seemed Gouzenko was fixed for life.

Defectors often have trouble adjusting to their new circumstances[8] and the sudden flood of wealth proved too much for Gouzenko. He came from a destitute background and was leapfrogged into a privileged position in an affluent society. Gouzenko was not accustomed to handling money and as a result he overspent. The fortune disappeared and Gouzenko was soon strapped for funds. He started charging for interviews as one means of making money.

Richard Jackson, a member of the Parliamentary Press Galley in Ottawa since 1943, bought one of these interviews for $500 on behalf of the London *Daily Express.* Jackson arranged the interview and agreed to accompany René McColl, the chief foreign correspondent of the *Daily Express,* to Toronto. The fee rose to $1,000 after Jackson and McColl arrived in Toronto.

"I went out thinking: 'What a dirty trick,'" says Jackson. "He knew he had us, so he squeezed. He was lucky it was the *Express*

[8.] Other defectors since Gouzenko have also had trouble adjusting. Polish Intelligence officer Michal Goleniewski defected to the CIA in April, 1958, with the first clues leading to the exposure of the Portland Spy Ring in Britain as well as providing other valuable information, such as the fact that 15 United States Embassy employees including all 10 Marines had been lured into bed by female agents of Polish Intelligence. The information proved accurate and resulted in recalls from the Warsaw embassy. Once an American citizen, Goleniewski claimed he was the Czarevich, the Grand Duke Alexei, and took out advertisements in the Washington *Daily News.* More recently Arkady Shevchenko, 47, the high-ranking Soviet administrator at the United Nations who defected to the United States in April, 1978, lavished between $35,000 and $40,000 on a beautiful 22-year-old woman he got from an escort service listed in the Yellow Pages.

because it didn't give a damn about money in those days."

Jackson borrowed the extra $500 from the manager of the Royal York Hotel and the two set out to meet Gouzenko. After being transferred from one location to another four times they arrived at a house in the Toronto suburb of Etobicoke where Gouzenko appeared without his famous hood. The interview produced no new information. Gouzenko essentially repeated the story he had told many times before. The only development to emerge was the fact that he could not get along on his allowance and was openly resentful toward the Canadian government for its alleged stinginess. During the interview Gouzenko indicated that he was living in a style that did not please him.

"The house looked very comfortable to me," says Jackson. "It was a good middle-class house. There was nothing wrong with it. It was nicely furnished and on a nice lot. He told us he had blown his money from the best seller. It was gone. He had bought a big oversized, overpriced luxury car and got rid of it. He didn't go into details about how he'd blown the money. He just said it had vanished."

Afterward Gouzenko voluntarily accompanied Jackson back to the Royal York Hotel and requested a drink in the room. There was little liquor in the bottle and when it was empty Gouzenko suggested drinks down in the bar.

"Christ, if you go down to the bar everybody in the Royal York is going to see you and know," exclaimed McColl. "Every reporter will be down to the bar in 10 minutes."

"Nobody knows me but the police, my family, and my close friends," replied Gouzenko. "I can go down with safety."

After a few rounds of gins in the bar, Gouzenko "bummed"—as Jackson put it—cab fare from McColl for the ride back home.

In October, 1953, the Chicago *Tribune* published a story quoting Gouzenko as saying he had further information and would be happy to appear before the United States Senate Subcommittee on Internal Security. On the basis of that story the American government requested an interview with Gouzenko. The request alarmed the Canadian government for several reasons. First, the RCMP was under the impression that all useful information had already been wrung out of Gouzenko. If there was anything else, the RCMP should have been told long ago. As well, Gouzenko had previously been interviewed on a number of occasions by American authorities, the last time by the FBI in August, 1950.

Second, the request came at the height of McCarthyism in the United States and the subcommittee, the initiator of the request, was an instrument of McCarthyism. Canadian authorities did not want the subcommittee to exploit Gouzenko in such a sensational manner, and it was clear the subcommittee's purpose was political and not informational. Third, Canadian authorities lacked confidence in Gouzenko. By this time his last contact with Soviet Intelligence was more than eight years old and over the years his accusations had shown a tendency to become broader and more strident. In the meantime the Canadian government was trying to prevent McCarthyism of the U.S. proportion from erupting in Canada.

The RCMP interviewed Gouzenko and was given his assurance he had no further information to offer beyond what he had already divulged. He claimed the Chicago *Tribune* had misquoted him and he denied having criticized the manner in which his evidence had been used. And, furthermore, he said, in no circumstances was he willing to be interviewed by a Congressional subcommittee. Canada was relieved and turned down the American request on grounds that it was based on a misunderstanding.

The subcommittee did not accept Canada's response and a second note arrived requesting an interview. Two days later the Chicago *Tribune* published another story quoting Gouzenko, upholding the accuracy of its first story and stressing that he wanted to testify. In the second story Gouzenko also criticized External Affairs Minister Lester Pearson for turning down the first American request. Based on this turn of events, Pearson agreed to the interview as long as it proceeded under Canadian auspices and was conducted in conformity with Canadian procedures. That would provide safeguards against red-baiting.

The interview was held January 4, 1954, in the 18th-century manor on the property of the Seignory Club in Montebello, Quebec, the lovely resort on the Ottawa River halfway between Montreal and Ottawa. The three American questioners were Senator William Jenner, chairman of the subcommittee, Senator Pat McCarran, the ex-chairman, and lawyer J. G. Sourwine. It was made clear that they were representing the United States government and not the subcommittee.

At 10 A.M. everyone except Gouzenko was in place for the start of proceedings. The room remained quiet for several minutes while the assembly waited for the man. There was no Gouzenko. People started getting restless. A ranking Mountie got up and left to see what was wrong. Gouzenko refused to appear unless he received payment and the money was to be paid in advance.

"Now listen very carefully, Gouzenko," the Mountie officer said. "If you don't come out right now I'm going to turn you over to our special disposal unit."

Gouzenko was scared witless and complied immediately. He believed the RCMP had a killer squad. The Soviet police had one, so why wouldn't Canada?

As expected, Gouzenko's testimony provided no new information. The Americans were kept firmly in place by the presiding judge, Mr. Justice McRuer, who disallowed certain questions. A witchhunt was avoided. There was speculation afterward that the whole exercise had been a public relations gimmick initiated by the publisher of Gouzenko's second book, which was released later that year. The book, a novel called *The Fall of a Titan*, became a best seller and a selection of the Book-of-the-Month Club and, in Canada, winner of the Governor-General's Award for best Canadian novel. It also earned the author another windfall.

Gouzenko's money disappeared again. The existing rift widened between him and the RCMP as well as the government. Gouzenko thought the government was shirking its responsibility in failing to provide for him; in turn, the government thought Gouzenko was an extremely difficult person to deal with. Justice Minister Stuart Garson had a prepared speech to be read in the House of Commons blaming Gouzenko for violating common-sense security rules in case something catastrophic happened to him. The government was not going to take the blame. Nothing happened and the speech was never given.

Gouzenko made frequent requests for more money. He claimed he could not take a regular job for security reasons and, besides, was busy working on another novel. He, indeed, was writing another book but he had very high standards and agonized over each word. His RCMP translator was gone and he could not find a replacement to satisfy his exacting demands. In the meantime the government was growing impatient with him, and on one occasion passing consideration was given to abandoning him, but wiser heads prevailed when the political consequences, both domestically and internationally in relation to attracting future defectors, were considered. Once even an audit was done to ensure that his financial plight was real and not contrived to fleece the government. The results revealed that Gouzenko was an honest overspender.

In the spring of 1965 Mrs. Gouzenko, an articulate and forceful woman, came to Ottawa and made the rounds of select offices on Parliament Hill to lobby for more money. In the foyer outside the House of Commons she met Richard Jackson of the Ottawa *Journal* and admitted her husband "blew" the income from the second book. She told Jackson her husband worked on occasion but quit in panic "at the first slightest suspicion."

"A strange face—almost any Slavic face, easy to spot, you know," she said. "He has an obsession it might be one of 'them.' And it might, so he runs, leaves the job, and as soon as we can, we move again."

As for the latest book, she said, "He tries—but not hard enough." The book, 11 years after the last one, was still far from finished.

"It's so long now," she said, "far, far too long. So long, nobody is going to read it, and I tell him he must cut it down before he goes any further. He says he's a new Tolstoy and when I wake him at six o'clock in the morning and he won't get out of bed, I tell him Tolstoy never got rich sleeping."

Mrs. Gouzenko said her life as a mother and wife was the same as any other Canadian woman's. "Although maybe I worry a little more," she said. "There's housekeeping and shopping and driving the children to their lessons, and pushing, pushing, pushing to get them through school. Then there's the husband—and mine is a problem."

Her request was direct: "If the government can spend millions to help complete strangers on the other side of the world, it should be able to spare a few more dollars for the family of a good Canadian who dared and did so much for his country."

A few months later Gouzenko gave an interview to Canadian Press staff writer John Tracy and rationalized losing his small fortune this way: "I don't say I'm a good investor. I'm a spy discloser, a novel writer, but not an investor. There are lots of people born and brought up in this country who can't keep their money. If I started a business I might lose it. If big business firms can lose hundreds of thousands of dollars, what do you expect from someone like me."

Gouzenko appeared on Radio Station CFGM in March, 1968, to plead his financial case. He said Prime Minister Pearson had refused to increase his stipend mainly because of the influence of counterspies in the government. He urged listeners to write the Prime Minister on his behalf.

Later Gouzenko recruited Conservative Member of Parliament Tom Cossitt (Leeds) to press his case on Parliament Hill. Gouzenko in 1975 claimed he was $13,000 in debt and had to borrow money at high interest rates to keep up with the cost of living.

"I should be the last person on whom the government should exercise economy," his letter to Cossitt said.

Cossitt put a series of questions on the House of Commons' Order Paper and they were answered by Solicitor General Warren Allmand on May 21, 1975. Allmand said Gouzenko was getting a tax-free pension of approximately $1,050 a month, which was reviewed each year to keep pace with the average industrial wage.

"Originally," Allmand's response said, "Mr. Gouzenko did live under special circumstances and there was fear for his life; however, the security requirements had greatly diminished and there is now no reason for Mr. Gouzenko not to seek employment."

In the 30 years since his defection, Gouzenko had gone from being a hero who alerted Canada to the Soviet espionage threat to being an annoyance to the government.

7

Growing Pains

THE GOUZENKO REVELATIONS heralded a new era in espionage.
The master spy disappeared and espionage became a bureaucratic
enterprise replete with guidelines and regulations. Rather than infest
enemy territory with a series of individualistic supersleuths who
procured enemy secrets by resourcefulness and instinct, the Soviet
Union turned the operation into a scientific process of management
practices and flow charts. The Soviet Embassy in Ottawa kept a form
for each Canadian espionage agent, listing basic information: name,
address, and other personal details including the unsubtle "Since
when in the net."

The Communist Party of Canada served as a pool of talent ready
to be enticed into "the net." Since the party operated clandestinely
(it was legally banned), the contact with the embassy was secret. It
was the party's practice to have hundreds of small "study groups"
holding regular meetings across Canada, with spotters like Fred
Rose and Sam Carr traveling from meeting to meeting and providing
the Soviet Embassy with reports on potential spy recruits who had
access or potential access to secret information.

"The Center" in Moscow set priorities and passed them on to the
embassy in Ottawa, where an agent-running officer passed them to
Canadian cell leaders, who in turn forwarded them to their contacts
whose positions in the civil service gave them access to classified
information. Like any linear organization the system sometimes

91

demonstrated bureaucratic insensitivity toward the agents in the field, but the Canadian traitors were ideological recruits and either did not notice or did not care, or else they were caught "in the net" and powerless.

The Canadian cell leaders did nothing without approval from the Soviet Embassy. The embassy in turn did nothing, or at least very little, without authority from The Center in Moscow. A recruitment attempt required written reports, including a psychological assessment that was passed up the line to be checked by The Center to ensure that everything conformed to standards and to make certain the individual was not already a Soviet agent in another network. If Moscow approved, the decision—along with instructions— was passed back through the chain and ultimately reached the Canadian conducting the recruitment attempt. The recruiter paused at each stage to write a report and await further instructions while Moscow scrutinized the latest progress report. The individual was secondary to the process, especially the co-opted Canadian at the end of the line. The agent-handlers working out of the Soviet Embassy also were numbers and were transferred from one country to another like interchangeable parts. When transfers occurred, the departing officer introduced the new officer to his Canadian contacts and told them to continue supplying information, which they faithfully did.

The Soviet Union had, and still has today, two primary organizations carrying out espionage: the KGB[1] and the GRU. The KGB, the *Komitet Gosudarstvennoi Bezopasnosti,* the Commission for State Security, is a civilian organization that dominates Soviet life and politics because it exercises responsibility for both external espionage and internal security and is the backbone of the notorious secret-informer system inside the country. The GRU, *Glavnoye Razvedy-vatelnoye Upravlenie,* is the intelligence arm of the Red Army and also operates abroad extensively. The two organizations operate independently, even though both make use of Soviet embassies, trade missions, and other state institutions in their international

---

[1.] The KGB as such was formed in 1954. Its predecessor at the time of Gouzenko was called the NKVD. Other forerunners were the Cheka, GPU, OGPU, NKBD, NKGB, and MGB. The designation KGB will be used throughout this book to avoid confusion.

operations. When espionage is involved, the embassies are divided into parallel and autonomous KGB and GRU sections reporting to different masters in Moscow. Gouzenko, a lieutenant in the army, was attached to the GRU. And while his disclosures smashed the GRU ring in Canada and retarded its activities in Canada for at least a decade, the KGB was left untouched since Gouzenko had no information about it. He knew only that it existed and was called "The Neighbors." (The KGB in turn refers to the GRU as "The Military Neighbors".) Since the KGB is the larger organization with more extensive espionage rings, the better established network in Canada was not affected by Gouzenko's disclosures. In fact, two of the principal talent spotters, Fred Rose and Sam Carr, were discovered only because they had been transferred from the KGB to the GRU to help build the GRU's infant espionage network.

At the time of Gouzenko, the RCMP Intelligence Branch had only a half-time investigator conducting what could be construed as counterespionage work at the field level in Ottawa (as distinct from headquarters). The Russian embassy went unsurveilled and Soviet intelligence met with members of the Communist Party with little fear of detection. The Force might have tripped across some Soviet activity if somebody had tried to recruit an RCMP informer, but the RCMP had no informers in valuable positions within the party. The entire Intelligence Branch, from one end of Canada to another, consisted of about two dozen men. The headquarters staff had two commissioned officers: Superintendent Rivett-Carnac and the well known Johnny Leopold. Sam Carr once asked his Soviet masters whether he should attempt to recruit an informer from within the RCMP and was told not to bother. Either the RCMP was so ineffective that Soviet Intelligence did not consider it a priority or it was already penetrated.

When Gouzenko defected, the RCMP enlisted the help of its criminal investigators to conduct the investigation because the Intelligence Branch lacked the manpower to do the job. Two senior criminal investigators were Inspector Cliff Harvison, who later became Commissioner, arriving from Winnipeg, and Inspector M. F. E. Anthony, later to become police chief of Edmonton, coming in from Vancouver. They were joined by many noncommissioned officers who were taken off police duties. The result was a police investigation when a security investigation was needed. When Gouzenko was finally interviewed on the morning of September 7, 1945, it was too late to turn him into a double agent, although that might have been possible had Justice Minister St. Laurent met Gouzenko the previous morning and promptly given him to the RCMP. Even then it likely would not have been attempted, given the level of sophistication of the Intelligence Branch and the fact it did not comprehend the advantages of running double agents. More significantly, there was no attempt to turn into double agents any of the Canadians exposed by Gouzenko. Only a few years earlier, during World War Two, British Security had neutralized the entire German espionage network inside Britain and got the agents to work for the Allies by doubling them. It was a masterful operation and the techniques were available to the RCMP.

Because the Gouzenko case was examined within the confines of the Criminal Code, the desire for legal redress was the central consideration. Wherever possible, the RCMP opted for prosecution, whereas Canada's larger interests lay in exploiting some of these agents for the purpose of frustrating further Soviet espionage. Not all code names mentioned in the Gouzenko documents were identified and it is likely that some of these undiscovered agents continued their operations once the trials ended. With the threat of prosecution as bargaining lever the RCMP could have possibly recruited double agents from among the identified agents. The Soviet Union would have soon detected this fact but would not have been able to distinguish between the double agents and the loyal agents and would have been forced to abandon the entire network, including the agents the RCMP never did identify. In one fell swoop the RCMP would have rendered useless agents it did not even know about. In such cases the need to preserve Canada's security takes precedence over the normal desire to inflict criminal punishment on wrongdoers. Police organizations are rarely sensitive to this distinction.

The irony is that when the prosecutions did go forward, half of those charged were acquitted. Of the 20 charged in Canada, 10 were convicted and 10 ultimately went free. Of the 10 who got off, seven were straight acquittals, two acquittals were on appeal, and one had her charges withdrawn. Prosecuted outside Canada was Allan Nunn

May, the nuclear scientist, because he was living in Britain at the time of the arrests. He was convicted and received the harshest sentence of all, 10 years.[2]

The RCMP bears responsibility for only part of the failure since the Justice Department officials were as inexperienced and inept in laying the charges as the Force was in investigating the case.

"I think there was sufficient evidence to get every one of them," says a former Mountie who is a student of the Gouzenko cases.

According to this expert, the failure to gain more convictions arose from the fact the RCMP did not know the trade craft. The Force treated the investigation much like another rum-running case and charged the defendants with the Criminal Code offense of conspiracy first and violating the Official Secrets Act second. The Soviet cell system, which was manipulated from the top and had each agent working in isolation, did not lend itself to conspiracy. When the conspiracy charges collapsed, the other charges under the Official Secrets Act were dropped. The former Mountie believes all would have been convicted had the original charges been laid under the Official Secrets Act.

The mistakes did not end with the trials. Once the prosecutions were concluded, the RCMP stopped the investigation and closed the file, much to the regret years later of second-generation Mounties who had to live with the consequences. The RCMP at that point did not fully realize the importance of continuing the search or understand that security cases are never closed, whether the courts have rendered a judgment or not. One officer continued to investigate informally and reached the point where he felt he had identified those unsolved code names. He had his knuckles rapped. The results of the Gouzenko investigation were given to the FBI, which continued the inquiry and traced unfollowed leads of interest to the United States. At one point in the early 1950s the mass of documents

---

[2.] Those convicted in Canada were Fred Rose, six years; David Gordon Lunan, five years; Philip Durnford Pemberton Smith, five years; Edward Wilfred Mazerall, four years; Harold Samuel Gerson, five years; Dr. Raymond Boyer, two years; John Soboloff, fined $500 and costs; Kathleen Willsher, who pleaded guilty, three years; Emma Woikin, who also pleaded guilty, two and a half years; and Samuel Carr, six years. Acquitted on appeal were Henry Harris and James Scotland Benning. Acquitted at their initial trial were Israel Halperin, Frederick Poland, Eric Adams, Matt Simons Nightingale, David Shugar, Agatha Chapman, and W. M. Pappin. Charges were withdrawn against Freda Linton.

appeared to be lost and a search discovered them in the basement of the Justice Building on Wellington Street.

Eventually the Force came to discover that compiling and analysing information was more valuable than gaining prosecutions, and the Gouzenko investigation was reopened sometime in the '60s. But the lost ground was never regained. Witnesses had died, others forgot details, and documentary evidence that once could have been compiled had disappeared entirely.[3]

Immediately after Gouzenko the Intelligence Branch was renamed Special Branch. It was a change in name more than in function. Special Branch did pick up more and better staff, gain some technical ability, and broaden its horizons, and it continued to do so over the years. But it remained a stepchild of the Criminal Investigation Branch and fell under the jurisdiction of the Director of Criminal Investigation. It took a decade for Special Branch to break free and become a directorate by itself.

The development of the security function within the RCMP was at a critical stage. The Gouzenko case had ended and the Force finally had time to sit back and decide what kind of organization the new Special Branch should become. The circumstances clearly called for a new approach and the response from the RCMP would largely reflect the priorities of the new officer in charge of Special Branch. Superintendent Rivett-Carnac was promoted and put in charge of police training at Regina. The new officer chosen in 1947 was a tough superintendent named George McClellan whose decisiveness would have been felt in Special Branch years after he left even if he had not eventually become RCMP commissioner.

What Special Branch needed more than anything else was somebody to loosen the paramilitary shackles that limited the Gouzenko investigation and would in future restrain the branch's efficiency. McClellan, a military-oriented man, was not the individual for this task. He not only attended Royal Military College in Kingston

---

[3.] One Special Branch officer interviewed during the research for this book disagrees with some of the above details. He says the Gouzenko documents were stored in the basement of the Justice Building (which also at that time happened to be RCMP headquarters) because it was the most appropriate place. He also stresses that the Gouzenko leads were being pursued after the trials but that they were done superficially. "There is no question we lost momentum because CIB was just skimming the surface. They didn't do an in-depth analysis. It put us back. That's really unfortunate."

(1929), he possessed all the traits of a military officer. He even looked the part. His bulky frame and square face resembled Stongehenge. He weighed nearly 200 pounds, was barrel-chested, broad-shouldered, and naturally had a military posture. His booming voice and rapid delivery packed authority into every word. In red serge his presence was intimidating. McClellan underwent extra police training in 1938 and was promoted to superintendent to take charge of Special Branch. His previous experience in security work derived from his police duties in Toronto where he put Gouzenko safely under cover and from intelligence work during the war, including liaison work with the British and the Norwegians.

An incident while McClellan was Commissioner demonstrated his allegiance to the chain-of-command structure. A constable in northern Manitoba phoned Commissioner McClellan's office in a sad plight. He was getting married and had already made all the wedding arrangements when his superior office refused to grant permission to marry. Would the Commissioner grant permission? "Give the guy permission to get married if he's gone this far," McClellan told his staff when advised of the phone call. "But as soon as he's back from his honeymoon put him under arrest for contacting the Commissioner unlawfully." McClellan sympathized with the constable's plight but was offended by the violation of the rank-structure system.

McClellan loved to display the authority that the paramilitary system invested in him as Commissioner. One year he was guest of honor at the annual levee in the sergeants' mess at headquarters and was overawed by the decorations.

"Who's responsible for these decorations?" boomed McClellan.

The room was buzzing with anticipation, for nobody knew whether he liked them or disliked them.

"Sergeant Barker," was the response.

"Sergeant Barker, please stand up."

A confused Sergeant Barker got to his feet.

"These decorations are magnificent," McClellan continued. "Congratulations, you are now a staff sergeant."

Promotions were hard to come by, especially in those years before the 1970s bureaucracy set in, and sergeants across the country put in hard work and long hours in the hope of jumping ahead one level.

McClellan treated the process like a circus prize. It was an awesome display of authority that nobody forgot.

McClellan was performing an inspection of the sergeants' mess in Montreal when he realized his chauffeur was not allowed to enter the room because he was only a corporal. But the corporal was already inside and violating the rules. McClellan was not perturbed for a minute. "You are now a sergeant," he proclaimed. And indeed he was.

There was more to George McClellan than pomp and authority. He was charming and likable "George B," raconteur and wisecracker. His grin extended from ear to ear and since his face was so big the effect was contagious. When he was not in a position to use his RCMP authority to get what he wanted, he relied on his storehouse of jokes, his polished knack as a storyteller, and outright charm. George B's staff gathered around and listened to the master spin out a yarn, and they all laughed at the funny parts. They had to laugh because he was the boss but usually laughed because the jokes were funny.

In many ways McClellan was a good choice as head of Special Branch. He was also an operator who had no scruples about manipulating events and individuals toward ends that suited his purposes. He possessed a willingness to forget some of his upright RCMP training and do unpolicemanlike things, which made him suitable for his new role in a way few Mounties were. McClellan took a liking to Special Branch work, and the failures of the Gouzenko affair soon impressed him that counterintelligence was not police work and that different techniques were required. He was one of the first commissioned officers to understand this fact and took steps to ensure that others would understand this elementary principle as well. It is this grasp of the uniqueness of Special Branch and the steps he took to give it a measure of sophistication that give him a claim to being the father of the modern security service in Canada.

One of McClellan's first acts was to circulate a memo advising all Mounties about Special Branch and inviting applications with the proviso that members with linguistic competence in Slavic languages would receive first consideration. This was a departure from procedure. One did not advertise for applicants. RCMP tradition held that men were transferred wherever and whenever it suited the needs of the Force. If McClellan wanted men with Slavic languages he needed only to check with the Personnel Branch to find them and transfer them before the month was out, although he required each man to have at least three years' police experience. This action did not become policy and men continued to be transferred in and out of Special Branch at the Force's will. But it did start the process of setting the branch apart.

Within six months McClellan, impressed by a visit to Great Britain, established a counterespionage branch. For the first time the RCMP had an organization whose purpose was to detect and prevent foreign countries from gathering intelligence and otherwise engaging in clandestine operations inside Canada. Previously the Force's sole security work consisted of countersubversive activity — investigation of such domestic groups as local Communist and Nazi groups. The counterespionage organization became B Branch and originally consisted of three Mounties: Sergeant Len Higgitt, who worked on the World War Two detention of German internees and later on the Gouzenko investigation and who 22 years later was appointed RCMP Commissioner; Corporal Jim MacMillan, who died shortly after; and Constable Charles Sweeny, who was transferred from police duties in New Brunswick and spent the next 16 years in B Branch before returning to police work and retiring in 1973 at the rank of Assistant Commissioner. These three greenhorns set out to learn counterespionage, and while their presence did not strike fear into the occupants of 2 Dzerzhinsky Square in Moscow, the headquarters of the KGB, it signaled the beginning of specialization and the eventual advancement toward professionalism.

Despite his military leaning McClellan had the good sense to realize he needed some academic minds, so he established within the Force a civilian group of individuals as an intellectual resource for Special Branch to draw on. Over the previous 30 years the RCMP had produced a mass of undigested intelligence left to collect dust in the filing system. There were reports from the Home Office in Britain early in the century about the movement of Marxist ideology into the colony of Canada. These had been sent to the defunct Dominion Police and were acquired by the RCMP in 1920. There were briefs on each of the major Communist organizations and known Communist front groups written by the Mounties themselves. However, the reports on Communist groups were worthless as constituted because they were compiled by individuals who did not distinguish between evidence of subversive intent and evidence of Communist sympathy. They automatically assumed subversive intent when members of the United Ukrainian Association of Canada, which supported the Soviet Union, visited the Soviet Union or when Canadian immigrants subscribed to Communist newspapers from the old land. McClellan understood that this information needed to be analyzed from a different perspective, and his solution was not to replace the military mind but to supplement the organization with a group of 12 civilian researchers to examine the material. Its chief task was to research the files and write briefs on known and suspected subversive organizations in Canada.

But of all McClellan's significant actions, none was more important than bringing into Special Branch as the fourth member of the counterespionage unit a lank sub-inspector by the name of Terry Guernsey who as a junior officer took charge of the unit. Guernsey hailed from Penticton, B.C., and joined the RCMP in 1933 because of the Depression. After a series of transfers to various parts of the country, including a stint in the Musical Ride in Ottawa, he was assigned to industrial security work in Toronto at the outbreak of World War Two. Guernsey, unlike McClellan, was quiet and his face always wore a thoughtful expression. He had a mind that absorbed detail without sacrificing imagination. While McClellan attempted to manipulate events through force of personality, Guernsey accomplished the same ends through intellectual prowess.

"Terry Guernsey was the most valuable asset the RCMP ever had in the counterespionage field," says Charles Sweeny, the third Mountie to join that group. "He had a completely analytical mind and had a genius for cutting through to the heart of any matter. At meetings he would sit back silently until the discussion was finished and then would make one or two comments that cut through all the verbiage. He was the biggest innovator in investigative matters. Without him, counterespionage development in Canada would have been retarded a long time. He was not an easy man to work with. He was so inquisitive and incisive you had to be awfully sure of yourself."

Guernsey and Sergeant Owen-Jones, who joined the counter-espionage organization the same time as Guernsey, were the first Mounties sent to Britain for intelligence training. Owen-Jones was a true policeman who never felt comfortable in security work and eventually drifted out of the Force. On the other hand, Guernsey at the outset displayed an instinct and a passion for the work. So impressed were the British that they offered him a job when Britain had one of the best organizations in the world. For years the British were said to have regarded him as the only professional security officer in Canada. Guernsey brought British experts to Canada to train Special Branch members. One of the instructors who came to tutor Mounties on interrogation techniques was the renowned William Skardon, the shrewd inquisitor who broke atomic spy Klaus Fuchs. (Fuchs was convicted in 1950 and sentenced to 14 years in prison for passing secrets to the Russians.) Guernsey also arranged to have individuals sent to Britain.

Guernsey was the driving force in assembling the Watcher Service which developed into one of the Special Branch's brightest beacons of technical expertise. Before Guernsey, Special Branch did very little physical surveillance and did even that badly. Surveillance was still a part-time occupation and was not taken seriously because most of the people doing the surveilling were Mounties waiting for an advancement to an investigative assignment. Guernsey led the fight for a professional surveillance team of civilians possessing the training and physical attributes enabling them to blend into the environment. Commissioner S. T. Wood was unsympathetic since he understood neither the concept of surveillance nor the need for a full-time civilian team of professionals. Guernsey had the backing of McClellan and when Commissioner Wood retired in 1951 a modest program was started. Guernsey was singlehandedly responsible for the adoption of a policy enabling Special Branch to wire-tap legally, something the Criminal Investigation Branch was never able to do until Parliament passed enabling legislation in 1974. During World War Two the RCMP, because of special authorization provided by the War Measures Act, was able to wire-tap at will and without requiring outside authority. The emergency powers lapsed shortly after hostilities ceased. There was no law forbidding wire-tapping but telephone companies refused to comply without specific legal authority. When Guernsey took over counterespionage duties, Special Branch did no wire-tapping whatsoever because of this stumbling block and thus lacked a valuable investigative tool. A dozen Department of Justice lawyers searched unsuccessfully for legal ways of wire-tapping short of introducing legislation in the House of Commons. Guernsey combed the Official Secrets Act, the Criminal Code, and the RCMP Act and by combining certain provisions in these statutes produced an interpretation that satisfied the Department of Justice but, more importantly, was accepted by the telephone companies. Consequently Special Branch was able to wire-tap legally and without a court order or the minister's approval. In contrast the Criminal Investigation Branch, which found no legal method, eventually started wire-tapping without legal sanction.[4]

When Guernsey joined Special Branch, field officers were not required to identify their sources in their reports to headquarters. A corporal in Saskatchewan might report that local Communists were planning a take-over of a local CCF youth group. His source might be a reliable individual at the center of the action, in which case the information was authoritative. On the other hand, the individual might be a dissident outsider picking up gossip and probably adding his own interpretation to the report, in which case the information was unreliable. The unreliable information may have been accepted at face value by a corporal in the field and passed on to headquarters. That information, although unreliable, was automatically accepted in Special Branch's filing system and given as much credibility as reliable information.

Guernsey realized it was impossible to appraise information at headquarters when each field officer had his own standard of reliability. As a police organization the RCMP had hitherto always relied on the courts to test the credibility of its sources. Guernsey's overseas training taught him that this practice was inappropriate and incompatible with the security role. Special Branch had to devise its own internal evaluation system, otherwise the entire filing system, for one thing, was vulnerable to a KGB disinformation campaign. If each piece of information in the filing system was not identified by its original source it would be impossible to flush out the bad informa-

---

[4.] The Guernsey interpretation was superseded June 30, 1974, when the Protection of Privacy Act and amendments to the Official Secrets Act became law. The Protection of Privacy Act for the first time provided a legal basis for the Criminal Investigation Branch to wire-tap provided a warrant—which contained limitations—was issued by a judge. These restrictions were amended in the police's favor in 1977. After 1974 security wire-taps fell under the Official Secrets Act and needed the signature of the Solicitor General of Canada.

tion in the event a contributor was later exposed as a double agent. There were other reasons why precautions had to be taken. People's careers were at stake. False allegations of a security nature could deny innocent people jobs in the civil service or ruin the prospect of career enhancement for existing government employees. Since there was no appeal to a negative security decision, Special Branch in effect had to combine the functions of the police and the courts. Guernsey introduced the system of identifying and evaluating sources that remains in use today. Like most of his innovations, he had to struggle to get the source evaluation system adopted.

Guernsey suffered in silent frustration from a system that was unimaginative and unwilling to change, and the tension eventually took its toll. Even if the Force had been flexible, inherent and basic institutional differences separated the RCMP's two sides and would have polarized the relationship. Guernsey came to believe that the RCMP should revert exclusively to its original function—law enforcement—and that Special Branch should be separated from the RCMP and be made a civilian organization. Separation was heresy in the eyes of the Force since it meant the break-up of the RCMP. Beyond almost anything else Mounties are trained to revere the institution as something sacred. The mild-mannered Guernsey never preached separation and always attempted to make the best of the situation, but the RCMP, with its accent on discipline and loyalty, would not tolerate nonconformity even if intellectual in substance and moderate in nature.

Guernsey never did become head of Special Branch. His rise stopped at the rank of superintendent, and underlings with less experience, less intelligence, and less imagination whom he tutored in the craft of counterespionage were promoted over him. First he was transferred out of the Counterespionage Branch. Then in 1962 he was put on pension early on medical grounds.[5] The hint of splitting off the security branch was a nightmare the Force would fight at any cost.

[5.] After leaving the Force, Guernsey received two offers from British Services, which he declined.

8

The Separation Fight: One

THE RCMP IN the early 1950s still was not putting much effort into security work. Ottawa had about a dozen field workers and Toronto about a dozen and a half, and those two cities comprised the majority of Special Branch members across Canada.[1] It was a vast improvement but not enough to generate respect for the RCMP as a security force either from friends like the United States or foes like the Soviet Union. Despite the Gouzenko experience and subsequent cold war hostilities the RCMP's priorities continued to be criminal work and events such as integrating into the Force the Newfoundland Rangers and the B.C. Provincial Police.

Special Branch was isolated. It was neither inside nor outside the Force. Its members, working on secret projects they could not discuss with their Mountie colleagues outside the branch, congregated into tiny groups and socialized among themselves. At these gatherings one subject inevitably arose: should Special Branch separate from the RCMP? Straw votes were taken and the results came out always the same. Most Special Branch members favored a split.

Special Branch Mounties were highly dedicated to their work. Men in all branches worked long hours for low pay and no overtime,

---

[1.] The term "across Canada" is not really appropriate in the sense that not a single Special Branch member was stationed in the Maritimes.

but Special Branch members worked even longer hours since they were hopelessly understaffed and underequipped. Added to their dedication as Mounties was a philosophical commitment to stop communism. In those days the Communist Party of Canada (and its front, the Labour Progressive Party) was a viable force and Special Branch was still an infant. The two sides were more evenly matched than they are today and the threat of Communist espionage in the shadow of Gouzenko was more pervasive. There existed hundreds of Communist front groups that Special Branch had to monitor, and, given the resources, scrutinizing all of them was nearly impossible. At first the amount of expertise consisted of taking down license plate numbers at a Ukrainian picnic. When a Soviet Embassy official traveled outside Ottawa he had to file an itinerary and thus enabled Special Branch to mount crude surveillance. The same burly Mountie who followed him to his hotel room at one o'clock in the morning would be back at the hotel at six o'clock to resume the operation. While following the Soviet official throughout the day the Mountie jotted down license plate numbers and descriptions of his contacts and hoped that next week there would be time in his 16-hour day to follow the leads. The investigators were so swamped with work they could not have functioned effectively even if they had had the training, which they didn't. In frustration they came to believe that only a separate security organization could provide them with the resources and the priority needed to fulfill the demands made on them.

Other factors fueled their impatience. RCMP policies and regulations prevented Special Branch from improving in key areas. Special Branch pursued countersubversion (i.e., investigation of the Communist Party of Canada) but essentially remained handcuffed in the counterespionage field (i.e., monitoring the Soviet Embassy). The Force was reluctant to establish a professional surveillance organization; but beyond that Special Branch was hindered in acquiring counterintelligence information by the police attitude of senior RCMP officers who held that investigation had to be precipitated by events. Thus Special Branch initiated no original investigations and only worked on cases passed on by either a friendly foreign service or volunteer sources of information. It still did virtually nothing to exploit the Soviet Embassy's Achilles heel, which was the susceptibility of its officials to defect. For almost a decade following the war the RCMP was in no better position to exploit would-be Gouzenkos than in September, 1945.

The RCMP's elaborate facility in Regina for training Mounties in a variety of policing subjects also provided a course for newly commissioned officers on etiquette, but supplied no training for members of Special Branch. McClellan was urged to bring members from Britain's security service, MI5, to Canada to teach courses on the differences between communism and socialism, but he feared that doing so would create desire for a civilian security organization like Britain's. Instead, for one or two weeks each summer the Force brought in outside lecturers for a one-time class. It was a good effort but was not effective since it involved no textbooks or homework and the students forgot the lectures soon afterward. There was no one to give instruction in the technique of security work except for the odd person like Terry Guernsey, who was fortunate enough to have been sent to England.

Then there was the old foe, the paramilitary structure, the symbol of rigidity and the single most durable roadblock to an effective Special Branch. The system stressed adherence to discipline and rank. Special Branch thought it was above such petty discipline. They were forced to wear uniforms and live in barracks (if single). To get married one needed at least seven years' service and permission from the commanding officer, who made you prove you had a minimum of $1200 in the bank—in those days one-third of a year's salary. Possessing $1200 worth of furniture would suffice but nobody living in barracks had furniture.

The paramilitary system discouraged originality and, more importantly, stifled independent thought. Orders were given and obeyed even when the order-giver was ignorant or out of touch. Special Branch envied Britain's MI5, whose members from all levels sat down and discussed objectives and tactics.

The paramilitary system induced more than an artificial order of behavior. Its promotion system prevented members from gaining the specialization and experience needed to perform their various tasks effectively. Each unit received an allotment of positions for every rank, which meant that promotions often caused a chain reaction of transfers. Every two years or so—often more frequently

—Special Branch members would be shuffled from one position to another. A constable on the Russian Desk might receive promotion to corporal and would be moved elsewhere because all the corporal slots were full on the Russian Desk. It did not matter that he possessed a particular gift for his work and had been studying Russian history and politics in his spare time, or that he knew intimately the characteristics of every potential intelligence officer in the embassy. The only corporal opening might be in a type of work for which he lacked facility. Meanwhile his promotion created an opening for a constable position on the Russian Desk, and the new man would have to learn his predecessor's job. Many transfers occurred not because the individual himself was being promoted but because he was involved in the chain of events to plug holes from somebody else's promotion. The system could not leave a specialist in place. The transfers resembled a game of musical chairs in which few people gained the opportunity to excel in any particular endeavor.

The authority of Special Branch in relation to the rest of the Force was not enhanced when Superintendent Jim Lemieux succeeded McClellan as head of the branch in 1953. The obvious successor was Terry Guernsey but he was passed over because he lacked seniority —then the single most important factor in the promotion of commissioned officers. Lemieux, latterly McClellan's assistant, possessed the appropriate rank and therefore was the logical choice according to the established procedure. Lemieux was a good police officer but was out of place in Special Branch. Unlike McClellan, he neither understood security work nor commanded sufficient authority with the senior police officers overseeing Special Branch.

The RCMP's natural inaptitude toward security work evidently came to the attention of outsiders, for the government actually toyed with the idea of splitting off Special Branch from the RCMP as early as the late 1940s.

"It's been talked about by Prime Ministers and by very senior civil servants going right back to the immediate postwar period," says Jack Pickersgill, who held key government posts throughout the period. "But in the early stages in which I remember participating in any of these discussions, the idea was to get a lawyer who would have legal training in the use of evidence and someone with rather more education than these policemen had because we used to be awfully worried about the inability of a lot of the policemen to distinguish between the CCF and the Communists. But there was always tremendous professional resistance from the Force. It would have been very difficult to do it without having considerable effect on their morale, because you had to give some reason. And what reason can you give?"

The Commissioner through most of the 1950s was Leonard Nicholson, fondly known as "Nick." Nicholson had a craggy face, gray hair, and a genteel military bearing. Although a shy and distant man, he was liked and respected. He was also a man of integrity and conviction, as demonstrated by the fact he is the only Commissioner in RCMP history to resign voluntarily over a policy difference with the government. Nicholson, never having done security work, had little feel for Special Branch but sensed the sentiment for a separate and civilian organization. A few years after becoming Commissioner in 1951, Nicholson requested a study on improvements in Special Branch and the task was assigned to Mark McClung, who headed the civilian group of analysts in that branch.

McClung was a cherubic man with a pleasant outlook on life. Behind his aging kewpie-doll exterior was a mind as sharp as a razor. The son of the famous writer and suffragette Nellie McClung, he was intellectually superior to anybody in Special Branch and this, in a civilian, caused some resentment among some members superior in rank but not in intelligence. The choice of McClung provided insurance that the assignment would receive penetrating analysis. McClung attacked the task with vigor and over a period of a year searched through files and interviewed every officer—except the two most senior ones—and most of the noncommissioned officers in Special Branch. He produced a weighty document known as the "McClung Memorandum" reflecting a consensus of Special Branch's opinions. All but one or two favored an increase in autonomy and civilianization in varying degrees, from a loose federation with the RCMP to complete severance. Not surprisingly, enlisted members and noncommissioned officers leaned strongly toward a separate service.

McClung proposed establishment of a civilian organization called the Canadian Security and Intelligence Organization (CSIO) to assume control over counterespionage and research. In today's environment it would also handle anti-terrorism. CSIO would be separate from the RCMP yet fall under the authority of the Commissioner. Regular Mounties wishing to join would resign from the RCMP and take off their uniforms. It would be run by a civilian director and housed outside RCMP headquarters. Since CSIO personnel would lack the power of arrest and other police powers, the RCMP would handle prosecutions arising out of CSIO's investigations. Special Branch would be reduced in size but remain in existence as part of the RCMP and be responsible for security screening and countersubversion, which CSIO would not do. Furthermore, Special Branch would retain its paramilitary flavor.

In 1955, shortly after McClung's report was finished, Assistant Commissioner Cliff Harvison replaced the good-natured Jim Lemieux as Superintendent of Special Branch. Although he had worked on the Gouzenko investigation, Harvison had spent his entire career on the police side of the Force and his reputation had been made on criminal work in Montreal. Nicknamed "Slim" because he was tall and thin, Harvison possessed an authoritative and booming voice and could be amusing, although not as amusing as his close friend, George McClellan.

Harvison, representing the established view of the Force, was hostile to McClung's proposal and saw no need for civilianizing or separating some of the functions of Special Branch. In fact he thought the civilians were already too dominant. As it turned out, Harvison was head of Special Branch for an even shorter time than Lemieux, but during his brief tenure he repulsed what seemed an inevitable tide. Harvison, contrary to McClung's recommendation, prevented the proposal from being officially discussed and wrote a searing memo to the Commissioner. McClung did not even get to see the Commissioner. He eventually left the Force and his civilian group decayed in size, spirit, and influence.

The episode forced the RCMP to review the status of Special Branch and it took some action. In November, 1956, Special Branch was upgraded into a more authoritative organization called the directorate of Security and Intelligence. However, S&I, as the directorate became known, still reported to a police officer—the Deputy Commissioner in charge of operations—who reported to the Commissioner. S&I would not get its own Deputy Commissioner until after the next fight for separation in 1970, when it was upgraded to its present standing and given its existing name, the Security Service.

The timing in the formation of S&I is intriguing. The RCMP had its own reasons for upgrading Special Branch other than the McClung episode. The Force dealt on a regular basis with high-powered foreign security agencies, such as the FBI and MI5, and felt somewhat abashed that Special Branch was run by a middle-ranking officer and rated only a single box in the RCMP organization chart. Foreign agencies tended not to take Special Branch seriously. Also, the RCMP wanted to impress the Treasury Board, holder of the government purse. By elevating the whole security organization, money would be easier to obtain.

The fight over separation remained an internal matter since the Force viewed it as dirty linen that ought to be kept from the government. In any case, the government throughout this period was absorbed by a more pressing concern in connection with Special Branch over the security screening of individuals with access to classified government information. During this time there was anxiety that Canada would follow the United States in adopting practices approaching the witch hunts of McCarthyism.

The Communist Witch Hunt

COMMUNIST WITCH-HUNTING flourished in the United States during the early 1950s and showed every sign of spreading north of the border. The pressures in Canada were similar to the ones in the United States and streaks of Canadian McCarthyism flared up occasionally but it was not as hideous or pervasive as the American experience.

The most overt symbol of potential Canadian McCarthyism was the Social Credit Member of Parliament for Lethbridge, John Blackmore, a Mormon schoolteacher from Alberta who stood up in the Commons each year and, with a handful of radio transcripts, called the CBC an active agent in communism.

"I think the people of Canada have a right to be protected against an absolute drenching of communism in program after program over the CBC," he bellowed.

Blackmore had a friend who logged CBC programming content and Blackmore produced the results from his pew at the far end of the Commons each year when the corporation's spending estimates were debated. For example, Blackmore produced a verbatim extract from a piece by commentator Max Cohen:

> My own guess is that if communist China could look forward to recognition by the United States and to a place in the U.N., communist China would go through with the motions of a deal.

111

"There we have a very definite pro-communist line," shrieked Blackmore. "... we have the CBC bringing in a man to preach that doctrine to us. Surely that is following the communist line. That is giving comfort to the enemy."

Another commentator suggested on the CBC that the United States should not support Chiang Kai-shek's troops because his government was discredited and the trouble it created for the United States outweighed the military advantages.

"How could you preach a communist line in a more concentrated form, in a greater variety of respects, and for the same length of time than is done right here?" asked Blackmore. "And we are paying men to say these things."

After listing a series of cases Blackmore concluded: "What is it about the CBC's organization, or who are pulling the strings behind the CBC, that causes them to be so emotionally exercised in favour of communism? ... in respect of all these matters that I have indicated here it is just as pro-Russian today as though it were being directed immediately from Moscow. It could not do any better job from Moscow than is being done right now."

Blackmore was isolated in the Commons and MPs openly sneered at him. However, his crusading served to inflame public opinion and exert pressure on the government of the day. It was not difficult to understand why Blackmore had appeal. Nobody knew how many active Communist agents were still embedded in the civil service because the Gouzenko investigation had not cracked all the code names. Furthermore, he never did have any information about the espionage operation, which was under the command of Vitali Pavlov, and Gouzenko did not work for him. Consequently the specter loomed that the Canadian government was penetrated by undiscovered Soviet spies.

The CBC was one of the most vulnerable targets and one of the first to be attacked. Within months of Gouzenko, checks were made into the loyalty of CBC staff, especially on-air personalities who could indoctrinate Canadians with Communist propaganda. The concern was heightened shortly after formal security screening began in 1948 when Special Branch discovered a former executive member of the Communist Party in Nova Scotia on the staff of CBC International in Montreal. He was dismissed but suspicion continued to smolder about subversion from within and later, when Blackmore made his allegations, suspicion multiplied to such proportions that an investigation was ordered. Fortunately for the CBC, Don Wall, a discerning Special Branch civilian and a member of McClung's group of analysts, was assigned to the inquiry. His report concluded that the fears were unfounded and cautioned the government that Canada was in danger of adopting some of the techniques employed in the United States. Wall's report set the government's mind at ease and helped it repulse the Canadian Blackmores.

The National Film Board (NFB) was also an open target. Established in 1939 to develop Canadian film making, the NFB flourished at the outset under the brilliant leadership of John Grierson, and its first half-dozen years created a legacy that stands today. The NFB attracted unusual individuals with peculiar lifestyles and eccentric views. Grierson himself, despite his background as a founder of documentary film-making in Britain, became the subject of an American Intelligence report while he was in Canada.[1]

As luck would have it, Grierson's secretary for a brief period was Freda Linton, who was charged with espionage during the Gouzenko spy trials, but the charges were dropped for lack of evidence. There is little doubt that she had a clandestine connection with the party but nothing linked Grierson to her activities or philosophy. In fact, Gouzenko's testimony tended to absolve him. Exhibit Number 37, one of the documents Gouzenko carried out of the Soviet Embassy, contained the curious notation "Freda to the Professor through Grierson." Gouzenko explained that "the Professor" was Dr. Raymond Boyer of the National Research Council and a Communist Party member subsequently convicted and sentenced to two years imprisonment.

[1.] After Grierson was given the added duty as General Manager of the Wartime Information Board the legendary OSS, the CIA's wartime predecessor, received an intelligence report from an Ottawa-based agent on February 17, 1943, saying: "John Grierson rates a lot of attention from yours truly. Right now the publicity folk in the armed services are hourly expecting an announcement that he has taken over their direction as well as his newly-acquired post of head of the Wartime Information Board. Cagily, Grierson has wrangled the appointment of a successor to Charles Vining in the person of Prof. Norman MacKenzie, but the latter is only a formal figure. John will run the show, with Dave Dunton, former managing editor of the Montreal *Standard,* as his right hand man. Grierson has NOT relinquished his post as Commissioner of the National Film Board. He is still very much the boss there, and rumour hath it that he will be deeply disappointed if the film board's next offering in the World In Action series, tentatively called "Not the Gates of Hell," does not win the Oscar for the best news documentary of 1943."

"The work Freda [Linton] was doing in the Film Board was not satisfactory to Moscow," Gouzenko testified. "Therefore they asked Colonel Zabotin to place her in some more important department. Therefore it looks as if Colonel Zabotin was to place Freda to work with the professor, using Grierson's influence to get her into the position."

Further evidence that Grierson's involvement was innocent and incidental was that the Soviets did not give him a code name. However, his name appeared in the Soviet document and according to the loose standards of the day that was sufficient for a guilt-by-association inference. In 1945 Grierson left the NFB to establish a production company in New York and returned to Canada the following year to testify before the Royal Commission into the Gouzenko disclosures. He was badgered and tormented and although he remained cool and answered all questions politely, he was visibly shaken afterward. All testimony before the Commission occurred behind closed doors and to this day most of it remains secret for the protection of individuals, including prominent Ottawa citizens who had innocent relations with the Soviets at the time. But Grierson's connection consumed six pages of the Commission's published report. Two years later Grierson was deported from the United States and never worked at senior levels again.

In the meantime the NFB fared only slightly better than Grierson. The Freda Linton involvement, whether the Soviets were satisfied with her work or not, stained the Board's reputation and left the stench of subversion throughout the organization. In 1949 the Department of National Defence refused to give contracts to the NFB for the production of classified training films and instead selected two private film-making companies. The stated reason was that the NFB's employees were not screened and could not be screened quickly enough since 200 individuals in the NFB's production unit needed checking. The two private firms, Crawley Films and Associated Screen News, each had only about half a dozen people needing screening. News of this humiliation leaked to the press and strengthened the suspicion that the organization was subversive. The NFB remained ostracized for almost a year while all 580 NFB employees—not just the 200 in the production unit having access to the military films—were checked by Special Branch before National Defence re-enlisted the Board.

Special Branch put in charge of the NFB screening an inspector who knew nothing about communism.

"Have you read the Gouzenko report?" he was asked.

He hadn't.

"Do you understand the Communists' talent-spotting system?"

"I know enough. I know enough," he insisted.

The inspector, now dead, produced the names of about 20 people he thought were security risks, and presented them to NFB Film Commissioner Ross McLean. McLean, a man who combined reason with principle, acknowledged that some had to go. At least two members of a secret Montreal Communist cell were discovered. But McLean would not accept a witch hunt and refused to fire most of them. Only three were ultimately dismissed although some resigned before the ax could fall. McLean himself became a witch-hunt victim. Within the year he was gone too. He read about the appointment of his successor in the newspapers before he was told. During the early 1950s, after McLean's departure, an atmosphere of hysteria reigned in the NFB as other employees were fired outright or pressured into resigning.

While overzealousness ruled in some government offices, there were occasional security breakdowns in others. A young lady who had worked in the women's army corps was dispatched to the Prime Minister's Office as a clerk in the file room without being security-screened. The Prime Minister's Office felt she was secure since she had come from the army and the army had assumed she was secure since she had enlisted in the aid of her country. Her superior in the Prime Minister's file room possessed a penchant for security and allowed her to see only routine correspondence and never let her stay late or work alone. The woman quit in frustration. It was learned afterward that both she and her husband were members of the Communist Party. Later a red-baiting Tory rose in the House of Commons and cited this incident and accused the Prime Minister (Mackenzie King) of harboring spies. The Prime Minister's Office was concerned for a time but the MP had got the woman's name wrong and nobody, including his own party, followed up the matter.[2]

2. The Conservative Member of Parliament was J. H. Ferguson, who represented Simcoe North. During a speech on May 22, 1947, he said: "Until recently, one Ruth McEwan worked in the office of the Prime Minister of Canada. She is the wife of Bert Hughes, an ex-employee of the Film Board at Ottawa, and Hughes is an openly confessed Communist and supporter of that bestial organization."

From the outset the staff of the Royal Commission into the Gouzenko disclosures was split over how aggressive an anti-Communist stance it should take. Some favored adopting tough tactics, as was done on John Grierson, while others foresaw the dangers of overkill. In the end the doves prevailed and the final report produced a relatively calm indictment of Communist espionage conspiracy that refrained from red-baiting. The commission made only seven general recommendations and each one was mildly framed. The most important recommendation urged the government to consider "additional security measures which would be practical to prevent the infiltration into positions of trust under the government of persons likely to commit acts such as those described in this report." In other words, the commission suggested a security-screening system for all civil servants in sensitive positions. Each time somebody was promoted or hired into a job with access to classified information the individual was to have his background checked to determine trustworthiness.

The commission's report was released June 27, 1946. A month earlier, the federal cabinet had already established the Security Panel, an interdepartmental committee of senior officials chaired by the secretary to the cabinet and reporting directly to the cabinet. The Security Panel lasted more than a quarter of a century and throughout its history had a small-l liberal bias. Its members on the whole were sensitive individuals—people such as Arnold Heeney, Norman Robertson, Jack Pickersgill, Bob Bryce, Gordon Robertson, Lester Pearson, and Don Wall—who abhorred McCarthyism and sought to contain its growth in Canada.

The Security Panel considered following Britain and the United States in establishing a loyalty board but rejected the idea. The RCMP opposed it since there would be hearings requiring the production of evidence and possibly the compromising of sensitive sources. Also, the idea of putting a civil servant before a board for the purpose of trying to assess political belief contained a totalitarian component repugnant to the liberal instincts of most panel members. There was also grave doubt that the system could be effective and the American experience soon proved these concerns valid. False loyalty was not susceptible to testing. The panel opted instead for a policy of transferring civil servants to nonsensitive positions if a doubt arose and firing them outright if a serious doubt came up. As for actual Communists, the government took the position that none should be in the civil service. This stand went further than Britain's policy of barring Communists only from positions of trust.

On March 5, 1948, the cabinet issued a directive that presented the government's position on security clearances. A widespread practice of formal screening started immediately in all "vulnerable" areas of government. The departments of National Defence and External Affairs were the first to be designated "vulnerable" because their secret information made them prime espionage targets. As Special Branch overcame the backlog other departments, branches, and agencies were added to the "vulnerable" list. The CBC was among the first and the NFB was included shortly thereafter.

The cabinet directive also widened the search beyond individuals with unfriendly political philosophies and included people with personal characteristics that made them vulnerable to espionage recruitment. After Special Branch began scrutinizing the activity of Canadian Communists, the Soviet Intelligence Services started targeting vulnerable individuals. As far as is known, the number of Soviet successes among these assailable individuals was never large, but they were sufficiently numerous to pose a security danger.

The government bureaucracy in some ways became one big machine that sought to purge from its ranks Communist sympathizers and other political extremists. The Security Panel established policy but lacked the administrative power to stop abuses. It could advise but not enforce. It rarely reviewed cases. Many loyal civil servants became apprehensive about their future. The anxiety was heightened when the United States began showing concern that American information lodged in Canadian government departments might not be secure. External Affairs and National Defence were particularly jumpy. At the same time Canadian departments were establishing their own security branches and issuing rules to protect confidentiality of information. Also, Special Branch's investigative techniques were not always subtle. All these factors, combined with cold war tension, exerted pressure on individuals to abandon common sense and the principles of natural justice.

The most deceptive danger, though, was the actual process of security screening. Many officers in Special Branch were militantly anti-Communist, but the RCMP never attempted to press its views on the political decision-makers. The Force understood that in a democratic society the police had to be subservient to the elected authority, and accepted this relationship without much complaint. To its credit, the RCMP always remained circumspect in keeping its political views private and not overstepping its mandate. The danger was more subtle. The security-screening reports compiled by the RCMP were supposed to be factual compilations of the subject's background and past activities. Special Branch was supposed to be the disinterested investigator while the deputy minister of the involved department became the judge who decided individual cases. There were no formal hearings or appeals because security work, being a secretive process by nature and requiring the protection of sensitive sources and methods, was jeopardized when the aggrieved individual had his day in court and could challenge the basis of the information against him. So if the individual was to be denied a defense, justice demanded he should also be spared a prosecution. The deputy minister was supposed to arrive at a decision in a non-adversarial atmosphere devoid of cross challenging. However, the system often broke down because the Mounties too often were ignorant of communism, moralistic in outlook, and lacking in training and judgment. Information in the reports was not always reliable and often irrelevant and some of it had to be challenged. This precipitated an adversarial encounter that should have been avoided. It was symbolical that Special Branch produced adverse reports on pink paper.

Too many Special Branch members did not understand what constituted good historical evidence. By nature they tended to look on the darker side of life. If the Force had accumulated a thick file on an individual, it was inclined to believe—particularly in the earlier years—that the person was dangerous. Despite its spotty record, there was no evil intent within Special Branch. In fact, there existed a genuine desire on the part of most members to be reasonable and just. Their failures reflected, not a lack of good will, but a lack of articulation and power of analysis.

Lack of experience on the part of the involved department played a contributing role in some of the decisions. Officially the deputy minister was responsible for deciding cases. However, the substantive decision was usually made by the department's security officer and the deputy minister became the arbitrator of last resort. The security officer in most departments represented a new concept and few of them had the training or experience to make consistent and judicious decisions. In all but the most sensitive departments the security officer was the personnel officer doing two jobs and had little rationale for decision-making. Too often he tended to accept the RCMP information unquestioningly. As late as 1969, when the report on security was published, the deficiency had not been completely corrected. "We have in fact found few departments where security officers and staff are adequate in strength, calibre, status, or training," the commission said.

For a time it seemed inevitable that Canada would follow the United States into a full-scale witch hunt—a few years late and with less intensity. The Security Panel, no matter how liberal its character, was largely powerless to prevent it. If it was to be stopped it was up to the departmental security officers to do it at the case level and, as just noted, they had deficiencies of their own. The Security Panel created the Security Subpanel consisting of departmental security officers who met every two weeks to discuss difficult cases. That proved to be a significant development and as a result security officers began exchanging experiences and scrutinizing Special Branch reports more critically. It provided departmental security officers a new non-RCMP perspective for arriving at decisions and the process became more sophisticated.

Coupled with the creation of the subpanel was the appointment of Peter Dwyer as its chairman. Dwyer, a former British intelligence officer, played a central role in halting the slide to McCarthyism. He was a humanist to the core yet his involvement in espionage gave him the experience that was needed. He was not merely following a code of rules but was trying to operate a system. Kim Philby, the famous Soviet double agent in the British Secret Service, replaced Dwyer as MI6's liaison officer in Washington late in 1949. "I knew him for a brilliant wit, and was to learn that he had a great deal more to him than just wit," Philby writes in his autobiography, *My Silent War*.

When the British Secret Service officially upgraded the position, the senior Philby replaced the middle-ranking Dwyer, which, Philby writes, was unfair to Dwyer since he had done an outstanding job that would be difficult to improve upon. Dwyer did not return to London. Instead he resigned and accepted a position as head of reporting in Canada's secret Communications Branch, which intercepted the Soviet Union's electronic signals under the cover of the National Research Council. Philby wrote:

> Peter Dwyer met me and explained, over our first bourbon, that his resignation had nothing to do with my appointment to succeed him. For personal reasons, he had long wanted to settle in Canada, where a congenial government post was awaiting him. The news of my posting to Washington had simply determined the timing of his northward move to Ottawa. So we started on a pleasant footing. Nothing could exceed the care and astuteness with which he inducted me into Washington politics.

Philby's book revealed for the first time that Dwyer was responsible for identifying atomic bomb spy Klaus Fuchs. The authorities knew a leak had occurred and had narrowed down the investigation to two scientists, Dr. Peierls and Dr. Fuchs, but could not advance it further. According to Philby, Dwyer's last service to the British before leaving for Ottawa was "a brilliant piece of analysis" that conclusively eliminated Dr. Peierls as a suspect. Dwyer was never proud of that achievement and rarely discussed it.

Nothing about Peter Dwyer pointed toward a career in security and intelligence. He was somewhat pudgy, wore glasses, and had slightly bulging eyes. He was an only child in an artistic family. His father was a symphony conductor and on occasion guest-conducted at the fashionable Glyndebourne Festival south of London. Dwyer himself was inclined toward the fine arts and took an intense interest in music, ballet, theater, and poetry while attending Oxford University, where he studied modern languages and was editor of the undergraduate newspaper *The Cherwell* and member of the Oxford repertory theater. After graduating he worked for Fox Films and is credited with discovering the English actress Joan Greenwood. At the outbreak of World War Two he worked with Movie-Tone News producing newsreels for theater showings until he received an unsolicited telephone call.

"My name is Dwyer," said the voice.

"That's odd, my name is Dwyer too," replied Dwyer.

"Oh no, I got it wrong. My name is not Dwyer."

The caller invited Dwyer to lunch. He was from MI6, the British Secret Service, and his purpose was to recruit Dwyer into wartime intelligence work. Since Dwyer spoke several languages and had achieved outstanding marks at Oxford, MI6's talent-spotting system picked him up. He was first stationed in France but before the war ended was moved to Panama and met the daughter of a British bank manager who became his wife. After the war he stayed on with MI6 and went to Washington as liaison officer. He was also the liaison officer to the Canadian security and intelligence community and visited Ottawa once a month or so from his Washington base. Dwyer had already made an impression on Canadian officials during the Gouzenko investigation and Norman Robertson sought to bring him to Canada. When he came eventually, after Philby replaced him in Washington, he received about $5000 a year, which represented a considerable pay cut. He was more concerned about raising his children in Canada than he was about money or seniority, although he occasionally prefaced a remark with: "When I was in Washington and rich ..." Bill Stephenson, the Man from Intrepid, loaned him money to buy his first house in Ottawa. In 1952, two years after coming to Canada, he moved to the Privy Council Office and occupied an office in the East Block on Parliament Hill.

Dwyer was concerned about Special Branch's lack of sophistication in preparing security reports on individuals, but he never betrayed his feelings to the Force and always tried to resolve differences in a friendly and diplomatic manner. He possessed the ability to encourage Special Branch to do better without being negative or condescending. He felt it essential to maintain good relations and the RCMP always invited him to its parties.

During Dwyer's six years at the Privy Council Office the quality of adverse screening reports improved remarkably, although it was by no means all his doing. There were other factors, such as Terry Guernsey's system for source evaluation and the fact that Special Branch was improving with experience. As well, Special Branch instituted formal guidelines for its investigators and this improved consistency. Dwyer's formidable presence as back-up referee to department security officers stimulated Special Branch into taking more care and assessing material more thoroughly before passing it on to the department. Special Branch knew bad preparation would be exposed and the file would be returned with a request for more investigation. Eliminating sloppy preparation was a key achievement in curbing McCarthyism.

Security work was merely an interlude for Dwyer. He disliked the whole business and wanted to get out. To escape the tension of his job, each day he lunched at the old Belle Claire Hotel with colleagues and friends like Mark McClung, Don Wall, Don Beavis, and Frank Milligan. His eyes always brightened whenever the subject of ballet, books, poetry, or music was raised and he begged his superiors for a transfer. The government had been consulting him on implementing recommendations from the Massey Royal Commission on the arts, letters, and sciences. In 1958, his final year at the Privy Council, he spent as much time drafting the Canada Council Act as he did on security.

Dwyer got his wish for a transfer and was named supervisor of the arts program when the Canada Council was born. He loved his new work and good-naturedly protested when somebody approached him for advice on security problems.

"That's all over," he'd exclaim. "It's done. Thank God."

One of the few times he became depressed was when his friend Kim Philby defected to the Soviet Union. He could not believe it; like everyone else, he had been fooled.

Dwyer rose to the position of Assistant Director, then Associate Director, and finally Director of the Canada Council. After becoming Director he suffered a stroke that left his face twisted and one side of his body paralyzed. His only concern was that he could not do his job any more. He learned to write left-handed and returned to work but died from a second stroke on New Year's Eve, 1972.

When Peter Dwyer left the Privy Council Office in 1958 the threat of anti-Communist witch-hunting had subsided. Not only was there a system of control over security-screening procedures but, more importantly, the hysteria that the civil service was full of infiltrators had subsided. The quality and the experience of departmental security officers were on the rise and new regulations giving failed security screening targets greater rights were on the drawing board. However, only red-baiting had abated and witch-hunting in other security areas remained alive. It would be up to Dwyer's successor to deal with the remaining problems.

The Homosexual
Witch Hunt

A NEW EVIL replaced Communist ideology as a potential threat to security and the attack upon it grew more pervasive. In the 1950s every homosexual in the civil service feared discovery because it often led to dismissal. Secret homosexuals—and in those days virtually all homosexuals were in the closet—were vulnerable to blackmail. Whether breaches of security did take place or could take place did not seem to matter at that time. Scores of people were fired who were loyal, patriotic, capable, and hard-working civil servants. Furthermore, it was freely acknowledged that this was the case.

One of the earliest firings occurred at the peak of the anti-Communist campaign in 1952. A homosexual was discovered working in a middle-management position at Canada's most secret institution, the Communications Branch, which intercepted radio signals mainly from the northern regions of the Soviet Union. The individual's loyalty or honesty was never in doubt, but the authorities feared more than anything that the Americans would find out, thus jeopardizing the arrangements for sharing intelligence, which would be a severe blow since Canada received more than it gave. The case was investigated personally by George McClellan, then head of Special Branch, and the man, who admitted his homosexuality, was asked to resign. There was no attempt to transfer him into a nonsensitive position elsewhere in the civil service.

Other homosexual cases were to follow at the Communications

Branch. At the end of the 1950s a senior manager was discovered. By this time the policy had been humanized and he was transferred to a nonsensitive position outside the branch. Then in 1963 a ring of homosexual code clerks who had arranged to be put on the same shift was uncovered in the communications center, the most sensitive part of the branch. Some were transferred and others fired outright. The Force managed to recruit informers among both groups.

However, the Communication Branch's problem with homosexuals did not match that of its American counterpart, the National Security Agency (NSA) at Fort Meade, Maryland. Two young NSA mathematicians defected to Russia in 1960 and held a news conference in Moscow, providing details of the United States' most secret institution. They were discovered to be homosexual and subsequently both NSA's personnel director and security director resigned and 26 other employees were fired for sexual deviation.

After Gouzenko, ideological spies were hard to find and recruit because the Communist Party of Canada was too closely surveilled and too well penetrated to be of use for Soviet espionage. The Russians were forced to shift to a new breed of spy, and began concentrating efforts on suborning people. The espionage priority was to find civil servants with access to classified information who had personal secrets to hide and put the squeeze on them. The process did not have to be subtle, for even people who refused often failed to report the attempt because that simply guaranteed they would be exposed.

Blackmailable civil servants included alcoholics, compulsive gamblers, large debtors, and people practicing a whole range of sexual taboos such as patronizing prostitutes, indulging in unusual sexual behavior, having extra-marital love affairs, engaging in bigamy, and, of course, homosexuality. The RCMP viewed homosexuality as a grievous moral offense and concentrated on this characteristic at the expense of the other practices even though the others posed equally great, if not greater, security risks. The Force's bias was reinforced by the departmental policy of arbitrarily firing all discovered homosexuals without bothering to determine whether they actually were a risk.

An investigative unit called A-3 was formed within the Force to concentrate exclusively on homosexuals. It was called A-3 because it was the third subsection of A Section, which was responsible for security screening. The special unit approached its task thoroughly as if starting at A for Agriculture and working its way through to Veterans' Affairs. The investigation spread far and wide and became far-reaching even by police standards. Informers watched favorite gathering spots such as informal gay bars and public parks. Ironically the RCMP had no trouble recruiting informers among homosexuals despite the Force's unfriendly attitude. Many male homosexuals seemed to get a weird satisfaction from turning in their fellows.[1] Each week dozens of new files were opened and more manpower added. A special digit was added to the code number of the file of every individual who happened to be homosexual.[2] Soon the Force had 3,000 cases and an administrative headache handling all the files. The investigation by this time had spilled out of the civil service and into the general public.

The CIA had used lie detectors to uncover homosexuals with devastating success, and the Force wanted to employ them. One sweep through the civil service would root out virtually every homosexual who came under suspicion. But the Security Panel recommended against their introduction and managed to keep them out of government in Canada. In some ways, though, it did not matter because individuals, when confronted, frequently confessed. The following excerpt from one of my interviews with a Mountie on the homosexual squad explains why:

Q: What happened if a civil servant denied being a homosexual?

A: I conducted hundreds of these interviews and almost never was there a denial.

Q: You would actually interview the civil servant?

A: Yes.

[1.] Lesbians, on the other hand, rarely cooperated and virtually never became informers. The Force attributed this to protective motherly instincts and the belief they just did not like men anyway. Since all RCMP investigators were men, the Force for a time considered hiring women investigators to handle lesbians.

[2.] The normal file number D939 followed by five digits indicates that the person has been subjected to a field investigation. Suspected homosexuals had their index read D939-7 followed by five digits. That extra digit, always a seven, identified the subject as a homosexual. It was not even necessary to open the file.

Q: Would they remain in their position if it was a sensitive position?

A: If they fought hard enough. Again, it happened so damn seldom that they would ever deny it. I couldn't understand it. I developed a technique of interviewing so that you knew right away if you were on the wrong track. It was done this way: "Well, Mr. X, it's nice to see you today. Now sit down. How long have you been practicing homosexuality in the city of Ottawa?" And if you get the wrong guy you'll get a reaction—now. And if you get the right guy, he'll stop and think for a minute. Then you know you got the right guy.

Q: Shock will be registered?

A: Yeah. Shock. If somebody calls me a fruit he's going to be wearing the desk. But if somebody calls me a reasonably enthusiastic heterosexual, I'm going to think for a minute: "Now what does he mean by that?" So you get a reaction one way or another.

Q: The guys admitting it would be either transferred or fired, would they?

A: Yeah. Resignation. That's a real bad deal, really.

Never did the campaign become public because most discovered homosexuals accepted their fate. Even the few who protested internally were frightened of possible public exposure. Most would sooner lose their jobs.

On one occasion the A-3 unit tried to plot the groupings of homosexuals on a city map. The theory was that people, particularly homosexuals, followed patterns, and if these exhibited themselves in definable physical movements, the Force would find the magic key for locating the whereabouts of other as yet undetected gay individuals. Every area with a concentration of homosexuals was identified and marked with a red dot on a map of the city of Ottawa. Civil servants spotted in these areas might be unidentified homosexuals or latent homosexuals needing investigation. The map, purchased from the National Capital Commission, soon contained so many colored dots that it was awash in red ink. A second and larger map was purchased, this time from the city of Ottawa—the largest one available.

It, too, was overcome by red ink. A third and last effort was made. A Mountie approached the Department of National Defence with a request to fly over the city with high-resolution cameras for the purpose of producing an extraordinarily large map. The department was experiencing an austerity program at the time and refused. The map exercise died.

The RCMP campaign against homosexuals was conducted essentially without the knowledge of the Privy Council Office or any outsiders. The Force did not volunteer that information and the victims did not complain. The Privy Council Office and the departmental security officers saw only the reports on individual's cases. However, they did know many homosexuals were being discovered by the Force and subsequently lost to the government.

Midway through his time in the Privy Council Office Peter Dwyer hired Don Wall as an assistant. Wall was a civilian analyst in Special Branch and Dwyer first knew him at the Communications Branch, where both were employed. Dwyer was later impressed with Wall's calm report concerning the Communist scare within CBC International. Wall looked like the farm truck driver he had been in his student days to finance his way through university. He was short and stocky and possessed unusually large hands that vise-gripped the hands of people he greeted. His rough-hewn face could have been chiseled by a sculptor. He had the same liberal instincts as Dwyer and the same love for music, especially opera, and the arts. When Wall graduated from the University of Saskatchewan in 1950 with a Master's degree in English he was approached by a federal employee.

"Do you want a job with the National Research Council?" he was asked. "I can't tell you what it is. It's confidential research in communications."

Wall accepted since no English-teaching jobs were available at the time. The job was not really with the NRC, it was with the Communications Branch under the cover of the NRC. Later he moved to the RCMP and worked with Mark McClung before Dwyer plucked him from Special Branch and put him in the Privy Council Office in 1955 as secretary to the Security Subpanel. As Dwyer worked less on security and more on the Canada Council, Wall took on more of the work and succeeded Dwyer when he went to the Canada Council in

1958. At first Gordon Frazer became Wall's assistant, but a short time later Don Beavis arrived and remained for more than a decade. Wall became the guiding light in the introduction of a new policy that gave some protection from firing based on tenuous and irrelevant allegations. Some of the most gifted civil servants were being driven out of government and Wall, disturbed by this loss of talent, expressed the regret to Bob Bryce, then secretary to the cabinet and chairman of the Security Panel.

"Surely we can make better decisions," said Wall.

Bryce agreed that the policy was arbitrary and should be studied. A research project was started to determine whether distinctions could be drawn between homosexuals who constituted a security threat and those who did not.

The research started late in 1959 and was finished in the fall of 1962. It concluded that sexual orientation was not a matter of choice. Although that finding today appears obvious and mild, it was crucial then since it removed homosexuality from the old character-weakness category and helped persuade the Security Panel that a nonmechanistic approach was needed for dealing with homosexuals. As a result, there were to be no more arbitrary firings. Each case required individual assessment as to whether the person was vulnerable. The difficult cases were left for Wall to deal with personally. Technically he could only make recommendations but they were invariably accepted by the department. He invited the individual into his office for a long and open discussion, during which it usually became clear whether or not the person represented a risk. People who discussed their homosexuality freely were generally safe and not likely to yield to blackmail attempts unless they feared their parents' finding out. The troublesome task, especially at the beginning, was gaining their confidence. They at first interpreted the new policy as a maneuver to obtain an admission so there would be grounds for dismissal. Eventually trust was established. The fact that homosexuals knew they had somewhere to go where they would receive understanding rather than punishment was the most effective security improvement possible, for it lessened measurably the prospect of successful blackmail.

Wall set the example by clearing two homosexuals in his own department, the Privy Council Office, where virtually everything was classified material. One of them worked in the sensitive cabinet documents center. The other worked in the Emergency Measures Organization. Both individuals were judged stable and not vulnerable but, in keeping with standard government policy, neither was permitted to travel abroad where the likelihood of a recruitment attempt was greater.

A renaissance in attitude toward the security reliability of homosexuals emerged. Abuses still occurred because not all security officers were converted at the outset, but in time the number of firings dropped almost to nil. The Communications Branch, which along with External Affairs and the Navy, possessed one of the least enviable records on firings, mellowed considerably and in one case backed down when a homosexual employee refused even a transfer to the National Research Council. The only alternative in such a case was to fire him. Instead, the individual was put under surveillance to ensure that he was not in contact with foreigners, and allowed to keep his job. In the old days he would have been fired automatically.

This new policy toward homosexuals occurred during the latter part of the Diefenbaker government and was approved personally by the Prime Minister and subsequently confirmed by his successor, Lester Pearson. The RCMP fought it. The issue was debated at length on the Security Panel on which the RCMP Commissioner was a standing member. The Force initially maintained that all homosexuals were security risks. When that argument was whittled away, Commissioner Harvison insisted that all homosexuals should be fired because homosexuality was illegal under the Criminal Code of Canada and the government of Canada was condoning illegal activity. Harvison, with that argument, was speaking as a policeman, not as a security officer, whereas the mandate of the Security Panel was to safeguard security and not apprehend criminals.

The RCMP held to its view that homosexuality was a criminal offense (which it was) and a character weakness (which it was not). To the horror of the Force a ring of homosexuals was discovered in its own central records section in the criminal division at headquarters and was, moreover, led by a commissioned officer. The officer, an inspector, was fired as were about six noncommissioned officers. This incident was followed several years later by another in which a single NCO homosexual was discovered and dismissed. Rather than moderate its hard-line stance, these incidents merely caused the

RCMP to redirect the homosexual hunt inward and escalate it to even more terrifying levels.

The RCMP has always believed—and still does—its own mythology that Mounties are beings of superior quality and character. If evidence of bad behavior or character defect reached the Force an ad-hoc investigation was established. If a Mountie fell too deeply into debt—in the Force's opinion—the individual was interviewed by a superior officer and told to change his ways. If the "fault" went uncorrected, the member was dismissed. The RCMP always punished its own severely because bad Mounties did more than break the rules: they violated a trust. Homosexuality, as a character defect, represented an aggravated disciplinary problem.

An internal homosexual investigation unit was established with the same goals and zeal of the earlier investigations. The two investigators who had been involved with the bizarre map experiment got leading roles in this inquiry. This time the Force was in complete control since the target was its own organization and no Security Panel or non-RCMP security officer could pass judgment on the results. The investigators compiled a list of known homosexual cases from outside the Force from previous investigations and prepared an inventory of the recurring characteristics found in homosexuals. These became "indicators" that were cross-indexed with descriptions of Mounties and any Mounties possessing some of those indicators became suspects and targets for investigation. Driving a white car was one indicator. Wearing a ring on the pinkie finger was another. Effeminate clothing was also one—with the RCMP devising its own definition of effeminate clothing, including the style of necktie. One Mountie fell under suspicion and was investigated because he possessed the following indicators: he split up with his wife, wore tight pants, let his hair grow, and became promiscuous. Promiscuity was considered a sign leading to homosexuality because the individual was trying to convince himself he was not one. The Mountie was transferred to another division.

A homosexual high-school teacher in the city of Ottawa who was an old informer and who claimed to be able to spot another homosexual on sight was tapped to quietly observe members of the Force. The internal investigation reached its peak at about the time Justice Minister Pierre Trudeau introduced the Omnibus Bill making homosexuality legal between consulting adults. The investigation continued and died out in the early 1970s. Homosexuality is still considered a character weakness and any employee of the RCMP, whether Mountie or civilian, whether in a sensitive position or not, is dismissed for it.

Homosexual witch-hunting came and went but a residue remained in the form of a permanent Internal Security Branch, which among other things systematically probed members of the Force. The internal homosexual investigation unit did not so much go out of business as it broadened its scope to include general internal inquiries, and from then on every Mountie fell under investigation at one time or another. In that regard the RCMP joined the ranks of other large police forces that have special units continually testing their own members. The Force's techniques included random tapping of office telephones without the knowledge of the commanding officer. These investigations were in addition to the thorough background checks done automatically when members join the Force. Upon enlisting, new members are subjected to a field investigation covering the previous 10 years. Another investigation covering 20 years is done when a person is transferred into the Security Service.

In the early 1970s a member of the Watcher Service in Ottawa fell under suspicion when a Soviet intelligence officer suddenly canceled a meet the Force had staked out. The Watcher was suspected of having tipped off the Soviet officer. The Internal Security Branch handled the investigation and, ironically, put under surveillance the suspected Watcher. No incriminating evidence was unearthed but, as a safety measure, the individual was transferred to a meaningless job.

Every Security Service needs an internal security system to discover the Kim Philbys of the world. The challenge is to devise a judicious procedure and find individuals to operate it who are efficient and thorough, yet humane and understanding of human frailty. The task is even more challenging in a paramilitary structure like the RCMP where the accent rests on discipline and order and not on discretion.

11

The Fruit Machine

ANY LOOK INTO the homosexual clamp-down of the late 1950s and early 1960s cannot fully capture the mood of the time without examining the so-called "Fruit Machine." Its purpose was to detect homosexuals among civil servants. The Fruit Machine is unknown and infamous at the same time. While the project was a secret and remained so, word at the time leaked out within the security community and rumors began flying. The RCMP tried to recruit members as guinea pigs but nobody would submit to the test. "I wouldn't go anywhere near it in case they put the electrodes on me and the machine blew a fuse," quips one Security Service officer. Jokes circulated and soon the device was dubbed the Fruit Machine, and the name stuck. "You'd better be careful or they'll put you into the Fruit Machine" was a popular refrain.

One of the Security Service's homosexual informers voluntarily took the test and reputedly was treated as a madman. "Keep him in the corner, don't let him get away," the machine's operator reportedly said. The bewildered homosexual, one of the few who did not hide his sexual proclivity, replied: "I volunteered for this. What's the matter with this guy? Is he crazy?" While the incident is undoubtedly exaggerated, and possibly wholly untrue, the story nonetheless made the rounds and soon members of the Security Service believed, as one member put it, that subjects would be confronted with flashing lights shrieking: "Fruit, fruit, fruit!"

133

There were no electrodes and no flashing lights. At the time the Fruit Machine was a sophisticated endeavor, representing the latest in the then-current technology. In retrospect it is a zany experiment that combines shades of George Orwell and Woody Allen. "I wouldn't do it today if somebody came along with a million bucks," says one of the participants. The Fruit Machine never did work. Possibly the most surprising element is how such a project could last nearly four years and involve respectable scientists and senior government people.

The principal group in establishing the research program which led to the development of the Fruit Machine—never called that by the people directly involved—was the Security Panel. To some extent Prime Minister John Diefenbaker played a role, although he was never told about the exact nature of the project. Diefenbaker, a civil rightist, accepted the advice of the Security Panel that homosexuals should not be dismissed from the civil service on innuendo and hearsay evidence. Both he and the Panel believed that objective evidence of vulnerability to blackmail was required. Given the fact that secret homosexuality existed and could represent a security threat, that the Americans were pressuring Canada to take a harder line against homosexuals, and that no objective method of discovering homosexuality was known, it was agreed that a scientific means should be found for testing one's sexual inclination.

The research project went forward in utmost secrecy. The Privy Council Office pulled it together. A psychologist was seconded from the Department of National Defence and some advice and assistance came from the Department of National Health and Welfare. An outside psychiatrist and a psychologist with an existing security clearance were recruited as consultants. NCOs from the Security Service were assigned by the RCMP. The staff of the Security Panel were consulted from time to time. There were scientists interested in pure science. There were men of conscience who wanted to protect helpless victims. And there were dinosaurs who wanted to purge, at last, homosexuals from the civil service. Secret funding was arranged through the Defence Research Board and office space was located in a psychology laboratory at the National Defence Medical Center where team members could come and go without arousing curiosity.

The team began compiling a program of conventional psychological tests and series of polygraph-like tests designed to check pulse rate, skin reflexes, and breathing rate. The plan was to monitor as many physiological variables as possible in the hope of finding a reliable method for identifying homosexuals without arousing the fear and anxiety involved with polygraph testing. Included in this series was a technique known as pupilary response: the examination of the human eye to measure how the pupil changed in size from visual sexual stimulation.

The technique was not entirely new. At the time, measuring the pupil of the eye was in vogue in academic circles, although for purposes other than to determine one's sexual tendencies. It had already been determined that the size of the pupil varied in proportion to a person's interest in what he was seeing. If a person saw something that provoked his interest, his pupil widened. An American university professor took the theory one step further and took subjects into a supermarket and attached to their heads a device with a camera mounted at the end of a pointer. The camera photographed the subjects' pupils as they roamed the aisles. The experiment produced scientific data that the subjects' pupils expanded and contracted from display to display. The experiment, conducted solely as a marketing tool so that manufacturers knew what kind of packaging appealed to consumers, was published in academic journals.

The team learned of these experiments and believed that if the packaging of a box of crackers caused a consumer's pupils to expand, the picture of a nude male would have the same effect on a male homosexual. Since earlier tests had already proven that the expanding and contracting process was involuntary, the team thought it might have found an objective and more reliable method for determining whether a male subject was stimulated by the appearance of another male body.

Work began on designing an apparatus to measure pupilary response. The subject sat in a chair similar to one found in a dentist's office. Above him hung a camera suspended from pulleys and pointed to his pupils. In front was a black box with a fluorescent screen and a projector beaming pictures inside.

"It looked like something out of science fiction," says one of the participants. "It didn't look as if it had been built on earth. I'm not trying to be sensational about that. It was a whole bunch of girders that were small flanges to bolt equipment together, and a screen in a box containing naughty pictures."

The pictures included a variety of humdrum scenes as well as sexually provocative pictures of males and females. The subject being tested was told it was an experiment to measure stress.

The practice of measuring pupilary response proved to be more complicated that anticipated. The technology for performing such tests in a sexual context was unknown and had to be invented, thus most of the experimenting was done on the technology and not the objectives. People were different heights, had different-sized pupils and different distances between eyeballs. Furthermore, the eye turned out to be one of the most difficult autonomic responses to measure. Pictures could not be taken head on since the camera blocked the subject's vision of the pictures. The camera had to be moved off at an angle but this made measurement more difficult. Fast-action cameras with high resolution lens were needed to maintain accuracy, and these eventually were secured from the Air Force, which had photographic equipment capable of taking pictures between the flashes of propellers. Each picture of the pupil had to be developed and magnified. It was a laborious process since each subject generated scores of these enlarged prints.

Each time one problem was solved, another emerged. The project always seemed to be tripping over stumbling-blocks. The months turned into years with no demonstrable results. The team even had trouble securing recruits. The Force produced none, mainly because, as noted earlier, word leaked out and nobody could be talked into volunteering. The Department of National Defence claimed it had no homosexuals. There were long discussions with the Surgeon General about using random samples of homosexual and heterosexual civil servants who were in the process of being dismissed, but no agreement was reached.

Soon the focus of the original project was derailed. What began as a comprehensive test involving a series of examinations got bogged down in the technical difficulties of measuring the varying widths of people's pupils.

Finally two problems defeated the Fruit Machine. The amount of light coming from the screen changed with each new slide, causing the size of the pupil to adjust accordingly—decreasing for bright pictures and increasing for dark ones—and compromising the results of the experiment. An attempt was made to hold the pictures to a uniform brightness but it was troublesome and went without complete success. The ultimate problem was even more basic: the change in pupil size was so small it was hard to measure. The researchers concluded that a 25 percent change represented a significant difference, but even a change of such magnitude represented less than one millimeter, and while the change could be observed it could not always be calibrated accurately.

Neither the lighting nor the measurement problem was insurmountable, but much more research was needed and the government's patience was wearing out. The end came when one of the government's recurring economy drives coincided with the request for more funds. The Defence Research Board had never been interested in the project in the first place and happily cut the funding when the government lost enthusiasm.

The Fruit Machine was doomed in any case. New technology involving telemetry was advancing rapidly and it no longer required the subject to sit in a lab. A simple device could be attached to the individual's body and a series of responses could be measured remotely as the subject went through his normal day. Measuring penal width was a simpler and more accurate method of measuring sexual arousal and with telemetry this could be accomplished with relative ease and accuracy.

When the Fruit Machine died its deserving death, with it went all other phases of the over-all program. By this time the Security Panel's program of dealing with homosexuals on an individual basis was already operating and the fear of homosexuality as a security weakness was abating. Today most people would rather forget their involvement with the Fruit Machine.

Domestic Discord

THE FRUIT MACHINE had been devised with the Department of External Affairs in mind. Concern touched all corners of the department but concentrated specifically on the embassy in Moscow, where several diplomats had been recalled. With the possible exception of the Navy, no department was believed to have more homosexuals during the big purge than External Affairs. And the homosexuals in no other department were so wracked by firings and fear. The sudden departures touched all levels, from senior administrators to lowly clerks. Lester Pearson, Under-Secretary of State for External Affairs from 1946 to 1948, described in Volume III of his memoirs how he advised an official in his department "to leave the foreign service since he might be subject to blackmail." Pearson helped the man establish a new career. Later, after Pearson was no longer Under-Secretary and when homosexuals became a primary target both of the KGB (as a means of conducting espionage) and the RCMP (as a means of stopping espionage), the gentlemanly practice of helping one find a new career was not followed.

External Affairs, influenced by RCMP pressure, did the same as other departments and demanded resignations. Dozens of foreign service officers, including senior individuals, were recalled from abroad and told to quit. The recalls came mostly from the embassy in Moscow but no center was safe. A young External Affairs officer attached to the International Control Commission in Vietnam was compromised by the Poles as a result of a homosexual relationship with a local Vietnamese.

Homosexuality was particularly troublesome for External Affairs because it had so many overseas postings. These postings presented special temptations and threats. It was difficult for a hostile country to discover homosexuals in Canada and also difficult to exploit them, although both can be, and have been, done. However, when the geography is reversed, the host country has an advantage and can mount elaborate operations through bugs, wire-taps, and local spies to pinpoint homosexuals among the embassy staff and, once done, to contrive circumstances to entrap them.

Later, when Canadian policy was liberalized and homosexuals were transferred into nonsensitive positions rather than being routinely fired, homosexuals at External Affairs were still prohibited from going overseas. While the restriction was necessary from a security standpoint, it limited External Affairs severely because the department was in the business of sending its employees around the world. It also acutely limited the career of the affected individual because one cannot prosper at External Affairs without gaining experience abroad. So despite the liberalized rules, homosexuals had an incentive to stay in the closet.

External Affairs concentrated on homosexuals during the late 1950s and early 1960s at the expense of heterosexuals, who were often equally or more vulnerable. The Canadian Embassy in Moscow was effectively penetrated through a heterosexual code clerk who worked in the cipher room. He was attending the Bolshoi Ballet and the seat next to him was taken by a glamorous woman named Larissa Fedorovna Dubanova. It happened that Miss Dubanova spoke perfect English and was more interested in him than in the performance.

The clerk should have spotted her as a KGB seductress because all External Affairs personnel are warned of recruitment and entrapment techniques before taking an Iron Curtain posting. However, External Affairs neglected its lower-echelon employees such as cipher clerks, messengers, secretaries, and the like. They were pseudo-servants and their superiors, the diplomats, did not socialize with them. So they lived in a foreign country with a strange language and an alien culture and were isolated in their own embassy as well. Cut off and lonely, they looked for friendship, which made them acutely susceptible to recruitment despite the warnings of the foreign service manual.

The KGB knows which individuals are susceptible since household staffs and some low-level, nonsensitive embassy staff members are Soviet citizens who frequently act as informers.[1] Supplied by the state employment bureau, they spot embassy personnel who are lonely, who fight with their spouses, and who may be homosexual. The KGB responds by producing a tailor-made sexual partner— either homosexual or heterosexual—and devising a pretext for an encounter and, possibly, courtship. Later a KGB officer produces photographs.

In the case of the Canadian cipher clerk, the Soviets used a variation of the classic blackmail attempt. Outright blackmail was inappropriate because he was single and his sexual encounter with Miss Dubanova did not break the law. There was nothing to hide. The KGB let the relationship grow until the two of them talked marriage—secret marriage, so that his job at the embassy would not be jeopardized.[2] The KGB arranged a fake marriage, which was concealed from the Canadian Embassy. From that point on he had something to hide and had become blackmailable.

The KGB had two levers. First, it could tell the embassy and he would be withdrawn and probably prosecuted. Second, the KGB could make arrangements so that he would never see his "wife" again. The cipher clerk became a Soviet agent. He disclosed all the traffic he was deciphering and enciphering and provided the cipher system itself. As an insider he was able to plant bugs within portions of the embassy and dismantle them when the bug sweepers arrived in Moscow for a periodic check. Through these listening devices the KGB overheard private conversations and monitored the clacking of typewriters. In those days, before the advent of the ball typewriter, each typewriter key made a unique sound and by listening to the clatter the Soviets knew exactly what was being written as if they

---

[1.] The Soviet Union in turn has a strict policy of employing only Soviet personnel in its embassies in Western countries and brings in its own people even for the most routine and nonsensitive chores.

[2.] The rare times a Canadian diplomat legitimately wants to marry a Soviet citizen, Canada's policy is to send the Canadian out of the country immediately and then try to get the proposed spouse out too. Sometimes it takes weeks and sometimes months. Sometimes it does not succeed and the two never see each other again.

were looking over the typist's shoulder. With bugs planted in the communications room, every message passing between Moscow and Ottawa was intercepted and deciphered.

The clerk, his loyalty unquestioned, was transferred to the Canadian Embassy in Tel Aviv and continued acting as a Soviet agent. By this time he was deep in the KGB net and was not about to be released. Fortunately, he became careless and telephoned an official in the Soviet Embassy in Tel Aviv who was a KGB suspect and therefore a target of the Israeli security service. The telephone call was tapped. After some investigation it became clear the Canadian was acting as an agent on behalf of Soviet Intelligence and Canada was notified.

Apprehending the code clerk represented a delicate problem. The first priority was to interrogate him suddenly and thoroughly and extract a confession. With time to think he was less likely to admit his role and, furthermore, External Affairs could never assess the extent of the damage since he was the only Canadian who knew that. However, the department took the view that it could not interrogate him in Tel Aviv for legal and security reasons. On the other hand, the department was reluctant to recall him to Ottawa since that might make him suspicious and cause him to defect. The clerk had been posted to Tel Aviv only a short time and no credible excuse could be found to recall him.

A scheme was devised whereby someone from the British Embassy approached him with an offer to transport sensitive papers to London on a free-lance basis. The British officer explained that the task was important and that the embassy was temporarily short of messengers through a series of circumstances. The clerk was told that the mission had been cleared by his superiors in the Canadian Embassy, and merely had to carry the package from Israel to Britain and receive a fee and a free weekend in London. The British offer was a ruse executed at Canada's request for the purpose of bringing him to British soil where External Affairs could take action. As the clerk stepped off the plane at Heathrow he was met by the director of security at External Affairs and brought to Canada. He confessed but was not prosecuted, although he was finished at External Affairs.

During those cold war years not a month passed in Moscow without at least one recruitment attempt against the American,

British, Australian, or Canadian embassies. The KGB trained beautiful young seductresses in one of several schools for that purpose. Sometimes they were ballerinas who themselves had been pressured.[3] To counteract this practice Canada adopted a policy of sending to Moscow only happily married men with their wives. The Americans sent virile young Marines but always kept attractive stenographers on hand.

There was a whole new series of successful recruitments in Moscow during the late 1960s and early 1970s. A Canadian corporal acting as chauffeur-assistant to the Canadian Military Attaché in Moscow spied for the KGB in the early 1970s. He was apparently caught black-marketing in the exchange of foreign currency and pressured into the role of an agent for which he was rewarded both financially and sexually. He did the usual things, like planting bugs within the embassy and reporting on the weaknesses of other Canadians, and continued to do so after being transferred to Peking. He was discovered by West German Intelligence after being posted to the Canadian military base at Lahr and put under surveillance in August, 1974. He was escorted back to Canada and confessed but also was not prosecuted. He resigned with a pension.

Many recruitment attempts were not successful. Another military NCO in December, 1975, was offered female companionship and an opportunity to exploit the black market. Ten months earlier, at a Moscow ski resort, his superior, a military attaché, was offered friendship and all the money he would need back in Canada. Both approaches were reported.

External Affairs was never security-conscious enough for the RCMP's satisfaction and the Force held a lingering suspicion that the department was penetrated by foreign agents. External Affairs

---

[3.] The ballerinas were kept on a tight leash by the KGB but one would occasionally fall in love with a subject or, in a fit of conscience, confess her real role. On one occasion in the early 1960s an External Affairs cipher clerk established a relationship with a junior ballerina. It appeared to be genuine and uncontrived. The KGB became aware of the relationship and began pressuring her to participate in a blackmailing scheme. The woman, a member of the Bolshoi and a future prima ballerina, refused and was transferred to a provincial town east of the Ural Mountains. A quick marriage was performed at the Canadian Embassy and a note was sent to the Soviet Foreign Minister notifying him that the dancer was now the wife of a member of the Canadian Embassy and deserved all the diplomatic protection of other Canadian personnel. The cipher clerk was transferred out of Moscow immediately following the marriage to await attempts to bring her out.

personnel often had the same kind of elite academic background as spies like Kim Philby, Donald Maclean, and Guy Burgess. Philby, through his liaison with External Affairs and the RCMP, probably damaged Canada's security more severely than any discovered agent and yet he nominally fell under the RCMP's jurisdiction since he was British Intelligence's liaison officer from 1949 to 1951, an irony External Affairs savored. Philby was stationed in Washington and concentrated mainly on establishing close links with the CIA and to a lesser extent the FBI. But he also held liaison responsibility with Canada and every month or so visited Ottawa for sessions with his two primary Canadian contacts, the RCMP and External Affairs. In those days Canada's security relations were closer to Britain than to the United States and Philby's role was to oversee the relationship and facilitate the exchange of information.

Philby was an impressive man by anyone's standards and tended to overawe his Canadian partners. To the RCMP he was a genuine intelligence officer who had operated in Turkey, developed a reputation, and headed MI6's anti-Soviet department. External Affairs was impressed by his intellectual depth and also taken by his charm and wit. When External Affairs started mulling over the idea of establishing a Canadian Secret Service, Philby was an adviser.

Nobody has ever been able to determine how much damage Philby did to Canada for nobody knows except Philby and his Soviet colleagues. Information was compartmentalized as a security measure but Philby easily overcame this barrier since as liaison officer he jumped from section to section at both External Affairs and the RCMP. He was one of the few who could do that. Reviewing the formal correspondence between Philby and his Canadian contacts was a simple exercise and, as expected, revealed a wholly proper exchange. What was difficult to assess, and where Philby would have made inroads, was the information be obtained from informal meetings and chitchats with officers of both organizations over a period of two years. Some External Affairs officers socialized with him and undoubtedly said things over drinks late at night they should not have.

The RCMP re-examined many operations and revised them in light of the Philby affair. Some defectors buried in Canadian society were jeopardized and measures had to be taken to protect their security. However, much of the damage that could be pinpointed was irreparable and some operations had to be abandoned. There are several schools of thought about what constituted the greatest damage to Canada from Philby's role as a double agent, the most common theory being that he developed a thorough knowledge of the RCMP's inadequacies for the KGB to exploit. The fact that the Russians could undertake certain activities in Canada with little risk of discovery was as important as positive information.

Philby was formally accredited to the RCMP but was personally much closer to External Affairs since he had more in common with the department's diplomats than with Mounties. Members of the Force usually were not university-educated, took a simplistic and conservative view of the world, and often lacked social graces. Members from External Affairs generally were well educated, articulate, sophisticated, and liberal in their views, as well as elitist. In keeping with the concept of departmental responsibility, External Affairs exercised authority for security within its department and usually was notoriously liberal—with the exception of the early homosexual period—while the RCMP watched its security-screening reports be ignored. Relations between the two liaison branches were good but this connection was not indicative. Deep down, the Force believed that External Affairs was not 100 percent loyal. The Force believed there had to be a spy at External. Its dream was to catch a Soviet spy and preferably a homosexual one.

The antipathy flowed in both directions. The RCMP resented the authority and attitudes of External Affairs while External felt affronted that on security matters it had to liaise with uneducated policemen and, worse, subject its personnel to the RCMP for routine security investigations. While snobbishness played a role in External Affairs' antagonism, the department nevertheless had genuine grievances because security-screening procedures, particularly in the early days, were crude. External was the first government department to complain about such failings. As the RCMP grew more sophisticated, the complaints became fewer and less formidable. However, the conflict never disappeared. On certain basic issues each side had institutional views. The RCMP would err on the side of caution while External Affairs usually sided with civil liberties. It was a fundamental difference in outlook that was never resolved.

Probably no single security-screening case aggravated these conflicting biases more symbolically than the Herbert Norman case. When Norman, Canada's Ambassador to Egypt, committed suicide April 4, 1957, by jumping off the roof of a nine-story Cairo apartment building, External Affairs was shattered. Lester Pearson, Minister of External Affairs at the time of Norman's death, wrote in his published memoirs: "The 1957 [election] campaign had not yet opened, but I was in Kingston talking to a Liberal assembly and meeting people when the message came that Herbert Norman had killed himself. My feelings never reached a lower point in my public career."

RCMP headquarters openly and unapologetically rejoiced at his death. When a civilian member rebuked them, a Mountie shot back: "Whose side are you on?"

The Norman investigation was started after the FBI, when sifting through the RCMP's mass of documentation from the Gouzenko investigation, discovered the diplomat's name in an address book belonging to Israel Halperin, a professor of mathematics at Queen's University who was charged and acquitted during the Gouzenko trials. The book contained many innocent names as well as the name of Klaus Fuchs, who as a British scientist of recent German descent had been interned in a prison camp in Sherbrooke, Quebec, in 1940. Halperin had sent him magazines from Kingston.

The FBI asked the RCMP for information in the Herbert Norman file and received it in October, 1950. The dossier contained a false allegation from an underground informer in 1940 that Norman had belonged to the Communist Party of Canada. The information was wrong—even the name of the university Norman had attended was incorrect—as the RCMP quickly discovered. Nevertheless the information remained on file and 10 years later was passed to the FBI without the correction. The FBI was informed some months later of the correction but that did not stop the United States Senate Subcommittee on Internal Security, chaired by Senator Pat McCarran, from accepting the bogus information and publicly releasing Norman's name in 1951.

Norman was Canada's Ambassador to Japan in late 1950 when the FBI was scrutinizing him. The fact the FBI was interested in him prompted a Canadian investigation and before the year was out

Pearson recalled Norman for the most thorough interrogation and investigation a Canadian civil servant ever underwent up to that time. The RCMP's inquiry lasted six to seven weeks, and according to one insider, "The RCMP took him apart and put him back together again." There was no evidence that Norman was disloyal or had ever been an agent of the Soviet Union or any other foreign power. But in 1951 the subcommittee publicized his name and be became a Canadian victim of McCarthyism. To Pearson's credit he stood behind his Ambassador and later made him High Commissioner to New Zealand; in 1956 he appointed him Ambassador to Egypt and Minister to Lebanon. Then in March, 1957, the same U.S. subcommittee, but under the chairmanship of Senator William Jenner, revived the same charge, with no new evidence. Three weeks later, Norman killed himself.

Norman's suicide became an international story and precipitated a wave of anti-Americanism in Canada and a mini-crisis in relations between the United States and Canadian governments. On March 18, 1957, four days after the subcommittee released Norman's name for the second time, Arnold Heeney, the Canadian Ambassador in Washington, sent the American State Department a note "to protest in the strongest terms the action taken by an official body of the legislative branch of the United States government in making and publishing allegations about a Canadian official. ... the repetition of such irresponsible allegations in the subcommittee and the publication on the authority of this official body of a record containing such allegations is the kind of action which is inconsistent with the long standing and friendly co-operation characterizing relations between our two countries."

On April 10, almost a week after Norman's suicide, the Canadian government received a reply saying in part:

> I wish to assure you that any derogatory information developed during hearings of the subcommittee was introduced into the record by the subcommittee on its own responsibility. As you are aware, under our system of government the executive branch has no jurisdiction over views or opinions expressed by Congress. The investigation being undertaken by the subcommittee lies entirely within the control of this subcommittee.

Ambassador Heeney sent a return note saying that Canada wanted a commitment that in future the United States government would not pass Canadian security information to third bodies over which it had no control, such as the subcommittee, without Canadian permission.

"Unless such an assurance can be given," Heeney's note said, "I am instructed by my government to inform you that the Canadian government must reserve the right in future not to supply security information concerning Canadian citizens to any United States government agency."

Canada was threatening to cut off the flow of intelligence to the United States—a threat that was largely empty because, as noted earlier, Canada received more information than it gave and ultimately would damage itself more than the United States. During the height of the storm the FBI, which had precipitated the conflict by giving the Norman dossier to the subcommittee without Canadian consent, pulled its Ottawa liaison officer out of RCMP headquarters and put him into the American Embassy, where he should have been all along.

Although Norman was a victim of McCarthyism,[4] the RCMP harbored a grievance that he was protected by External Affairs, and this indeed was the case. Norman, although never a member of the Communist Party of Canada, was once a Communist.[5] He formally joined the Communist Party at Cambridge University around 1935 and for several years prior to that had been sympathetic to communism. In 1936 he wanted to fight for the Loyalists in the Spanish Civil War but was so physically and mechanically inept that he concluded he would cause more harm than good. By this time he was studying at Harvard University and, although poor, contributed

---

[4.] The McCarthyist forces in the United States also attempted without success to smear other senior Canadian officials, the most notable being Lester Pearson. Another was Bob Bryce, who at university had been a member of the Cambridge Socialist Society and introduced Herbert Norman to the Japanese Marxist scholar Tsuru Shigeto, an association that later haunted Norman. Bryce belonged to the social democratic wing of the socialist society and was active in the debate against communism, but in the 1950s these distinctions mattered little. For a decade, including the period of Norman's death, Bryce, as Clerk of the Privy Council and Secretary to the cabinet, was Canada's highest-ranking civil servant. Even more significant from a security standpoint, he was chairman of the Security Panel.

[5.] The information in this paragraph is taken from Charles Taylor's *Six Journeys: A Canadian Pattern,* which provides a detailed and scholarly essay of Norman's career.

part of his Rockefeller Foundation scholarship money to the Loyalists. He also defended the Stalin purges and the show trials in Moscow. In 1939, with no evidence that his devotion to communism had diminished—although there is also no public evidence he was still a member of the party—he joined External Affairs and the following year was sent to Tokyo as language officer and third secretary at the Canadian Legation. At that time there was no established and regular system of security screening. After the war he was returned to Japan at a senior level and worked closely with General Douglas MacArthur on Japan's reconstruction before becoming Canada's Ambassador to Japan.

Mounties viewed Norman as a clear security risk. Many believed he was a Communist agent. The fact that Norman at one point attempted to conceal information about his Communist past from the FBI convinced them even more. External Affairs' approach was to attempt to gauge how deeply he had been committed to communism during his university days and ascertain if his commitment to the cause ever overrode his other loyalties. External concluded that Norman was loyal and trustworthy. Since External Affairs was the employer, and the RCMP merely the collector of information, External Affairs prevailed.

While External Affairs' decision to keep Norman probably was the correct one, it fueled resentment within the RCMP for understandable reasons. In this case External Affairs kept an officer with access to sensitive information who had been a committed Communist stalwart. The established policy during that period was to remove such people from sensitive areas, if not entirely from the civil service. Most other people in the same circumstances would have been dismissed. But Norman was a friend of External Affairs Minister Pearson, who had attended university with Norman's older brother, and he was given the benefit of the doubt others would not have received. This favoritism increased the RCMP's resentment. On the other hand, External Affairs resented the RCMP's role in the affair. The Force had been sloppy in accumulating bad information and then had not corrected it sufficiently when discovered. Furthermore, the Force's *carte-blanche* willingness to give the information to the FBI precipitated the case in the first place.

Relations between the two were not helped by External's desire to see the security function taken away from the RCMP and placed with an independent civilian agency. The Force was particularly sensitive to such suggestions. External Affairs even consulted Sir William Stephenson (the man called Intrepid) over the matter. It succeeded only in raising suspicion.

External Affairs fired another salvo when the RCMP began dispatching liaison officers to foreign postings.[6] When the Force requested diplomatic status for the Mounties involved, External, which had authority over such things, balked. The issue gnawed at relations for years, beginning in the early 1950s and festering through most of the 1960s. Being on the diplomatic list provided Mounties with status that gave them access to higher officials in the host governments and this enabled them to do their jobs more effectively. The RCMP's function was "representative"—representing one government agency to another—and clearly deserved diplomatic status and foreign service allowances. But External Affairs was reluctant to admit rank-and-file policemen to the club. It was a class conflict featuring striped pants versus uniforms.

The RCMP's miserly attitude toward bureaucracy was also partially to blame for External's refusals. The Force in those years was a lean organization and had very few commissioned officers. Most liaison officers were noncommissioned officers and External Affairs relied on the excuse that they were not real officers and therefore should not get diplomatic status. External divided its employees into two categories: "foreign service officers," who had representational duties, and "foreign service employees," who were the support staff. The NCO liaison officers were classified as support staff on the same level of secretaries, code clerks, messengers, and the rest. External Affairs told the RCMP: "You wouldn't expect us to send support staff to your department and insist they be made commissioned officers, would you?" It was a problem of definition. External would have been denied this excuse had the Force played the bureaucratic game and raised the ratio of commissioned officers to enlisted men.

[6.] The RCMP posts liaison officers abroad in various Canadian embassies for three functions. First, they act as immigration-vetting authorities to screen out subversives, criminals, espionage agents, terrorists, or any others barred from Canada. Second, they act as liaison for the host country's security service regarding the exchange of information. Third, they perform the Interpol function of liaising with local police forces on common matters of international crime.

Eventually the RCMP did just that, and when all foreign postings became filled by commissioned officers the problem disappeared.

The biggest dispute between the two organizations revolved around External Affairs' policy of expelling—or not expelling— foreign "diplomats" the RCMP caught spying against Canada. This issue never vanished since it represented an ongoing institutional conflict in roles. The RCMP's role was to unearth espionage and External's role was to keep relations friendly with foreign governments, and frequently one could not be achieved without violating the other. An NCO labored a year identifying the Soviet cultural attaché as a KGB officer, working weekends with no overtime to build his case. The only satisfaction was knowing his toil contributed to the security of Canada. Then the case went to External Affairs for action and it refused to expel the Russian. The Mountie brooded and started believing the Soviets carried more weight with External Affairs than the Force did and that the priorities of the country were all wrong.

External made other decisions the RCMP viewed as unfriendly. When foreign intelligence officers were expelled it too often was done quietly, without mention in the press. A silent expulsion disturbed the Force because they were thereby denied the publicity that gave them good public exposure and a boost in morale and, most importantly, generated additional evidence of Soviet intelligence activity. Each time newspapers announced an expulsion the RCMP received phone calls providing further information that was often valuable. The publicity caused Canadians in contact with Soviet Embassy personnel to put into an espionage context details they had never particularly noticed before. Publicity also had a secondary benefit in that it served as effective propaganda for Canadians to be on guard against recruitment attempts.

The RCMP was also distressed over the decision by External Affairs to increase from 42 kilometers to 125 the travel limit for members of the Soviet Embassy, thereby making physical surveillance, the Force's most effective method of scrutinizing Soviet activity, all the harder.

If External was not always cognizant of the RCMP's tribulations, neither was the Force aware of External Affairs'. The department had many difficulties and the Mounties, especially members down in the ranks who had little exposure to larger concerns, made little effort to understand them. External had to consider a variety of vested interests arising out of numerous government departments, and on balance expelling a foreign intelligence officer could be contrary to Canada's over-all interest even though a clear case of espionage was established. If Canada was negotiating with the Soviet Union for a sale of wheat that would boost trade and reduce surplus stocks, External usually took the view that Canada's interests were better served by completing the wheat sale. The espionage operation was uncovered in any case and posed a minimized threat as long as the RCMP monitored it. In such clear-cut cases even the RCMP did not object. However, most cases were not so sharply defined.

For the RCMP an expulsion marked the end of a case, whereas for External Affairs it could be the beginning of series of consequences the Force knew nothing about. External Affairs itself sometimes had to absorb Soviet reprisal, which could come in the form of a retaliatory expulsion from the Canadian Embassy in Moscow on contrived charges. Occasionally petty harassment was involved; sometimes it involved thuggery. So when expulsion cases arose, External Affairs usually attempted to arrange some compromise that satisfied the RCMP while avoiding diplomatic backlash—although External was more successful with the latter than the former. Sometimes expulsions were delayed prior to a critical Canadian-Soviet treaty-signing. Other times, expulsions were done quietly since complications were avoided if the Russians did not have to save face by retaliating. Sometimes when the Soviet intelligence officer's term in Canada was about to expire he would be allowed to serve out his remaining time. Or—and this particularly angered the RCMP—External Affairs informally advised the Soviet Embassy and it would voluntarily pull back the intelligence officer without a ripple.

While External's low-key nonconfrontationist approach worked well for individual cases, it backfired in the long run. It represented softness, which the Soviet Union interpreted as weakness, and the Russians soon sought to incorporate this perceived Canadian tolerance as an intrinsic component in the Canadian-Russian relationship.

Relations between the RCMP and External Affairs have improved in recent years as both sides have drawn nearer to each other on expulsion cases. However, few people could have forecast the events of February, 1978, when the Canadian government announced the biggest diplomatic expulsion in Canada's history. Eleven Soviets were expelled outright and two others away on leave were barred from returning. There was a statement in the House of Commons, a special press conference, an outline of details, the naming of names, and even an official release of pictures. External Affairs could not have been more accommodating. February, 1978, represented a unique state of affairs in which the interests of the RCMP and External Affairs temporarily and coincidentally corresponded.

Countering the KGB

AT 3:05 P.M. Thursday, February 9, 1978, External Affairs Minister Donald Jamieson rose in his front-row seat in the House of Commons and triumphantly made a statement.

"Mr. Speaker, at noon today, on my instructions, the Under-Secretary of State for External Affairs requested the Ambassador of the Soviet Union to withdraw 11 Soviet nationals from Canada for engaging in inadmissable activities in violations of the Official Secrets Act, and ... two other Soviet nationals who were involved have already departed Canada but will not be permitted to return. A strong protest has been conveyed to the Soviet authorities about these activities.

"The Soviet Ambassador was informed that the Canadian government had irrefutable evidence that all 13 persons had been involved in an attempt to recruit a member of the RCMP in order to penetrate the RCMP Security Service."

It was the biggest diplomatic expulsion in Canadian history. Jamieson spent 10 minutes on his speech and then an hour answering questions from Opposition Members of Parliament, after which he walked across the street to the National Press Building for another hour-long question-and-answer session with reporters, who were given copies of documents detailing the times, locations, and conditions of the ballyhooed espionage meets and color photographs of a hollowed-out stick and cut-out package of Marlboro cigarettes for

153

concealing microfilm. ABC News in New York dispatched a television crew to Ottawa for the first time in years. For the next two days Canadian reporters and photographers gathered outside the Soviet Embassy on Charlotte Street for glimpses of the fingered KGB officers. When a Soviet convoy of five vehicles left for Mirabel International Airport north of Montreal, a procession of reporters, photographers, and television crews followed, stopping only for the Soviets to fuel up their vehicles for the final time in Canada.

The Soviet Union accepted the expulsion in good grace. Relations were back to normal several months later. Not one Canadian was expelled in retaliation from Moscow on a trumped-up charge although that might have been because the Soviet Union was warned in advance that expulsions of Canadians would be met with additional Soviet expulsions on a one-to-one basis. The Soviets had been flagrantly exposed and offered only the meekest public denials and were even apologetic when speaking privately. The world of espionage has its own sense of ethics and one of them is not to fume or complain over the fact that some of your people have been declared *persona non grata* (although you are perfectly free to trump up reverse charges in your country and then not expect the other side to complain). However, another ethic is that the country doing the expelling should not publicize these affairs. It is based on reciprocity. Don't divulge the other person's embarrassments and he won't reveal yours. It is particularly unethical to blow your horn just for the sake of doing it.[1]

The Soviets eventually did respond, not to the expulsions, but to the publicity, by publicizing several Canadian embarrassments. The Security Service over the years attempted its quota of penetrations of the Soviet Embassy and, not surprisingly, most of these high-risk ventures failed. The Soviets, true to the unwritten rule, never publicized these failures at the time they occurred. But a month after Jamieson gave his performance in the House of Commons, the official Soviet newspaper *Izvestia* in Moscow made some revelations of its own by publishing an account of two failed RCMP recruitment

---

[1]. Although Canada clearly violated the rules I am not suggesting it was wrong to do so. Canada is not a member of the league of countries with espionage organizations and therefore should not feel bound by its rules.

attempts aimed at Soviet officials in Canada. In 1976, I. V. Zakharov, the Second Secretary in the Ottawa embassy, was approached, and earlier the Security Service gave gifts of thousands of dollars and rubles to a Soviet trade official and even opened a bank account for him in a branch of the Bank of Montreal in Ottawa, and later in a major bank in Switzerland, as an inducement for him to defect. Furthermore he was promised a false passport, birth certificate, social insurance number, and a letter signed by Solicitor General Warren Allmand guaranteeing political asylum. Clearly, the RCMP had been doing to the Soviet Union what the Soviet Union had just finished attempting to do to the RCMP and failed equally badly.

The Soviets mentioned the name of only one RCMP officer, Tom Quilley, who they said was in charge of the operation. To ensure the point had not been missed, the Soviet Embassy in Ottawa a week later released more details, including the names of the two alleged go-betweens who supposedly conveyed the offers to the Soviets. And a week after that, *Literaturnaya Gazeta,* the official Writers' Union weekly in Russia, published more details about the operation, including the false name on the Canadian passport and the names of two more Mounties allegedly involved. Both the RCMP and External Affairs, which is responsible for issuing passports, refused to discuss the matter.

"Even if it were true I wouldn't say it," Jamieson said.

Interestingly, the Soviets did not release the name of the Mountie they had attempted to recruit as that would have embarrassed the RCMP since the individual was a dissident. In fact, it was his unguarded criticism of the Force that had drawn Soviet attention. He faithfully reported the recruitment attempt but was not trusted by the Force and was placed under surveillance during periods of the operation. He was transferred out of Ottawa when the case ended.

There is no mystery or surprise over the fact the RCMP wanted to expel the principals amid fanfare. Expulsions and publicity were actions the Force had historically advocated in such cases. But a mass expulsion of 13 exceeded even the Security Service's wishes since such drastic action created more problems than it solved. If 13 KGB officers were expelled, 13 new ones take their place. Through the process called Residency Analysis the Security Service seeks to determine which individuals on the Soviet Embassy staff are intelligence officers. Some individuals are identified within months; others may take a year or longer. Some are never discovered. Once the individual is identified, the Security Service can scrutinize him with relatively little effort and possibly set him up for recruitment as a double agent or defector. In terminating a case of Soviet espionage the Security Service wants only one or two principals expelled so that it needs to start over on the identification process of only a few new officers and not expend resources on lower-level staff.

Normally even the RCMP would have resisted an expulsion of 13 but the Security Service was embroiled in a political controversy and was the subject of a Royal Commission investigation into illegal acts and improper conduct, with the result that both morale and effectiveness were sagging. A big expulsion would create good publicity and possibly revitalize spirits. So contrary to good counterespionage policy the Security Service sanctioned the expulsion decision.[2]

As strange as it seems, the impetus for the big expulsion came from External Affairs itself. The department had already concluded that its earlier policy of appeasement had only aggravated the problem with the Russians, and the events of the past 14 months had underlined this conclusion. In December, 1976, Major Vladimir Vassiliev, under cover as Assistant Air Attaché in the embassy, was expelled for attempting to buy classified information from a contact acting as a double agent for the RCMP. Two months later Lev Grigoryevich Khvostantsev, a Soviet exchange scientist working at the National Research Council, had to be deported after spending only three months in Canada for trying to buy secret information from another exchange scientist. In July, 1977, Lieutenant-Commander Valerie Smirnov, who was listed as the Soviet Naval Attaché, was publicly rebuked by External Affairs for seeking to purchase industrial information from a Bell Northern Research scientist in Ottawa. Smirnov, away on home leave at the time, never returned. After each incident External Affairs called in a Soviet representative and advised him that such activity must stop—or else.

The Soviet Union did not really believe the Canadian warnings

---

[2.] The expulsion so outraged one former member of the counterespionage branch that he phoned me long distance that night to denounce the action. "There is not a month in the year in which the government could not throw out 13 Soviets for engaging in intelligence work," he said. "It is strictly a political action."

and not without reason. Since the Russians had been caught many times and External Affairs always reacted diplomatically rather than forcefully, the Soviets had come to believe that Canada was weak. On the last three occasions External had issued stern warnings but had done nothing and was in danger of crying wolf too often. In February, 1978, External Affairs had to act and had to do it overwhelmingly to impress the Russians that the policy had changed.

In May, 1977, Allan Gotlieb had been named Under-Secretary in External Affairs. Gotlieb, a sharp and tough-minded friend of then Prime Minister Trudeau, was an unapologetic hawk. As Deputy Minister in the Department of Communications he had controlled some of the most security-sensitive operations because the department figured in every cipher operation Canada had. When he became Deputy Minister of Manpower and Immigration he had earned the admiration of every security official by make politically unpopular decisions in the name of security and cleaning up a backlog of immigration cases postponed by previous deputies. As the civil servant in charge of External Affairs he did not fret over possible Soviet retaliation when he proposed to his minister that 13 Soviets be expelled.

Which side actually triumphed in the expulsion case is one of those nagging curiosities that nobody can answer. History may answer only if both Canadian and Soviet files become available. On the surface the case has the markings of an open-and-shut RCMP victory. But appearances can be deceiving, especially in the security and intelligence world because it is based on deception. Successful operations often hinge upon the fact that one side has been fooled into thinking it triumphed. Current and former Mounties interviewed during the research of this book expressed doubt about the case.

"I think it was set up," says a senior NCO, "but you have to start wondering why. Why would the Soviets do that? It almost seemed as if they were helping out."

A former member says: "I just can't see them getting sucked in like that. It involves so many of their resources. All kinds of their people allegedly carrying out countersurveillance measures and this sort of thing. They put so many eggs in that one basket. I can't see them doing that."

Other Mounties believe the case was genuine. They point out that, while the KGB is ingenious and astute, it nevertheless is a bureaucratic organization that is not above bumbling from sheer size.

The Vasily Tarasov case in 1964 is an example of a situation where the real outcome may differ from the apparent one. On the surface no case was more clean cut than Operation Carton, the code name for the case, for here, too, evidence apparently revealed an RCMP triumph.

Tarasov was ostensibly a journalist for the Soviet newspaper *Izvestia* and as such belonged to the Parliamentary Press Gallery. Tarasov was short, stocky, and blond; his thick glasses gave him an owlish look. The 36-year-old Soviet spent an inordinate amount of time socializing in the National Press Club and always smiled and displayed a mouthful of gold teeth when he laughed.

Tarasov developed a contact in the patent office whom he wined quietly in various establishments in Ottawa. Through surveillance the Watcher Service discovered the rendezvousing and consequently investigators on the Russian Desk pressured the civil servant into becoming a reluctant double agent. Under RCMP supervision the civil servant passed worthless documents to Tarasov while setting a trap. An important transaction was arranged for April, 1964. The civil servant was to meet Tarasov at a motel on the Prescott Highway south of Ottawa and pass information on a secret videcon tube. In return he would get money.

The motel was staked out with Mounties, a photographer, and even a powerful car to force Tarasov off the road and into a steep ditch in the event he tried to flee. The car was not necessary because Tarasov surrendered quietly and was taken into custody for questioning and released. As a journalist he lacked diplomatic immunity and was legally liable for prosecution.[3] Instead he was expelled with publicity.[4]

[3.] Canada and the Soviet Union have an agreement that neither side prosecutes each other's embassy staff members who do not have diplomatic immunity. The pact protects Canadian nondiplomatic staff in Moscow from wrongful prosecution. The main advantage to the Soviets is that they can provide their intelligence officers with a wider range of cover positions without fear of prosecution.

[4.] It was almost impossible to evict Tarasov quietly because he was known to journalists in the Press Gallery. It also happened that Peter Dempson of the old Toronto *Telegram* tripped across Tarasov at two of his meets with the civil servant and Dempson deduced from Tarasov's embarrassment and note-taking that he was a spy. Dempson's inquiries threatened to ruin the double-agent operation, so Commissioner George McClellan promised Dempson an exclusive story when it broke. At least that is Dempson's version in his book *Assignment Ottawa*. Dempson, as stated in an earlier chapter, was also an RCMP informer and was given exclusive information for this activity.

Was the Tarasov case an example of Soviet bumbling or good counterespionage work by the RCMP? The Soviets made no attempt to disguise Tarasov's role as an intelligence officer; if it was not obvious from his unabashed efforts to cultivate friendships everywhere, it was by his open attempt to get technical maps from the library at the Department of Mines and Technical Surveys.[5] Before Tarasov left, the Soviet Embassy held a going-away party — a joyous affair with uproarious laughter. Tarasov was congratulated and patted on the back. Had the Soviets been expecting a failure, or even desiring one? Had the KGB learned or accomplished something from the case, or was it a diversion? While newspapers congratulated the RCMP with stories on the case, the Security Service pondered these questions.

As Tarasov was leaving, three Soviet intelligence officers were arriving who were to make Tarasov look absolutely discreet. They were Yuri Perfilyev, Boris Bukaty, and Victor Myznikov. They were dubbed "the stud squad" since their purpose evidently was to throw parties and invite women with the hope of seducing them for espionage gain. They rented a cottage in the Gatineau Hills but were always so drunk and obnoxious their efforts met with little success. Intelligence officers sometimes feign drunkenness but in this case there was no doubt. They lunged at women in swimsuits and missed. The cottage was on a slope and had a balcony. Bukaty, in one of his more spectacular moments, stumbled backward into the railing and somersaulted over the deep side with cocktail glass in hand. The trio created some concern for the Security Service when one of the guests was discovered to be working for a cabinet minister. When interviewed she said her first party was her last since she could do without the boorish Russians.

Myznikov, officially an attaché and the most sedate member of the trio, was in his mid-30s. The next chapter will describe how he led the Security Service into an escapade that lasted six years and absorbed thousands of man-hours of resources without yielding any

---

[5.] Tarasov's quest caused the government concern since the maps, although public, contained information the government did not want the Soviet Union to have. He was eventually denied them. Tarasov sought them in a heavy-handed manner, asking for them directly and never bothering to hide the fact he was a Soviet national. The maps could have been obtained routinely through a go-between.

significant counterespionage results. Perfilyev and Bukaty were slightly younger, more outgoing, and previously identified as intelligence officers. They had been stationed at the United Nations in New York together and both were active and subjects of thick FBI files.

Perfilyev was a second secretary with press responsibilities and wore stylish western clothing. He was tall, about six-feet-two, and had an athletic build and a handsome face. Perfilyev, like Tarasov, spent much of his time in the National Press Club across the street from Parliament Hill, and when doing so left his car in the diplomatic parking zone next to the East Block, within radiation distance of External Affairs' sensitive communications operations. Why Perfilyev did not park his car in the Press Gallery zone near the press club aroused official suspicion. His car was bombarded with electrical impulses while an individual, pretending to be loitering in the vicinity, listened for electronic feedback that would betray the existence of eavesdropping devices. There was no response. The tests were repeated over and over. The power was turned high and not one high-pitched squeal was produced.

The anxiety grew more acute when the House of Commons recessed for the summer and cabinet meetings were moved to the East Block, within range of Perfilyev's car. Then a real panic developed. The car was there when cabinet was in session. Once a cabinet meeting was even rescheduled without public knowledge and the car was there for the revised time. Some of the best available technical brains studied the problem but without success. Several options were considered, such as moving cabinet meetings back to the Centre Block, tearing up the East Block meeting room and shielding the premises from radiation, and even, in jest, stealing Perfilyev's car and dismantling it piece by piece, including the engine.

After all the scheming a consensus developed that the car was clean. It was learned that Perfilyev loaned his car to embassy personnel who used it for shopping. They parked it on Parliament Hill because downtown parking was scarce and the diplomat zone happened to be convenient, which explained why the car was so far away from the Press Club where Perfilyev was drinking.[6]

---

6. This incident occurred while Lester Pearson was Prime Minister. A few years later, during

Boris Bukaty, also second secretary, was the most senior of the three and the most suave-looking. His most notable romantic conquest while in Ottawa implicated a female diplomat in the French Embassy. The woman was recalled over the liaison and during interrogation admitted she had fallen in love with Bukaty but had been put off by his behavior. At critical moments in her apartment Bukaty would throw up from drinking too much. Bukaty's driving habits were legendary and on several occasions he became involved in automobile accidents that were usually the result of alcohol and on at least one occasion he left the scene. Although his diplomatic immunity protected him from prosecution, External Affairs complained to the Soviet Embassy and threatened to revoke his driving privilege. The embassy responded by recalling him.

What was Bukaty up to? His record in the United States suggested he was a KGB officer. Yet his performance in Canada was elephantine as he repeatedly drew attention to himself. Bukaty's wife was a tall, striking woman with a lovely body kept fit with regular workouts at the health studio. She was one of the first women in the Soviet Embassy to get a Canadian driver's license. Often Bukaty left the embassy in his car and she left shortly after in another car. He got coverage from the Watcher Service and she was left alone. If Bukaty was a decoy for his wife, the Security Service was fooled to the very end.

All agencies involved in security and intelligence work bungle sometimes and neither the RCMP nor the KGB are exceptions. The earliest known case of KGB blundering in Canada occurred during World War Two when Soviet intelligence officers walked into the Canadian Patent Office and asked for information on a secret radar invention. They looked foreign and spoke with thick accents and were detained as German agents. They were released but it set off a quarrel between the two intelligence networks in the Soviet Embassy.

the time of Pierre Trudeau, cabinet meetings for a period were actually moved back to the Centre Block out of fear that the Soviets were bugging the East Block cabinet room. A pair of Soviet nationals had moved into rooms on the west side of the Chateau Laurier overlooking the East Block and were in perfect perpendicular line for shooting an electronic beam at the cabinet window and have it bounce back to their suite at the hotel. A beam could pick up the vibrations on the East block window and thus enable the Russians to understand conversations in the cabinet chamber.

GRU head Colonel Zabotin dashed off a telegram to Moscow complaining of the "hooligan" methods of the KGB.

The Soviet Embassy in Ottawa sits as a fortress on Charlotte Street protected by the Rideau River on the east, Strathcona Park on the south, a solid brick wall topped with prison-style barbed wire on the north, and an imposing wrought-iron fence with an electronically controlled lock in the front. It was built in 1956 to Soviet specifications and features the drab utilitarian architecture of Communist Bloc countries. When fire destroyed the original building on the same site on New Year's Day, 1956, the Soviets made no attempt to call the fire department. Instead, they lit a fire in the cipher room on the second floor to ensure that secret information was destroyed. Neighbors, fearing the fire would spread, eventually called the fire department and firemen pushed their way into the building while ducking blows from the Russians. One enterprising newspaper photographer was thrown out of the building several times. In his last entry he reached the sensitive second floor and took shots and escaped only because he outran his pursuer. Later in the evening he was visited by two Mounties requesting copies of his pictures.

The amount of information a host-country security service can acquire by observing an embassy is surprisingly large. By examining the personnel it is frequently possible to distinguish the intelligence officers from the diplomats and thereby increase the effectiveness of counterintelligence investigations. The counterespionage branch of each Western security service commits considerable resources to the process of identification. The RCMP concentrates on the Soviet Embassy but other countries with known espionage capability, such as Poland, Czechoslovakia, Hungary, Cuba, and China, are also targets.

Because the Security Service exchanges information concerning Soviet Embassy personnel with friendly foreign security organizations, it often knows whether a Soviet is an intelligence officer before he sets foot in Canada. Each "diplomat" requires a visa from External Affairs, which routinely vets the name with the RCMP before issuing one. The Security Service in turn checks with its counterparts in other countries for traces on that individual. If he had a previous posting in one of these countries, chances are there is a file with information about his activities. Even if he had never been posted abroad before, the CIA or FBI might be able to identify him since these organizations have

Soviet defectors who supply the names of all the KGB or GRU officers they know. This information is traded freely and free of charge.

Even without outside help the Security Service usually can identify
part of the intelligence corps in short order. The lifestyle of an
intelligence officer sets him apart from genuine diplomatic officers.
Regular employees, especially lower-ranking ones, are restricted in
their movements and associations with Canadians. They tend to live
in spartan housing, usually near the embassy, and often share quarters
with their colleagues. They often speak flawed English and sometimes
do not speak the language at all. Intelligence officers speak good
English and are encouraged to mix with the locals (if for no other
reason than to complicate life for the Security Service). They wear
fashionable Western clothing, have good apartments, and are free
with their money. If an embassy figure has a personal car, chances
are he has intelligence duties. Intelligence officers tend to socialize
with their colleagues despite warnings from their superiors not to do
so. Likewise genuine diplomats tend to flock with their ilk and stay
away from intelligence personnel.

There are other weaknesses in the cover system that provide clues.
Individuals are sometimes moved from one cover position to another in
a way that is inconsistent with true professional traditions. For example, an individual will be a commercial representative in one posting
and a cultural attaché two stops later. Sometimes the heavy hand of
bureaucracy is the officer's worst enemy. Military attachés once were
invariably intelligence officers with the GRU, the KGB's cousin
responsible for military intelligence. The Central Committee in 1958
directed the GRU to de-emphasize that cover position and exploit
civilian positions more frequently. The directive was designed to improve secrecy but had precisely the opposite effect because the ensuing
mass transfers of GRU officers to nonmilitary positions was noticeable
and exposed rather than concealed the identity of GRU staff. There
are other indicators. A demotion in position is a sure sign an individual
has intelligence functions since regular personnel who are demoted
cannot serve abroad. The KGB and GRU sometimes must "demote"
an individual when an appropriate cover position is not available.[7]

[7.] It is not unknown for the GRU chief to assume cover as a chauffeur. This leads to inevitable
problems. The officer being chauffeured sometimes forgets and salutes the chauffeur.

Intelligence officers adopt a variety of habits designed to give them protection. Ironically, many of these measures serve to betray their function. When they go somewhere, by car or foot, they perform strange and observable exercises to determine whether they are under surveillance; they also avoid fixing an established daily routine. Normal people do not behave this way. While such lack of consistency creates hardships on the surveillance team, it also is an indication that an individual is an intelligence officer since virtually everybody falls into patterns. He is likely to shun the red diplomatic license plates that announce one's foreignness and to shy away from being photographed (as well as use old photographs on passports). Such passion for establishing a low profile offers them protection when dealing with local contacts but is another sign for the Security Service.

The Soviets refer to some of their embassy personnel as "three-hour men." They devote the minimum time to their cover occupation. They arrive at work and leave at various hours and perform work outside normal hours partly because of the demands of their intelligence functions. They also travel frequently to various parts of the country, but their trips are easily monitored because of the full itinerary they must submit in advance if they are going beyond the 125-kilometer radius of Ottawa.

Even when the cover is technically perfect, lapses in security still occur because intelligence officers are only human. Sometimes breaches are inexcusable. Cultural attachés can be quite uncultured and economic attachés may be ignorant about Canada's economy or about economics in general. Such failures are not too common because Russian intelligence officers come from the Soviet elite and possess the education and sophistication to carry their covers. A more frequent mistake occurs from overconfidence and a willingness to talk too freely. This can lead to contradictory statements about experiences, backgrounds, and duties from posting to posting and even from meeting to meeting within postings. An intelligence officer lies readily to ingratiate himself with potential sources, who are often interviewed later by the Security Service, who notices the discrepancies.

Once the Security Service has identified an individual as an intelligence officer it concentrates on determining whether he belongs to the KGB or GRU residency. The two organizations work autonomously but have overlapping responsibilities and often compete with each other. There are several distinguishing features but one of them is not the type of information they seek. Although the GRU is the intelligence arm of the Red Army, its espionage goals are not limited to military information. Likewise the KGB, although a civilian body, seeks military intelligence as fervently as political and economic material.

As already noted, a social demarcation exists between the real diplomats and the intelligence officers. This division exists within the intelligence community as well. The KGB does not associate with the GRU and vice versa. The partitioning even stretches to the social lives of the wives. Each service celebrates separate anniversaries: the KGB commemorates December 20 as the anniversary of the founding of the Soviet security organization; the GRU observes Soviet Army Day on February 23.

There are other telltale indicators. The KGB and GRU each have their own fleet of cars which they share neither with each other nor with the general embassy staff. Thus some vehicles becomes identified as KGB or GRU cars and while the individual may be transferred outside Canada the vehicles stay behind to help identify the successor. However, the method is not infallible because each residency draws upon the embassy car pool from time to time.

Both organizations establish different patterns in using embassy positions as cover for their personnel. The KGB has about twice as many people as the GRU in any given embassy. An intelligence officer whose wife works for the military attaché is likely to be with the GRU. Officers rarely move from one organization to the other and the two seldom support each other's operations. For instance, since it was established that the Soviet attempt to recruit a Mountie in February, 1978, was a KGB operation it is safe to assume that all the individuals providing technical assistance and backup support were also KGB. It demonstrates why the decision to expel all 13 participants was a political rather than a security decision since some of the 13 were inconspicuous and identified by this operation for the first time. As a result, no sooner were they identified than they were thrown out of the country. The Security Service never got the opportunity to study what they were doing and thereby possibly uncover a new case. Also, the Security Service sacrificed an opportunity to mount an operation against them in the hope of recruiting a defector or a double agent. They may have been stalled in their careers or disillusioned with communism and ripe for defection. The expulsion forced the Security Service to start over again with the identification process on the replacements in the hope that the future will provide sufficient information to undertake a recruitment.

It is not uncommon for intelligence personnel to escape identification completely. Those whose activities occur mostly inside the embassy are subjected to limited observation. They include the internal security officer, technical support officers in charge of photography and concealment devices, cipher clerks, and those who monitor communications intelligence. As well there is the "co-opted worker," a legitimate diplomatic employee who occasionally is recruited for specific intelligence tasks.

The rule of thumb used by Western security organizations is that intelligence personnel comprise 40 to 50 percent of total Soviet representation. Those figures are considered so reliable that if the number of suspects drops much below that level the Residency Analysis is assumed to be faulty. Until the mid-1960s the figure was 60 percent, but Soviet diplomatic representation abroad has grown so dramatically that the ratio has fallen even though the number of KGB and GRU officers has also expanded substantially. Segments such as press representatives are still predominantly intelligence officers and the formal diplomatic list itself—as opposed to support personnel and low-ranking officers—still comprises about 75 percent KGB or GRU personnel. The RCMP's figures for Soviet personnel in Canada generally fall into the 40 to 50 percent category.

Year	Diplomatic Establishment	Estimated Number of Intelligence Officers
1970	60	30
1971	60	27
1972	59	30
1973	54	24
1974	59	24
1975	59	24
1976	61	28

The size of the Soviet Embassy in Ottawa was 64 as of 1979, making it significantly larger than the Canadian Embassy in Moscow. The intelligence activity of the KGB and the GRU accounts for most of this difference.[8] Under international convention Canada has the right to determine the size of the Soviet contingent, and exercises that right by imposing a ceiling. No so-called friendly countries are restrained in such a way and many Communist countries are also not restricted. It is a crude but effective restraint on espionage activity and serves as an ever-present reminder of the permanent lack of trust between Canada and Russia. The Soviets complain from time to time that the ceiling deprives them of essential services and prohibits them from undertaking legitimate functions in Canada that non-Communist countries perform. Furthermore, they claim, it crimps their diplomatic style. External Affairs replies by advising them to stop relying on high-cost imported Soviet nationals for every service and hire local people the way Canada and the United States do in Moscow. The Soviets will not consider it and are thereby caught in their own dilemma.

The Soviets have countered by increasing the number of intelligence officers in nondiplomatic establishments, such as the International Civil Aviation Organization (ICAO) in Montreal, which in 1976 had five intelligence officers on its staff of 40 Soviet nationals. No travel restrictions are imposed on the ICAO secretariat, and for that reason one KGB officer was believed to have been transferred from the ICAO delegation—a diplomatic posting—to the ICAO secretariat.

The weak link in the Soviet espionage chain is communication. The KGB and the GRU face no overwhelming obstacle recruiting Canadians with access to confidential information to betray their country. In turn, an agent with access encounters little difficulty

---

8. There are also several legitimate reasons having nothing to do with espionage why the Soviet Union should have a somewhat bigger embassy. The USSR, being a larger country, can justly claim it needs a bigger embassy because its range of interests is broader. American embassies around the world also tend to be large. As well, the Soviet Union has stricter security standards than Canada and, because it employs no locally engaged staff as Canada does in Russia, it must bring in its own people to do janitorial and kitchen help work and routine stenography. The Soviets also require more employees for the same amount of work because their labor efficiency is significantly lower than that of Western countries. While these factors are noteworthy, they do not in themselves account for the exaggerated differences in embassy size that presently exist.

copying reams of secret information that once required months of laborious hand-copying or, more recently, special cameras to duplicate. Now it is done in minutes by office photocopying machines. No tools are needed. It is only necessary to have access to secret material—and as the federal bureaucracy gets bigger, more people have access—and the espionage target itself will supply the photocopying machine. But at some point this intelligence has to be passed on to the Soviets and while the process has been refined it still represents a considerable risk. The information can be communicated through dead drops, live drops, secret rendezvous, brush meetings, mail or radio communications, but it must move somehow. Since this stage represents the Security Service's one big chance, it does everything to exploit this opportunity.

Intense scrutiny of the Soviet Embassy has placed limitations on the Russian capability of communicating without detection. Consequently the relative importance of the embassy is declining in the over-all intelligence effort.[9] The danger of "running" agents out of the embassy is becoming too great. The Soviets have been relying increasingly on ships as an espionage base, and port cities such as Montreal—a two-hour bus ride from Ottawa—and Vancouver are playing greater roles. Intelligence officers posing as sailors disembark when a ship docks at a Canadian port and make their contact. Monitoring ships is difficult because the Security Service can only guess which few of the disembarking throng are intelligence officers. There is no Residency Analysis to fall back on in selecting surveillance targets. Each outing is essentially a stab in the dark. The intelligence officer may never set foot on Canadian soil again, the next contact is made by a different "sailor."

There is no border at the forty-ninth parallel as far as intelligence officers are concerned. One of the Soviet Union's principal interests in Canada is the proximity and easy access to the United States. The fact that agents in Canada can cross the border along with millions of tourists each year and meet their contacts in the United States

---

[9.] I am not suggesting the role of the embassy in espionage cases is becoming unimportant. The embassy still is the nerve center for operations and likely will continue to be. Its role in "running" agents may have declined, but it still predominates in recruiting agents as well as conducting functions such as an illegal support program—collecting information for the purpose of constructing legends for future Soviet illegals.

without arousing suspicion gives Russia sufficient reason to operate in Canada. However, even if there were no reason the Soviets would operate in Canada nonetheless because the Soviet Union has an obsession about the outside world's hostility that can be traced back to the conspiratorial origins of the Communist Party. At one time Communists were hunted and Russia possesses a paranoic fear that other countries plot confrontations against it and genuinely believes the KGB and the GRU are defensive organizations helping to preserve a threatened state.

There are also other reasons why the KGB would continue to function, most notably because it has grown so large and become so entrenched that it has developed a powerful bureaucratic justification. Virtually every Western country has diplomatic relations with the Soviet Union and to have diplomatic relations with the Russians is tantamount to having an espionage problem.

14

Non-Soviet Espionage

ON SUNDAY MORNING, October 3, 1965, Victor Myznikov stood along Highway 16 on the outskirts of Ottawa trying to thumb a ride south. The circumstances were unusual since Myznikov was listed as an attaché in the Soviet Embassy and had his own personal car. He was also a known KGB officer and part of the infamous troika that crudely pursued women who had access to secret information. On this occasion Myznikov was not drunk and had not been drinking the night before. His destination was Brockville, an eastern Ontario town tucked beside the Trans-Canada Highway about 108 kilometers south of Ottawa and nicely within the 125-kilometer travel limit for Soviets. At 1 P.M. Myznikov was to meet an agent who was to have a copy of *Look* Magazine in his left-hand pocket outside the Brigadier Inn restaurant in Brockville.

The procedure fit the Soviet espionage pattern for that period. Intelligence officers started out late Saturday or early Sunday in the hope that the Watcher Service was off duty or under strength. However, hitchhiking was a departure from normal practice and was later the source of discussion: was it clever or did it attract unnecessary attention? In any case, traffic was light that morning and Myznikov had trouble securing a ride. He arrived an hour late, by which time his contact was inside eating lunch. Myznikov sat down across the aisle and gave the code: "Have I by chance met you in Brno?"

The agent was a 34-year-old salesman from Edmonton named

Anton Sabotka[1] who had flown under a false name to Toronto and taken the train to Brockville.

Sabotka was an interesting spy because he was not the classic illegal who adopted a new identity and entered the country with a false passport and detailed KGB-concocted legend. Sabotka used his real name and was who he said he was: a Canadian-born Czech who in 1946 at age 16 emigrated with his father to ancestral Czechoslovakia. He returned to Canada on May 29, 1961, and landed in Montreal with his real wife and real six-year-old son. What he did not tell immigration authorities was that the wood-carved toy truck his son was carrying through customs was hollow and contained unbreakable one-time cipher pads, a series of microdots with instructions, a microdot reader, and a Minox camera used by agents around the world for spying; and that the valise he was holding was lined with $5,000 in Canadian currency. Nor did he tell the authorities that off and on for four years he had received espionage training both in Czechoslovakia and in Moscow and had come to Canada to act as an agent for the KGB in Edmonton.

The fact that Sabotka traveled to Brockville in 1965 to meet a KGB officer attached to the Soviet Embassy was unusual. The Security Service had no traces on Sabotka and he already possessed a direct and safe communication link with Moscow. He knew how to pick up messages from agent drops and relay them. He also knew how to receive enciphered instructions, decipher them, and drop them for later pickup. He also possessed microdot capability and was able to communicate safely by mail. It violated standard practice to have such an in-place, self-contained agent meet someone from the embassy who was surveillable and identified, especially a notorious intelligence officer like Myznikov. The circumstances grew stranger when it became obvious that the Brockville meeting served no crucial purpose. Sabotka was told to pick up $4,000 at a dead drop in Belanger, Quebec, and was given an address in Port Credit, Ontario, and instructed to use his job as a salesman to discover if permanent guests lived there. Both items could have been handled safely through normal channels — the way he had been instructed to come to Brockville in the first place.

[1.] Anton Sabotka is not the agent's real name; it is a pseudonym created by the Security Service.

The meet with Myznikov was not Sabotka's first high-risk rendezvous. Six months before, on March 28, 1965, he had been contacted in Edmonton by Oleg Khomenko, another KGB official in the Soviet Embassy. Khomenko, listed as a consular official, took on the temporary role of guide and adviser to the Soviet Moiseyev Dance Ensemble touring Canada which gave him a plausible reason for traveling outside the 125-kilometer limit. In Edmonton he telephoned Sabotka and after giving him the code—"Greetings from Peter"—arranged a brief meeting. It was Sabotka's first face-to-face meeting with another KGB official in the nearly four years he had been in Canada and Khomenko took advantage of the opportunity to inform him the organization was not pleased with his performance.

Sabotka was having second thoughts about his role as an agent and wished to remain in Canada as a loyal citizen. Whether the KGB at this point realized its spy was falling away is not known. During his four-year settling-in period Sabotka had shown little initiative, and this may explain why the KGB authorized direct embassy contact. Perhaps it believed that personal contact was necessary to salvage this agent. Or it could be that the KGB had already abandoned Sabotka and was handing him to the RCMP for the twofold purpose of putting him into legal trouble with Canadian authorities and diverting the Security Service's attention and draining its resources on a dead-end case. The latter might explain why a known officer like Myznikov was put onto the case and why he hitchhiked to Brockville.

If the KGB had not written off Sabotka before the Brockville meet, it must have done so after the event because he failed to pick up the $4,000 and did not carry out his assignment in Port Credit. If the KGB sought to beguile the Security Service, it succeeded. The first meeting in Edmonton had gone undetected, but the Brockville meet fell under surveillance.[2]

As Myznikov hitchhiked back to Ottawa the Watcher Service was in a minor frenzy trying for a fix on the unidentified male who stayed overnight in Brockville and then took the train to Toronto. Sabotka caused further tension when he booked a flight to Thunder Bay to

---

[2.] Ironically it was at this point that Sabotka started to feel he was being followed and started spotting suspects. The KGB was unperturbed. As it happened, none of the people Sabotka suspected were following him in fact were. The Watcher Service surveilled him so professionally over the next two years that he began doubting his fear of surveillance.

visit a relative. Should a Watcher board the plane with him? Or should he be met at his destination? And who in Thunder Bay would meet him on such short notice? Thunder Bay had no Watcher Service. It was a critical part of the operation since Sabotka was unidentified and once lost he vanished for good. The target had to be surveilled closely until he was positively identified, at which point the Watchers could sit back and afford to lose him occasionally.

The Security Service decided not to board the plane and assembled local Security Service members at Thunder Bay as a makeshift Watchers' unit. Sabotka was successfully followed back to Edmonton and identified. He became one of the Security Service's prime cases of the late 1960s and over the next six years absorbed time and resources in the form of wire-taps, bugs, and surveillance. The case drained thousands of man-hours and hundreds of thousands of dollars. The KGB left him idle for nearly two years while the Security Service monitored his daily activity and investigated his social contacts.

Sabotka received a microdot message in August, 1967, directing him to a meet at St. Joseph's Oratory in Montreal the following month. There he was contacted by Anatoli Shalnev, who posed as an official from the Russian Pavilion at Expo 67. Shalnev gave him $400 and a new schedule of shortwave broadcast transmissions for receiving instructions. The next spring a message arrived over the radio instructing him to fly to East Berlin. He ignored it and instead climbed onto his roof and dismantled the antenna and received no more broadcasts. The Security Service maintained its expensive but fruitless vigil for three years after that. Finally in April, 1971, while Sabotka was driving home from work he was intercepted by the Security Service and taken to a motel. He readily divulged everything but by this time he was of little worth. It was too late to turn him into a double agent and even his debriefing information was dated.

The purpose in relating the Sabotka incident here is not to attempt to measure the effectiveness of one side against the other but to demonstrate how the intelligence services of Eastern European countries cooperate with the Soviet Union. Sabotka started as a police informer who told the STB, the Czech state security organization, about resistance to the government's land collectivization program in his village. This association brought him in 1957 to the attention of a KGB representative, who recruited him. After the STB taught him the fundamentals—Morse code, surveillance, and countersurveillance—at night while he worked as a truck driver during the day, he went to Moscow for advanced training. In effect the KGB was using Czechoslovakia as a farm system to find talent.

The various Bloc intelligence agencies are developing increasing autonomy but still share information, personnel, and technical assistance and act as an intimate network, which is neither surprising nor improper since Western intelligence services do the same thing, although with more subtlety and with a more cultivated sense of autonomy.

The Security Service of a middle power like Canada is not expected to measure up to an awesome organization like the KGB. The RCMP is more evenly matched against the intelligence services of satellite countries whose intelligence resources more closely approximate Canada's security capability in terms of experience, resources, and breadth of vision. Both demonstrate serious lack of innovation— the RCMP because of its stifling paramilitary structure, which stresses order and discipline, and the East European organizations because of their stifling political system, which also stresses order and discipline.

The level of sophistication on both sides is demonstrated by a double-agent case involving the RCMP and Czech Intelligence during the late 1950s. František Svoboda[3] left his native Czechoslovakia after the Communist coup in 1948 and settled in Canada. He graduated from a Canadian university in 1952 and joined a federal government agency, and shortly thereafter approached the Czech Embassy in Ottawa seeking permission to bring his mother to Canada. His request would have fallen on deaf ears but by coincidence the third secretary, Milan Klenik, was once a schoolmate of Svoboda's sister and a conversation began. Klenik, an intelligence officer, told Svoboda that he had a reputation as an anti-Communist and asked him why the Czech government should do him, of all people, a favor. On the other hand, he added, something could be arranged if he was willing to work for it. It was simple blackmail. The

---

[3.] Svoboda is a pseudonym to protect his identity. All other information is unchanged.

attempt also showed the inadequacy of Czech Intelligence in trying to co-opt an obvious opponent as an agent for communism. Such cases frequently become double-agent affairs and an astute organization either avoids them or proceeds extremely cautiously. But the Czech officer was mainly interested in being able to tell Prague he had recruited an active agent. Svoboda did exactly what many intelligence officers could have predicted: he pretended to succumb to the blackmail but went straight to the RCMP and volunteered to become a double agent.

From there on the battle resembled the Original Amateur Hour. Czech Intelligence displayed its ineptitude by overlooking Svoboda's employer as a source of intelligence. Evidently the Czechs had not told the KGB about Svoboda's recruitment because the agency he worked for was a mine of top-secret information that the KGB would have loved to tap. Instead, Svoboda's assignment was to penetrate Czech refugee organizations and political organizations and report their activity. Klenik, the officer who handled him, would phone once or twice a week and ask: "How about a game of cards? Meet you at 7 P.M., usual place." Svoboda would drive to a shopping center where the Czech officer picked him up and produced a bottle of liquor and drove from one small town to another in the Ottawa Valley. The conversation would not begin until Svoboda pretended to be drunk.

The officer himself was an alcoholic and started getting so drunk he became increasingly careless. Once, while making a meetwith Svoboda, he ran into a pair of Americans he knew to be Air Force officers, and he was in the process of deliberately precipitating a confrontation when the two Americans—upon Svoboda's whispered urging—left. Svoboda felt he could not afford such incompetence and when Klenik returned to Prague on leave in 1958, he complained to Klenik's temporary replacement, Miloslav Čech. Klenik never came back to Canada and Čech, who was listed as second secretary, became Svoboda's permanent handler.

The RCMP's handling of Svoboda was not much more accomplished. His RCMP officer took him to headquarters, itself a violation of professional procedures, and had him sign in at the front desk. Svoboda submitted a phony name.

"Good thinking," the Mountie said later when Svoboda told him what he had done.

"This lack of professionalism pissed me off," says Svoboda.

After that they met regularly at a sand pit near Ottawa.

There were other amateurish traits. The Force evidently did not fully appreciate the double-agent role. Double agents should not only prevent legitimate information from leaking but also spread disinformation for the purpose of confusing and misleading the other side. This process should be exploited so that maximum damage is inflicted. The RCMP gave Svoboda complete freedom to invent his reports although he always told them in advance what false information he would pass. Fortunately, Svoboda was bright and innovative and seemed to understand his role better than his RCMP handlers. In three years his lies to the Czechs were never caught.

Svoboda's first written report to the Czechs was carefully typed out but he deliberately did not sign it.

"František, you're stupid," said his Czech contact. "Don't you think they can identify the typewriter?"

"Oh, I never thought of that," feigned Svoboda.

"We've got you now," boasted the officer. A few months later Svoboda was made to sign an oath of allegiance to Communist Czechoslovakia. He pretended to protest, but signed.

Svoboda's mother came to Canada in 1958, permitted to leave by a tough Stalinist regime at a time when nobody was leaving, not even illegally. It raised suspicions that perhaps Svoboda was a Communist. With his mother safely in Canada, Svoboda ceased his activity. Both sides protested and claimed they needed him, the RCMP even more than the Czechs. For about four years Svoboda had posed as a traitor and a drunk. Now he told the Force he was at his wits' end always fooling the Czechs and, besides, was tired of getting drunk twice a week and acting like an alcoholic. When the Force appealed to his patriotism, Svoboda reluctantly agreed to continue on one condition: he was to have official status with the Force and be paid $1 a year in case his "cooperation" with the Communists became public. The Force refused and Svoboda quit in 1959. His over-all assessment of the RCMP in the late 1950s is that the organization was very honest, clean-shaven, straightforward, but without imagination. In fact, it was similar to the Czech organization but somewhat better.

One of the worst examples of ineptitude on the part of the RCMP is the Tomasz Biernacki case. It was all the more embarrassing because it happened in public view.

Biernacki, born in Grodziec, Poland, in March, 1924, was a tall, reasonably handsome engineer who attended technical schools in Warsaw during World War Two and later studied in Milan, Italy, before distinguishing himself in his profession. One of several papers he wrote was given at the World Power Conference in Montreal in 1958, and it so impressed engineers in Canada that they invited him to immigrate to Canada. An organization called the Polish Engineers of Canada provided federal immigration authorities with proof of his professional qualifications and a guarantee of initial financial support. It lined up a job with the local Montreal engineering firm Surveyer, Nenniger and Chenevert, and arranged accommodation with a Polish family in Montreal. The association had done the same for hundreds of Polish engineers over the previous 20 years but this was the first time it had brought somebody directly from Poland.

Biernacki debarked from the SS *Batory* in Quebec City on May 6, 1960. Soon after arriving in Montreal he moved into a basement suite in Westmount and took language classes at night to improve his English. (He was already fluent in French.) He was quiet, never discussed politics, had few friends, and seemed totally immersed in his work. It seemed odd that his wife Elzbieta, a surgeon, and two daughters remained in Gdansk, Poland, although Canadian authorities had not barred his family and employment for his wife had been guaranteed in a Montreal hospital.

Biernacki had been recruited as an agent for Polish Intelligence before taking up residence in Canada. He had been schooled in the science of secret communications and knew how to make dead drops and use code phrases in routine correspondence. He carried in his pocket diary the number 430-52, a telephone number in Warsaw for direct emergency contact with his superiors. Within weeks of his arrival he started gathering information about Montreal and the individuals he worked with at the engineering firm.

One Friday evening 11 months later Biernacki was eating dinner in his suite when members of the Security Service knocked on his door and asked to examine his passport, which had expired two days previously, and to find out why he had changed his status from visitor to landed immigrant. It was the beginning of a 52-hour marathon interrogation, during which Biernacki readily confessed. He said he knew this would happen eventually and was happy to be relieved of the burden. Furthermore, he expressed a desire to remain in Canada. It was evident that Polish authorities had recruited him unwillingly.

Biernacki turned over four pages of closely handwritten notes on onion-skin paper describing his progress in establishing himself in Canada and providing personality assessments on fellow workers and 14 members of the Polish community in Canada who were potential recruitment targets because they had either socialist or homosexual tendencies—the latter "a quite common symptom" in Canada—or access to confidential information. His report concluded with "a general comment":

> I estimate that, in the circumstances, besides the good pro-
> gress of the case or a suitable "guidance," based on additional
> information, obtained outside—the period of acclimatization,
> which would make possible the establishment of rather closer
> contacts—especially with non-Poles—would take 3-4 years. It
> would also be necessary to pretend that one has completely
> severed his ties with Poland and, during that time, at the most,
> one trip to Europe could ensure a good contact on neutral
> grounds.

Biernacki was charged with spying for a foreign power and with his confession, his own notes, and other incriminating documenta-tion, the Security Service believed the case was open and shut. When Biernacki appeared in court on April 18 the original charge was withdrawn and he was charged instead with collecting information "preparatory to the setting up of an espionage and intelligence ring ... useful to a foreign power." The word "preparatory" had been inserted. It was a sign that maybe the case was not so strong after all.

The preliminary hearing stretched into several weeks and often was held in secret. Even when it was open the press was barred from reporting the evidence although it covered the legal maneuvering prominently. On May 9 the preliminary hearing turned against the Security Service. Mr. Justice Peter V. Shorteno ruled that two key documents which were critical to the Crown's case could not be used as evidence and also accused the RCMP of "bungling" Biernacki's interrogation. The judge said he "was literally shocked" by the "contradictions" and "discrepancies" in the evidence given concerning Biernacki's removal to a midtown hotel the morning after the RCMP began questioning him.

The courtroom was frozen as looks of mutual contempt rebounded between the faces of the judge and the half-dozen Mounties sitting in the chamber. Special prosecutor Jean Miquelon, Q.C., informed the judge at the next session that the Crown disagreed with the ruling.

"I would like to have it put on the record that the Crown respectfully states that it takes exception to the judgement and the reasons for it," said Miquelon, despite the fact there was no appeal against such a decision.

"What does that mean in legal terms?" retorted Mr. Justice Shorteno. "Do you intend to go on with the preliminary inquiry?"

"Yes, M'Lord, I do," replied Miquelon.

One of the rejected documents contained Biernacki's confession. It lacked legal authority as evidence in court because it had been made to the Security Service and not the Criminal Investigation Branch. The Security Service had assumed that a confession made to a security investigator held the same legal authenticity as one given to a criminal investigator. That error altered the nature of the trial and Biernacki, who by this time had four defense lawyers, including the noted trial lawyer Joseph Cohen, Q.C., and was remaining silent, found his prospects for winning the case radically improved.

A few weeks later Mr. Justice Shorteno issued a 44-page judgment rejecting the laying of charges and ruling that the Crown had not established sufficient grounds to warrant a trial. Biernacki was a free man—but for only a few seconds. Prosecuter Miquelon stood up and announced that, having anticipated the judge's decision, he had obtained a preferred indictment from the Attorney-General of Quebec which placed Biernacki back under arrest. (A preferred indictment was a legal device that gave the Attorney-General the authority to send individuals directly to trial without a preliminary hearing.) Biernacki was given bail[4] at $4,000 while his lawyers appealed the preferred indictment.

[4.] In granting bail Mr. Justice Wilfred Lazure assigned the RCMP to watch Biernacki so that he would not flee the country.

In January, 1962, Mr. Justice J. S. P. Trottier ruled on the side of Biernacki, saying that he could not be sent to trial if a preliminary hearing had already determined there was not sufficient grounds for the laying of charges. Thus Biernacki was absolved; he returned to Poland.

The Security Service's bungling of the legal technicalities of Biernacki's interrogation was not its worst error in the case. A more fundamental miscalculation was made, one that betrayed a serious lack of professionalism: the Force failed to let the case develop to the stage where it was prosecutable—that is if it ever should have been prosecuted. Biernacki, in Montreal less than a year, was still going through his familiarization rituals of making contacts and gathering information that was mainly public such as bridge locations and the like. He was still training and had not reached the stage of seeking official secrets. There had been no recruitments.

Mr. Justice Shorteno concluded: "I am rather of the opinion that the most which can be said on behalf of the Crown, is that the accused committed *preparatory acts* toward the commission of *other preparatory acts* ..."[5] Besides, the judge ruled, none of the information constituted a state secret and therefore did not fall under the jurisdiction of the Official Secrets Act.

There is also the underlying question of why the Force did not attempt to turn Biernacki into a double agent, the accepted practice of security organizations better and more experienced than the RCMP. Biernacki was classic double-agent material. First, he confessed his role and handed over his handwritten notes, which showed his willingness to cooperate. He turned silent only after formal charges were laid against him. Second, his wife and daughters were still in Poland. Once exposed, he could normally expect a prison sentence and prolonged separation from his family. As a double agent he would remain free and be able to seek to bring his family to Canada. Third, and most convincing, was the fact that Biernacki said he wanted to remain in Canada.

The fact that the RCMP is primarily a police organization and by its nature does not appreciate the benefits of doubling an agent and has minimum resources for such operations provides part of the

---

5. Italics belong to Mr. Justice Shorteno.

answer. The other part of the answer lies in events that had recently happened in Britain and the United States.

The preceding years were active in the international security and intelligence field. With great publicity the FBI arrested the infamous Soviet illegal Colonel Rudolf "Red" Abel, who was sentenced to 30 years imprisonment (but later swapped for American U-2 pilot Francis Gary Powers). And only months before Biernacki's arrest, Scotland Yard rolled up the Portland Spy Rink and procured impressive convictions on espionage charges. Because the leader of the Portland Spy Ring, Gordon Lonsdale, was really a Soviet illegal by the name of Konon Trofimovich Molody who posed as a Canadian businessman whose family records had been destroyed in the forest fire that swept the Haileybury area of Ontario, the RCMP was involved in the investigation but received none of the publicity.[6] The Force had been dry since Gouzenko and wanted to demonstrate it could catch spies too.

The Biernacki proceedings were probably followed with some interest in the Montreal newspapers by Anton Sabotka, who happened to land in the city from Czechoslovakia during the preliminary hearing en route to his role as immigrant espionage agent in Edmonton. The Biernacki and Sabotka cases show how the separate jurisdictions of immigration and security intersect and why one function needs cooperation from the other.

There are scores of other cases although not always as elaborate as the Biernacki and Sabotka examples. The Soviet Union commonly allowed citizens to emigrate only on condition that once in Canada they perform low-level intelligence tasks such as infiltrating local ethnic groups. Family members in Russia became hostages to ensure the fulfillment of that commitment. Many of these immigrants contacted the Security Service upon arrival in Canada and explained their predicament. The Security Service, to its credit, set up these immigrants as double agents and in one fell swoop ran a disinformation

---

[6.] The conclusive evidence that proved the man claiming to be Gordon Lonsdale was an imposter was produced by the RCMP. Dr. Elmer Mitchell, who had delivered the real Gordon Lonsdale, born in Cobalt, Ontario, August 27, 1927, had retired and was tracked down in Toronto. Dr. Mitchell said he remembered circumcising the baby. The Soviet imposter was not circumcised. That was the one thing the Soviets had overlooked.

operation to confuse the KGB and protect the relatives in the old country.

Security screening became an important factor in admission of immigrants. Without clearance, no one, no matter how desirable his attributes, was accepted. While the Immigration Department made the final decision the RCMP controlled the security-screening procedure and played a crucial role in the process. The RCMP's input was always conservative and sometimes retrogressive.

There was no effective security-screening program for immigrants until 1947. Until the end of the 1920s Canada was too eager to attract settlers and, besides, the threat of espionage through immigration was small. Immigration virtually ceased in 1930 for economic reasons and continued to be frozen through World War Two. Only in 1947 did the immigration doors reopen. By this time countries like Canada had become security-conscious as a result of the Gouzenko experience and the cold-war tensions. The security problem was considerable because there were no records for many of the displaced persons in the European refugee camps, making genuine security screening impossible.

As postwar immigration continued, Commissioner S. T. Wood, attempting to save the expense of sending an officer to England, tapped the part-time services of a retired Mountie already living in London to coordinate immigration-checking for Europe. He received little or no pay and effectively was the RCMP's first liaison officer. Then in 1952 Inspector William Kelly, later to become head of the Security Service and then a Deputy Commissioner, was posted to London and replaced the ad-hoc arrangement with the retired officer. Noncommissioned officers were later posted to other centers generating heavy flows of immigrants.

The Security Service had a representative on both the Immigration Committee and the Citizenship Committee and a hand in examining every case that came before either body. When doubts arose, the Security Service as an institution usually took the negative view, which was not surprising since its only mandate was to protect Canadian security. The Force's representatives were adamant that any affiliation with a Communist organization, no matter how peripheral or how long in the past, or how youthful the individual at the time, should preclude admission.

Sometimes the cases were absurd. One committee member interviewed during the research for this book said that for a long time he could not understand how an ordinarily reasonable Security Service representative could take a hard-line position on case after case. Then he discovered the Mountie was ordered to keep a box score of his won-lost record for his superiors to peruse.

One of the factors contributing to the RCMP's sensitivity about passing judgment on immigrants was the United States, which viewed Canada as an open door for spies. The Americans exerted pressure at several government levels but most of all on the RCMP. The American claim that Canada represented a weak link in its fortress was not without justification since border-crossing was easy, Canada's passport system more easily abused, and its immigration policies more liberal.

When checking the background of a potential immigrant the RCMP relied almost entirely on the security agency of the originating country since it provided the information. This arrangement obviously worked only when the foreign countries were friendly and trustworthy. For that reason the RCMP could not do any security screening behind the Iron Curtain since the countries there were primarily the ones that security screening was directed against. In any case, there was little immigration from Eastern Europe largely because of the restrictive emigration policies of the countries themselves. When the Polish government relaxed its tough prohibition in 1956 and permitted some emigration, Canada had to decide whether or not to accept Polish emigrants. The Security Service wanted to exclude them all and probably would have prevailed had it not been for the intervention of Jack Pickersgill, the liberal-minded Minister of Citizenship and Immigration who viewed such a policy as unacceptable. Pickersgill decided that immigrants directly from Poland were acceptable if they had a relative in Canada who was not a security risk. However, the Polish government reversed its policy the following year and again clamped down on emigration.[7]

Security screening of Hungarians was virtually abandoned for the brief period of the Hungarian Revolution in 1956 and even the

---

[7.] Since the adoption of new immigration regulations in 1967, the ban on sponsored immigration from Eastern European countries has been relaxed and immigration offices have been opened in Budapest and Belgrade.

RCMP did not fight the policy. The revolution created thousands of refugees and Canada opened its doors despite the security risks. The RCMP took a very correct approach: it pointed out the risks and graciously accepted the government's decision to let the people in and just hope there were no spies. The government's policy enjoyed widespread public support. Citizens' groups were formed to lend assistance to displaced Hungarians. The effort was spearheaded by the energetic Jack Pickersgill, who made the decision to cut the red tape and do the security-screening checks after the Hungarians arrived in Canada.

It will probably never be known positively whether the Hungarians or Russians exploited the flow of Hungarian immigrants because if they did and were successful, the RCMP would not know about it. However, circumstances suggest there were no significant breaches. The first stream of refugees consisted of hard-line Communists who fled because they thought their side had lost. Later the fortunes of the revolt were reversed and the next flow of immigrants were the losing revolutionaries who were anti-Communists. Both wound up in the same refugee camps and the Security Service distinguished itself with effective security screening by interviewing both factions. In no time hard-line Communists were being exposed and denounced. A number of these individuals voluntarily left Canada, some for their own personal safety. Some returned because the Communist regime regained power, others because they were homesick. Some probably returned because they were agents who had been compromised. Of approximately 37,500 refugees arriving in Canada, about 600 returned. The usual security-screening requirements were also waived for Czechoslovaks in 1968.

The biggest immigration headache involved the Chinese and reached a peak in the 1950s and 1960s. An organized illegal immigration industry in Hong Kong brought Chinese people into Canada and under false identities for a price. So many Chinese immigrated deceptively that the system broke down and on several occasions the government simply gave up and offered amnesty to illegal immigrants. There were several reasons for the breakdown. The Chinese had an identification system that baffled Canadian officials and made falsification relatively easy. Members of the Chinese community in

Canada were close and willing to hide their fellow members and, most importantly, Hong Kong liaison officials were corrupt and willfully supplied Canadian officials with false information.

The widespread illegal immigration gave Chinese Intelligence an ideal opportunity to plant agents in Canada. Historically, the Chinese have been unusually successful in using the Chinese living in other countries for intelligence work. One can only surmise they did the same in Canada because the Chinese are so unhurried, patient, and farsighted in enlisting agents that they seldom backfire. Chinese Intelligence defectors, unlike the KGB, are virtually unknown.

Despite its methodical and quiet approach, Chinese Intelligence can be belligerent and, when so, can outstrip the KGB in aggressiveness.

> While China is typically "unaggressive" in her overall espionage, she does on occasion embark on "aggressive" espionage in an extreme manner. This may seem a total contradiction, but it needs to be stated that the two techniques are quite separate. One can put it this way: ninety-five per cent of Chinese espionage and intelligence work is low-key and unaggressive, five per cent of it is violent, open and brutal aggression. Often such tactics may appear to have nothing in common with secret service work.[8]

Canada experienced some of this belligerence during the 1960s after the two countries exchanged journalists in what was to become a prelude to opening diplomatic relations in 1970. China accepted a reporter from the Toronto *Globe and Mail* while Canada admitted two representatives from the notorious New China News Agency. Consequently, China got a legitimate Canadian journalist and Canada got four Chinese intelligence officers, since their wives were also believed to be active. The foursome immediately and with little subtlety set out to obtain recruits among the Chinese community in Ottawa. The Security Service vainly attempted to monitor the activity but the Force's only Chinese expert was a WASP member of the Russian Desk (there was no Chinese Desk) who spoke no Chinese. He followed their trail, interviewed their contacts, and soon learned

[8.] From *The Chinese Secret Service* by Richard Deacon (New York: Ballantine Books, 1976).

that a white man is out of place in the Chinese fraternity.

The Security Service was lacking in Chinese staff because Chinese Canadians at the time were effectively prevented from joining the RCMP. Security-clearance regulations excluded people with relatives in Communist countries, and most Chinese Canadians, even third-generation ones, had relatives in China. The Security Service had infiltrated virtually every ethnic group in the country but had failed to make inroads with the Chinese and were at a loss in investigating the activities of the New China News Agency. Eventually the Force did achieve limited success because the Chinese officers were so aggressive and created so much resentment and fear within the Chinese community that a few Chinese Canadians approached the Security Service to volunteer information. They were only interested in curbing these Chinese nationals, and refused to become permanent informers.

By the late 1960s it was obvious that Canada and China would be extending diplomatic recognition. Negotiations began in Stockholm in February, 1969. The Force viewed this development with suspicion and grew alarmed at the prospect of inundation from a yellow wave of espionage officers. All Chinese looked the same. Mounties did not know the language.

The RCMP lobbied against Chinese recognition within the councils of government. The first tactic was to dramatize, quite legitimately, the increased threat to Canada's security that diplomatic representation would present. While expressed in alarmist tones, the argument was substantially accurate. The establishment of a diplomatic base always provides an important mechanism for intelligence-gathering. The broader the relationship, the broader the scope for espionage activity. This argument held particularly true for China since it had at the time neither an embassy in Washington nor a seat at the United Nations in New York and therefore the embassy in Canada was certain to become its intelligence headquarters for North America. Although the RCMP position was valid the drawbacks did not outweigh the benefits of diplomatic recognition.

The RCMP's second tack was to dramatize the financial expense of recognition. Bolstering security capability would cost millions and the RCMP budget would need enriching. On that point the RCMP won the battle but lost the war. China was recognized and the Force managed to secure increased funding beyond strictly China-related needs which was used to compensate for past deficiencies.

The Security Service did not create a long-overdue Chinese Desk. It created instead an entire branch called H Section, which ostensibly covered Southeast Asia but operated almost exclusively against China. Not even the Soviet Union had such status. Russia was a mere desk in B Section (Counterespionage), although the Russian Desk was bigger than all of H Section. The Security Service sent members to Washington and elsewhere for Chinese language training. It also ordered across-the-board budget increases for support sections such as wire-tapping, bugging, and surveillance since these units would have increased workloads because of H Section's activity. One noncommissioned officer in charge of a technical section was told to submit new higher estimates for his establishment and refused because he did not think he needed more staff. He was then ordered to submit enlarged estimates.

While the New China News Agency was near the height of its aggressive recruitment efforts within the Ottawa Chinese community, a gruesome incident involving Chinese Intelligence was unfolding in Amsterdam. A Chinese engineer attending an official convention in Holland tried to defect and was found lying outside the three-story residence of the Chinese third secretary and taken to hospital despite attempts to prevent it. The man was discovered to have a fractured skull, broken ribs, and spinal damage. The Chinese claimed he had fallen out the window. While in the X-ray department the engineer was kidnapped by a team from the Chinese Embassy and a little later the embassy announced he had died. The Dutch surrounded the office where the engineer's eight colleagues were staying to keep them from leaving the country without being interviewed by the police. In effect the eight became hostages. The Chinese government in return declared the Dutch chargé d'affaires in Peking *persona non grata* but refused to let him out of the country. In effect he was under house arrest. The stand-off lasted nearly six months before a compromise was reached and each side allowed to return home.

The Security Service was primarily aware of the aggressive 5 percent of Chinese Intelligence and tailored its counterintelligence program predominantly to this segment. The wave of Chinese espionage never materialized—at least not in the form the Security

Service had anticipated. Once diplomatic relations were established, the Chinese did relatively little detectable intelligence work, although there have been a few diplomatic expulsions, mainly in regard to activities aimed against the United States.

The relationship between Canada and Cuba is truly outlandish and reveals the colonial status of both countries in the international security and intelligence community. For the Cuban Directorate of General Intelligence, otherwise known as DGI, Canada is primarily an opportunity to secure either espionage against the United States or armed insurrection against third-world countries. To the extent that Cuba is interested in Canada itself it is a tool of the Soviets since they manipulate and, to a large degree, control the DGI. Conversely, the Security Service runs aggressive counterintelligence operations against Cuba which are not always primarily aimed at Cuba but at the Soviet Union. According to information from defectors, Cuba and the Soviet Union made a pact back in the 1960s that Cuba would carry out intelligence functions on Russia's behalf in countries where the Russians are oversurveilled. Furthermore, since the Cubans, unlike the Soviets, are not restricted by the 125-kilometer limit they are therefore harder to surveil. One report suggested that a subsequent agreement in 1976 gave Cuba responsibility for subversion (as opposed to espionage) in Canada. As for the times Cuba itself is the target, the operation is usually done on behalf of the CIA since the Cuban intelligence headquarters in North America is located in Montreal and the CIA, for defensive purposes, is interested in what the Cubans are up to and provides favors if Canada conducts an operation on its behalf.

These events are staged on Canadian soil but both Cuba and Canada are bit actors. The real performance features the CIA and the KGB. Sometimes it is the CIA versus the DGI, or the RCMP versus the KGB. Rarely is Canada pitted against Cuba.

In 1976 a Cuban official was told to leave Canada for engaging in unacceptable activities involving the Cuban community in Canada. In January, 1977, four Cubans were expelled—three with diplomatic status plus a postgraduate student at McGill University without diplomatic status—for recruiting agents to work in Africa. The Cuban Embassy did not deny the claim but issued a press release saying that none of the operations was directed against Canada and should not affect Canadian-Cuban relations since the objective was to assist Angola protect itself against "a group of bandits."

Canada became a war zone of sorts between North Korea and South Korea for a brief period in the early 1970s. South Korea's notorious KCIA, the Korean Central Intelligence Agency, an organization with extreme aggressive tendencies, had grass roots connections with Korean groups in Canada. Relations were so close that legal title to the Korean-Canadian Cultural Association's $202,000 center in Metropolitan Toronto was held directly by the South Korean government. When China was recognized in 1970 North Korea thought it deserved recognition too and mounted a propaganda campaign within the Korean community for the purpose of inducing them to lobby the Canadian government for North Korean recognition, as well as to conduct a little intelligence-gathering on the side. The KCIA liked neither the possibility of Canada recognizing North Korea nor North Korea's muscling into the Canadian Korean community, hitherto its exclusive domain. The KCIA brought additional officers into Canada to counteract the effort and the battle was on. The jousting reached the Security Service's attention in 1972. The RCMP investigated and for the first time realized the extent of the KCIA's involvement in Canada. The inter-Korean rivalry became prominent enough for the federal cabinet to be briefed. In the end External Affairs decided against extending diplomatic recognition to North Korea. Its crude lobby-cum-espionage campaign did more damage than good.

In March, 1978, Yung-man Yang, the Vice-Consul in South Korea's Consulate-General in Toronto, defected and went into hiding and was debriefed by the Security Service about the KCIA's role in Canada. He claimed to have knowledge of blackmail and harassment of South Korea's critics in Canada and said his superior, Shin-chung Park, was an undercover KCIA official. Park was recalled shortly after Yang's defection. The Security Service and External Affairs conducted an investigation and, according to a statement from External Affairs Minister Don Jamieson, turned up nothing illegal or strictly improper in diplomatic terms.

Lately even the Iraqis have been getting into the intelligence act, and when caught have accepted expulsions less gracefully than other countries. Abu Al-Khail, Minister Plenipotentiary at the Iraqi Embassy, was expelled in August, 1977, and in May, 1978, Second Secretary Abdul Latif M. Al-Niaimi was ousted. Both men had bought information on the Canadian Kurdish community and were involved in efforts to disrupt Kurdish organizations. Iraq retaliated both times. Following the second incident W. A. McKenzie, the first secretary and chargé d'affaires at the Canadian Embassy in Baghdad, was expelled although there was no allegation that he had done anything improper.

The Iraqi incidents demonstrate that the practice of espionage and pseudo-espionage is increasing and is not limited to the big powers or countries that have traditionally been hostile. The countries cited in this chapter are not the only ones who actively gather intelligence in Canada. Rumania, Yugoslavia, East Germany, Bulgaria, and others have operated in Canada. Egypt once engaged in an embarrassingly amateurish spy attempt.

To some degree every country collects intelligence from its embassies, even countries like Canada without intelligence-gathering agencies. One of an embassy's prime functions is to gather information; it is an accepted and entirely legitimate activity. The point at which information becomes intelligence defies definition. Allen Dulles, the renowned Director of the CIA, is reputed to have said: "Intelligence is information that is hard to get." Some countries strive harder than others.

The Separation Fight: Two

THE MID-1960S saw the minority government of Lester Pearson bounce from scandal to scandal and each time the RCMP seemed to play a starring, if reluctant, role. Cohorts of the drug-running ruffian Lucien Rivard attempted to bribe with $20,000 the lawyer representing the United States government not to oppose bail in the attempt to extradite Rivard to face a dope-smuggling charge in Texas. The lawyer, Pierre Lamontagne, reported the bribe to the RCMP, which responded with an investigation that was sometimes dim-witted and often inept.

The criminal investigation side of the Force reacted slowly and then proceeded to interview suspects in the wrong order, giving conspirators time to coordinate stories. It also initially assigned a unilingual Anglophone investigator when all the principals were French. Richard Gwyn, whose book *The Shape of Scandal* details every twist and turn in the case, concluded that the RCMP acted inefficiently.

> At least one incident brought the image of the RCMP peri-lously close to that of the Keystone Cops. This was the moni-tored conversation of August 20th between Lamontagne and [Raymond] Denis. If it had been properly intercepted, this call could have ended the case. Instead, one of the officers sent to listen in on the conversation took no notes at all, because, as he

explained, he had to use one hand to hold the receiver of the telephone extension and the other to cup the mouthpiece so that he would not be overheard. The other officer was only able to scribble down a few exchanges on the back of a gasoline bill envelope; he had forgotten to bring a notebook with him.

Then there was Hal Banks, the brutal labor leader who headed the Canadian branch of the Seafarers' International Union. He was sentenced to five years in prison for conspiracy to commit common assault but, strangely, was granted bail and promptly disappeared into the United States, where he was located living luxuriously by Toronto *Star* reporter Bob Reguly.

There were also the Furniture Scandal and the controversy over the government's decision to revoke pension benefits from Vancouver postal clerk George Victor Spencer after his exposure as a Soviet agent. In defending the government, Liberal Cabinet Minister Lucien Cardin let drop news of a sex-and-security scandal during the previous government headed by John Diefenbaker. Gerda Munsinger, a prostitute and alleged former Russian spy, had had an affair with Pierre Sévigny when he was Associate Minister of Defence, and she also knew George Hees while he was Minister of Trade. The RCMP told Prime Minister Diefenbaker of the liaisons and he put an end to them but did not fire anybody. When the story broke, the press went looking for Mrs. Munsinger but the RCMP told the government she had died of leukemia in East Germany. Bob Reguly tracked her down in Munich, where she was very much alive and working in a bar. It was suggested the government dispense with the RCMP and hire the Toronto *Star*.

The minority Pearson government could have fallen on any number of occasions. It was shaken but not defeated. Part of the trouble stemmed from the relationship between the Minister of Justice and the RCMP. The minister's main function was drafting legislation for Parliament. In addition he had responsibility for the penitentiary system, the Parole Board, the superintendent of bankruptcy, and the combines branch. The task of overseeing the RCMP was added as well.

Even if the minister had the time to supervise the RCMP he usually lacked the inclination. The RCMP would always beg its minister to come to headquarters for a tour. Only Don Fleming in the Diefenbaker government accepted the invitation. The RCMP was looking for a friend at court and wanted to impress the minister, in part because he controlled the Force's budget allotment. The situation was further aggravated by the fact that the Justice Department had responsibility for criminal matters and the Prime Minister for security. If there was one minister busier than the Justice Minister in those days, it was the Prime Minister. So the RCMP had two part-time ministers, with neither giving it much attention.

John Diefenbaker was the most frustrating Prime Minister; the Force could not get a decision out of him. Diefenbaker returned top-secret security files totally unmarked; not even a JGD was initialed into the margins to indicate he had seen them. Diefenbaker was unable to make the hard decisions required in security work. Prime Minister Pearson when possible avoided the files because he was a gentleman and detested the seamy side of the business. Pierre Trudeau proved different. He never shirked a tough decision. He read the files and returned them with crisp instructions on what to do, which made him popular with the Force.

The RCMP was most neglected when Guy Favreau was Justice Minister in the mid-1960s. On top of his existing responsibilities Pearson gave him two other highly demanding positions: House Leader and Quebec lieutenant, each demanding virtual full-time attention on its own. The overworked Favreau rarely saw his agency heads and fumbled immediately and soon resigned in disgrace for exercising bad judgment.

The tragedy of Guy Favreau alerted the government to the circumstances the RCMP had lived under for years, namely that there were not enough hours in the day to enable the Minister of Justice to fulfill his responsibilities as overseer of the RCMP. Parliament responded in 1965 with the Government Reorganization Act, which stripped the Justice Department of five responsibilities and combined three of them—the RCMP, the Parole Board, and the penitentiary system—into a single ministry called the Solicitor General. Although the ministry was new the name was old because the Solicitor General had existed for years as essentially an Associate Minister of Justice whose only significant duty was bringing to cabinet notices of death sentences that could be commuted to life imprisonment.

The series of parliamentary fiascos as well as the need to define security requirements in a modern context moved the government to re-examine the general issue of security, with the result that in 1966 Pearson told the Commons a Royal Commission on Security headed by Maxwell MacKenzie was being established "in order to assist the Solicitor General in his particular and new responsibility." The theory was that policies appropriate during the intense 1950s might be incompatible with the liberalism of the emerging détente. One of the three members of the Royal Commission was former CCF leader M. J. Coldwell, for years a critical vigilante on security. The third commissioner was Yves Pratte, a liberal-minded Quebec lawyer who later became Chairman and Chief Executive Officer of Air Canada and then a judge on the Supreme Court of Canada.

Shock waves went through the RCMP when Coldwell was placed on the commission. The Force had a file on the former CCF leader. He was a lifelong civil libertarian and defender of the downtrodden, and at one time was considered a subversive by the RCMP. The apprehension grew when the commission requested access to RCMP files; the individual expressing the greatest interest was Coldwell himself. The Force hesitated at first.

"Turn them loose," Commissioner George McClellan finally declared. "They can't lug papers out of here anyway. Maybe it will do some good."

Coldwell blitzed the fourth-and fifth-floor filing system and when he saw his own file he was disappointed to discover that it consisted mainly of newspaper clippings. In the end Coldwell became the conservative anchor on the commission and often argued against some of the more liberal proposals of his two fellow commissioners.

The Royal Commission spent the next 18 months rummaging through the RCMP's top-secret files and hearing witnesses *in camera*. The commission was forbidden by its terms of reference from holding public hearings and became a captive of RCMP information. It produced a report in September, 1968, shortly after Pierre Trudeau succeeded Pearson as Prime Minister, and the bulk of it—160 pages—was published in June, 1969.

The report was not what Pearson had envisaged when he established the commission. Bothered by cases like the unfortunate George Victor Spencer—a pitiful individual who was more a victim of the KGB than a collaborator—Pearson hoped the commission would propose a more humane way of dealing with the Spencers of the world. However, its recommendations were anything but progressive. Rather than softening the restrictions it advocated a hardened attitude. It recommended security checks for every federal government employee, whether the individual had access to confidential information or not. That meant a man cutting grass for the National Parks Branch in some remote region would be checked. Not even the RCMP was that severe. The report also recommended the fingerprinting of every government employee.

There was more. The commission also recommended that the RCMP have a voice in determining which individuals should be denied security clearances. The Force's traditional role was to collect information and turn it over to the relevant department for decision-making. Even though the RCMP had long felt frustrated since its information was not always heeded, the arrangement placed an important check on its power and played a crucial role in containing some of the excesses of McCarthyism during the 1950s. The commission wanted the RCMP to comment "on the validity, relevance and importance of the information it provides and make a formal recommendation on whether or not clearance should be granted." The recommendation, if implemented, would upset the old balance and make the police the imposing factor on decisions.

The federal government would have had to revive some of the old policies toward homosexuals to abide by one of the commission's recommendations. "Homosexuality should not always be a bar to employment in the public service, but should normally preclude clearance to the higher levels of classification and certainly preclude posting to sensitive positions overseas," the report said.

It would have required External Affairs to recall some of its officers abroad. Although External already had a policy of not sending homosexuals to sensitive positions behind the Iron Curtain, the commission wanted homosexuals excluded from all foreign postings, which was tantamount to denying homosexuals a decent career in the department.

The commission's conservative recommendations pleased the RCMP—with one exception, which happened to be the most important one. Reviving the festering wound of civilianization and separation, the commission recommended that the Security and

Intelligence Division, as it was then called, be split off entirely from the RCMP. This recommendation surpassed the relatively mild proposal of Mark McClung in the 1950s. McClung had advocated a separate organization under the authority of the RCMP Commissioner. The Royal Commission advocated total divorce.

The RCMP was not prepared to preside over the dismemberment of its empire. It would lose about 20 percent of its manpower. Connections with the CIA would dry up, as they would with the British, French, Australian, and other foreign security services. Even the strong link with the FBI would be whittled down to criminal matters.

"I hope to Christ we're not going through with this recommendation for a civilian service," said John Starnes, Assistant Under-Secretary in the Department of External Affairs. "It will be infiltrated from the start and there's no way you can get around that. You'd have a Philby on your hands in no time."

Since Starnes was a senior diplomat and former ambassador, his vehement denunciation of the commission's main recommendation gave hope to RCMP officialdom. As far as the Force was concerned, it was the most serious attack since the 1920s, when it was almost disbanded. RCMP senior officers held strategy meetings and resolved to fight by lobbying the government. Leading the fight were Deputy Commissioner Bill Kelly and soon-to-become-Commissioner Len Higgitt. Each had once headed up Security and Intelligence. The articulate Kelly was particularly persuasive. Their main political ally was George McIlraith, a wily cabinet minister and a friend of the Force who fortuitously happened to be Solicitor General at the time.

The government's deliberations stretched into months and during this time departments with an historical desire for civilianization, such as the Privy Council Office and the Department of National Defence, had an opportunity to press their case to a seemingly obvious conclusion. But several factors intervened on the RCMP's behalf. First, the Force lobbied with unexpected vehemence. Second, the RCMP was such a revered institution that the government hesitated to push it and so the cabinet became divided. Third, and possibly most significant, the RCMP's old nemesis, External Affairs, the department that had clamored loudest and longest for a separate organization, could not pull together at the critical moment, especially since John Starnes, one of its most senior officers, opposed the split.

In the end a compromise was reached. Security and Intelligence would be given more autonomy, a measure of civilianization, take the new name of Security Service, and have a civilian head. As well, for the first time in history, the officer in charge of the security organization would hold rank equal to Deputy Commissioner and report directly to the Commissioner without having to go through some policeman first. In return the RCMP got to keep the organization.

The RCMP brass was relieved that the new head of the Security Service would be John Starnes. Of all the possible civilian heads Starnes was the most palatable since he had always held its respect, one of the foremost External Affairs officers to do so. The arrangement received little debate in cabinet. It was a compromise that left the RCMP empire intact. It was also acceptable to Prime Minister Trudeau, who favored a civilian security service but wanted the separation to occur slowly. On June 26, 1969, Trudeau unveiled the compromise in the House of Commons.

"The Security Service, under the Commissioner of the RCMP, will be increasingly separate in structure and civilian in nature," Trudeau said.[1]

Well before Trudeau's statement the RCMP realized it was vulnerable to the charge that Security Service members were unable to differentiate between subversives and dissidents. The issue had been raised often enough in the Commons, particularly in the mid-1960s when Mounties had been discovered investigating innocent protest groups. Although the Force as early as the 1930s had sent a hand-picked few men to university and increased the numbers steadily over the years, most Mounties had no education beyond high school and had formed their political views within the paramilitary environment of the RCMP. When this lack of education developed into an argument supporting a civilian security agency, the

---

[1]. One of the interesting sidelights during the internal struggle concerned the publication of the Royal Commission's report. The RCMP opposed publishing any portion of it because the report criticized the Force for its lack of education and, more specifically, its lack of sophistication in distinguishing between differing left-wing political philosophies. Trudeau himself favored publishing as much of the report as possible and from there on a committee was formed to decide what portions to delete. The time between the submission of the report to the government in September, 1968, and its publication in abridged form in June, 1969, was spent mostly on the debate of what sections to publish. In the end most of it was published.

Force responded with a program of sending selected individuals to university as if to say: "See, our guys have education too."

Mounties were sent to university at RCMP expense and invariably received outstanding marks since they studied diligently. Others took night courses and had their tuition fees paid by the Force. It was a 180-degree shift in attitude. Officers were suddenly promoted on the basis of education and ambitious Mounties everywhere started striving for better education and studied a variety of subjects, from technical to liberal arts, including the political theories of Marx and Lenin. The trend was encouraging but its impact in terms of changing the philosophical outlook was minor. Mounties who studied full-time returned to their duties four years later better educated but just as conservative. Their political convictions had been formed in the first years of their career, when they were impressionable, and formal education rarely changed that. The only change concerned their views on management style. Here they became significantly more liberal and the educated ones grew to dislike the chain-of-command philosophy and its insistence on unquestioning discipline. The Force still did not get many recruits out of university. By and large they continued to come from high schools with the prospect that they might be sent to university years later—after their political outlook had been nurtured within the Force.

The arrival of John Starnes in January, 1970, was viewed with optimism and anticipation. He was the right man at the right time, so it seemed. He had the confidence of both the government and the RCMP and the support of the rank and file. Since most Security Service members favored a civilian organization, they considered Starnes a messiah of sorts who would lead them to the promised land. The new university-trained Mounties were returning from school and dissatisfaction was growing over the sheer arbitrariness and harshness of the paramilitary system. This increasing disenchantment within the Security Service was based on two factors: that it hampered effective security work and that it was inconsistent with the freedom of modern society. Starnes disliked the structure and understood the dissatisfaction but lacked the authority to cast off the paramilitary shackles. However, he tried to make the system more humane and informal. He banished uniforms for the Security Service and defied the chain-of-command procedure by directly soliciting the advice of NCOs. More importantly, he started little think tanks and encouraged members to understand why they did certain things. His aim was to make the Security Service more thoughtful and less reflexive.

Starnes was more qualified to head up the Security Service than many Mounties even though he had never been in the RCMP. His grand-uncle, Cortlandt Starnes, joined the NWMP at the time of the Louis Riel Rebellion and was RCMP Commissioner from 1923 to 1931. His great grandfather, Henry Starnes, was a Loyalist who became Speaker of Quebec's Upper House before it was abolished in 1867. The son of a wealthy Montreal grain dealer, John Starnes was educated at private schools — Selwyn House in Montreal and Trinity College in Port Hope — before continuing his studies in Switzerland and Germany. He joined the Black Watch as a lieutenant in 1939 but his knowledge of the German language propelled him into military intelligence, to which he took an instant liking. It marked the beginning of a career in the security and intelligence field, which continued after he joined External Affairs from England in 1944. He became a member of the Security Subpanel and would often sit in for the Undersecretary on the Security Panel itself. By the time Starnes assumed his post as Director-General of the Security Service in 1970 his finger had been in virtually every security pie in Canada.

Experience aside, the characteristic that most suited Starnes for the position was his ability to amalgamate the divergent qualities of toughness, conciliation, and sensitivity in proper proportions. On the one hand he was so tough that, as one close friend put it, he would turn in his wife. Yet he was fair and sympathetic. Starnes impressed many with his broadmindedness when he had titular responsibility for the Communications Branch, which intercepted electronic signals. Starnes, at the expense of his own department, External Affairs, refused to play the partisan role in the customary interdepartmental bickering over who got priority. Although External had nominal control, Starnes considered his responsibility was to act in the best interest of Canada and backed off External's dominance while trying to mediate among the warring factions within the Department of National Defence.

Starnes had great ambitions for the Security Service. No matter how busy he was, members could see him simply by dropping over to his office after 7 P.M. when he was working alone. Despite all the hope, plans, and dynamism created by his appointment, Starnes fulfilled neither his own ambitions nor the expectations others had. When he arrived Starnes discovered he had no allies in senior positions. His upper-class background was antithetical to a police background and, soon after his arrival, he became resented and somewhat feared. The officers he worked with were the very ones who had prospered from the paramilitary structure and wanted to retain it the most. Any move to reduce authoritarianism undermined their authority, so they distrusted his aspirations. Clashes were almost immediate with his superior, Commissioner Len Higgitt, who once headed the security organization and liked it just the way he had left it.

Starnes suffered his first setback in the Security Service as a result of the FLQ Crisis in 1970. He spent the first six weeks of the crisis flat in bed with pneumonia while his organization floundered under the critical watch of the government. Starnes had been Director General only 10 months. The failure, as described in Chapter 19, was only partly his fault, but it was so complete that his image suffered both inside and outside the Force. In the aftermath of the FLQ failure, the mood turned ugly and the Security Service, especially the Quebec Division, committed scoundrelly acts and engaged in roguish attempts to recruit informers. The acts were strategically unsound as well as illegal and this legacy would forever haunt Starnes. He was in charge during the three years of barbarism and personally authorized some of the illegal acts. Also by giving the Quebec Division unprecedented autonomy he created the administrative circumstances for other illegal acts that he did not know about.

Starnes found the organization too big and too entrenched to change easily, especially by the efforts of one person. He could not fight 100 years of tradition. He was handcuffed in other ways as well. He had responsibility without authority. He lacked his own budget and was limited by RCMP restrictions in recruiting the type of people he wanted and in promoting the good personnel already there. He was unable to revise the pay structure. Starnes, accustomed to the genteel style at External Affairs, subtly attempted to wean the Security Service from the RCMP's rigid grasp. His RCMP colleagues were oblivious to such subtlety.

Lacking the base of support for a knock-down, drag-out fight and having no desire for one so late in his career, the ex-diplomat decided he had had enough. He had not accepted the post for power or vanity. Originally he had been offered the Commissioner's job and refused. His role was to remold the organization into a more effective and modern operation and if he could not accomplish that objective, which he became convinced he could not, he had no reason to stay. He already had a good pension and yearned for a civilized and relaxed life at his cottage in the Gatineau Hills. So before the summer of 1973 arrived, Starnes quit, telling the Solicitor General only that he wanted to read, write, and tend his garden.[2]

Ironically, after Starnes's departure, the Force gave the Security Service the increased autonomy Starnes had sought. It received its own budget, its own personnel department, and a clearer administrative separation from the rest of the Force. However, the measures were superficial and there was no movement toward civilianization. Trudeau's dictum for a Security Service "increasingly separate in structure and civilian in nature" had been checkmated.

Starnes nevertheless left the Security Service a different and improved organization. A measure of creativity was injected into a stolid body. He instilled into members the concept that they were professionals and not merely foot soldiers carrying out others' orders. He also, to some degree, broadened their horizons.

"He took us out of our provincial milieu and introduced us to the international scene," says one former Security Service NCO. "We had many visitors to headquarters from friendly foreign agencies but very seldom did any one of us go to these other countries to exchange information. He changed that."

Starnes also worked to improve the quality of reports sent to government departments, for years a source of conflict, particularly with External Affairs and the Privy Council Office. Reports became more concise and contained better information.

Few people understood why Lieutenant-General Michael Dare succeeded Starnes, for he epitomized the worst of two worlds. As a career military man he represented precisely the military tradition

---

[2] One of the few quirks in Starnes' personality emerged after his retirement when he started writing ascerbic letters to the editor of local Ottawa newspapers.

the government was committed to eradicating. And as an outsider he lacked the experience to run the Security Service effectively. Unlike Starnes, he had no background in security except what he had picked up in his normal duties as a general staff officer in the army.

With Dare as Director-General the Security Service reverted to the old style of running on a day-to-day basis. Senior officers in the organization lacked respect for their new boss, who in turn displayed a lack of interest in the job. Behind his back he was called Martini Mike and stories echoed throughout the service about how he fell asleep at his desk in the afternoon.

Dare looked like the soldier he was. Not a handsome man, he had a big brandy nose, harsh facial features, and wore shabby clothes. A staunch Roman Catholic with a military outlook on life, he was unimaginative and wooden. He had commanded an armored regiment in northwest Europe at the end of World War Two, remained in the regular army, and risen through the army promotion system. He was a hard man even by army standards. As vice-chief of the defense staff he represented the Military in the East Block situation room during the 1970 October Crisis and impressed cabinet ministers with his decisiveness and effectiveness while the RCMP fumbled about. At one meeting Defence Minister Donald Macdonald asked how fast troops could be moved to a given location.

"Let me make one phone call," replied Dare.

About five minutes later he produced a list of units and the times needed to put them on the ground. It was an impressive performance.

After his success in the FLQ Crisis he was moved into the Privy Council Office and worked on emergency planning—preparing for natural disasters such as earthquakes and dam bursts. He had just finished that task when John Starnes resigned unexpectedly.

As Director-General of the Security Service, Dare adopted a policy of refusing to talk to the press and stuck to it without exception, even in 1977-78 when his organization came under public fire and needed somebody to defend its interests.[3] His rigidity in handling

---

[3.] Dare's policy was sorely tested when Ian Urquhart of *Maclean's* Magazine called his office to ask about a list of alleged subversives the Security Service had compiled known as the Extra Parliamentary Opposition.

"Mr. Dare doesn't talk to reporters," replied his secretary.

personnel had a detrimental effect on the Security Service and one of his most tragic intrusions involved the firings in 1973 of two of the organization's best investigators, Staff Sergeant Don McCleery and Sergeant Gilles Brunet.

"That's interesting," replied Urquhart. "Maybe you'd like to tell General Dare why I'm calling. I'm calling because I understand that Mr. [Michael] Pitfield's office checked with General Dare a few months ago about the existence of this Extra Parliamentary Opposition list and was told that no such thing existed. I wonder why General Dare would tell the office of the most senior civil servant in Canada such a thing when in fact it did exist."

The secretary put Urquhart on hold and came back a minute later.

"Mr. Dare had no comment but would like to know who told you such a story."

"Michael Pitfield told me that."

Urquhart was again put on hold while the secretary consulted with Dare. This time there was a long wait before she returned.

"Mr. Dare still has no comment," she said.

Getting Their Men

MITCHELL BRONFMAN COULD have clipped coupons all his life and lived very comfortably. He was born a Bronfman and that fortunate piece of happenstance gave him wealth, security, and prestige. Life's only requirement was cashing the monthly check from his inherited trust fund. But such predestiny did not suit him. He possessed the same restless spirit of Sam, Allan, Abe, and Harry, the four entrepreneuring brothers who two generations earlier had built the Bronfman family into a financial dynasty. "I don't feel I was entitled to be given anything," he says, "it's something you have to earn." Collecting a measured financial dropping each month was like collecting welfare. Besides it was just plain dull. Life had more to offer than comfort and security.

Bronfman never worked for Seagram's except as a 10-year-old errand runner for Sam, the chairman. For a short time in his early adult years he was groomed for the dairy chain owned by Uncle Gerald. He started as assistant general manager of a milk plant and liked the job but left because he found it difficult to be a Bronfman and be treated like everybody else.

Bronfman was intrigued by how things worked; he possessed an insatiable curiosity to experiment and learn. While visiting western Canada as a young man in the 1950s, he received a ride in a small private airplane and thereafter became fascinated with the concept of defying gravity and soon acquired his pilot's license. Then the

204

mysteries of air-to-ground communication caught his interest and he immersed himself in the study of radio communication until he was a layman's expert. Once he went shopping for a German Shepherd his sister wanted to buy as a gift and became so involved he wound up a dog breeder and an executive member of a foundation breeding guide dogs for the blind.

Young Bronfman ignored the practical advice from both family and business associates and entered the aviation business in the late 1950s in London, Ontario, where he had worked briefly for the family dairy. His first attempt to establish a flying school, charter service, and airplane distributorship was unsuccessful and in the early 1960s he returned to Montreal where, along with a partner, he purchased a one-airplane company for the price of the airplane, with the goal of establishing a charter service and maintenance base for corporate aircraft. Bronfman's plans were too big and the partner dropped out. Bronfman wanted big airplanes in the hope of attracting major corporations. For companies with corporate jets, his company, Execaire, offered to store and maintain the craft and even provide the pilot. For other companies, Execaire provided executive charter service, a concept that had never been tried before in Canada. The first year, Execaire grossed $16,000, which did not even cover salaries for the three employees. Revenue the next year tripled to $45,000, tripled again the following year to $150,000, then nearly tripled again to more than $400,000.

Execaire grew so rapidly that the financial demands for servicing the continual round of corporate expansions became formidable. With each heavier piece of equipment Execaire needed a new license, more employees, and a costly upgrading program. The capital requirements outpaced even Bronfman's resources, which, ironically, were limited when raising money for Execaire was involved. Banks and other financial institutions refused to provide loans because aviation was considered a high-risk venture in the first place. Execaire was an even greater commercial risk because it was pioneering a market that had yet to prove itself. The financial institutions financed only the purchase of aircraft since they were secured assets. When it came to running the business, Execaire received nothing.

For a man like Bronfman a seemingly obvious source of money was his family. But as it turned out, it was no source at all. First,

Bronfman was proud and unwilling to make the request. But even if he had asked for money it is unlikely he would have received any. The Bronfman clan have a rule that family ties and business decisions do not mix. Every business venture must have financial integrity regardless of who is behind it. And Mitchell Bronfman was not convinced that the family saw the possibilities for Execaire.

One other source of money remained — one that put to the test the value Bronfman placed on his wealth and security. The source was his trust fund. If Bronfman really believed in Execaire, he would tap the fund for capital and gamble secure money on a company that might not succeed. That is precisely what he tried to do.

Bronfman was only eight when his father died without leaving a will. The estate was distributed according to the prevailing law, with one-third going to his mother and two-thirds divided among the children. Since he had two sisters, Bronfman received two-ninths of the estate, which was placed into a trust fund and administered by his uncle, Gerald Bronfman. Years later the trust was reconstituted and jurisdiction was shifted from the Bronfman side of the family to his mother's side. Under the new provisions a 75 per cent vote was needed to withdraw capital, and when Bronfman sought to withdraw principal for Execaire he was vetoed by his mother's one-third share.

"We would deal with my uncle — my mother's brother," says Bronfman. "He never believed the aviation business was any good and always wanted to keep his fingers on everything. He would never release the monies. Or he would make a commitment to release the monies and then it wouldn't happen. So based on that commitment you would go out and do something or commit yourself to an expenditure, and then the money wasn't there. It would take six, eight, or 12 months to get what you're supposed to get at a given time. In the meantime I was getting my income out of it but I wasn't able to get the capital. And the shares that I had in the fund, while they were worth a lot of money, were not good as collateral. Because it was a private company with this voting trust, no bank would touch that as collateral because everybody else needed to agree."

It was shortly after his plunge into full-time aviation that Bronfman first met Willie Obront. Obront would later be identified as the Montreal Mafia's "money mover" — the person who hides the identity of Mafia money and then puts it to work accumulating more.

Back in 1960, when Bronfman met him, Obront evidently was a successful front man for the Mafia since nobody, including the police, viewed him as an underworld figure. He was simply "Obie," the successful proprietor of a meat packing plant and a friend of politicians, judges, and even one Mountie who would later become the RCMP Commissioner, Maurice Nadon.

Both Bronfman and Obront had a habit of frequenting nightclubs and became good friends. The police themselves did not become convinced of Obront's involvement in the underworld until 1969 and thereafter Bronfman, too, became leery. When Bronfman asked Obront about his friendship with Vic Cotroni, Obront explained that he was in the meat business and Cotroni was in the restaurant business and that they did business together. Bronfman once threatened to cut off the relationship if Obront was involved in drugs. Obront swore up and down he had nothing to do with drugs, which was probably true. Eventually when it became obvious that Obront had underworld connections Bronfman terminated the friendship although they continued doing business.

One day in 1962 Bronfman was complaining how nobody would help finance Execaire when Obront volunteered that he "could probably help out." And he did—with no questions asked. The loans started as nickel-and-dime advances designed to tide Bronfman over until the next trust fund payment. There were many loans and most lasted about 90 days. The money was available without lengthy negotiations or months of form-filling. Obront provided the cash; Bronfman simply turned over a series of weekly checks covering interest payments plus one large check equaling the principal which Obront promised to put aside until the loan was due. Interest rates as such were never discussed. The policy was "5 for 6," which meant the borrower would return $6 for every $5 borrowed. When tabulated, the rate often exceeded 100 per cent. Bronfman knew it "wasn't bank financing"—as he puts it—but he needed the money so badly he did not care about terms. "This may be very naïve on my part," says Bronfman, "but I used to think he was doing me a favor by arranging financing. I didn't know who or where the money was coming from. It has since come to my attention the money was coming from him. I was under the opinion he was into the money lenders himself because of his gambling habits. He was a compulsive gambler."

The loans got bigger, longer, and more numerous as Execaire grew. At the same time Bronfman stepped up his fight to withdraw his capital from the trust fund but was blocked. It would be a decade before the trust fund was broken and he got access to his own money, and by that time the future of Execaire was secure. His victory with the trust was Pyrrhic since much of the money was passed on to Obront in interest. More than $1 million was paid out in interest alone and while Bronfman had built a successful company he had also sacrificed much of his inheritance. "If I had had all my money from day one," he says, "I would still have some of that money in the bank and have a very successful business today. As it is, I have a successful business but I haven't got that money in the bank."

Robin's Delicatessen on St. Catherine's Street West in downtown Montreal was a half-block from RCMP headquarters, and for many Mounties the only good steakhouse within walking distance of the office. The restaurant, located next to the Montreal Forum, at one time had been enormously successful; its seating capacity turned over three times every time the Canadiens played at home. Bronfman purchased shares in the restaurant so that his brother-in-law would have a job managing it, but Robin's began to slide. The restaurant was in danger of collapse when Bronfman reluctantly assumed the debts for one dollar and became sole owner. From his table at the back Bronfman spent many evenings in the early 1970s watching the Mounties come and go.

Policemen had always intrigued Bronfman. His first encounter with the police came at age four when members of the Westmount force frequently visited his parents' home and played with him. When his father died a few years later, Westmount policemen stopped by every day to take him and his two sisters to the park. He often visited the police station; in fact some people say he hung out there the way youths hang out at a pool hall. His desire was to become a Mountie. Later as an adult he acquired and trained police dogs for the Westmount force before it merged with the Montreal force.

The connection with Robin's allowed Bronfman to reunite this old police bond and he became an RCMP informer and even passed on information learned from Willie Obront. When Obront learned that the RCMP rented a secret apartment in Montreal's Alexis Nihon Plaza it was Bronfman who informed the Force that its existence had been compromised. The apartment was a safehouse used by E Special as a top-secret base for conducting illegal break-and-enter operations to avoid connections with the RCMP.

In the early 1970s Bronfman established a private security agency called Securex which obtained two large contracts at Dorval International Airport, one screening airline passengers and the other guarding foreign detainees for the Immigration Department. Through Securex, Bronfman personally turned over information to the RCMP squad at Dorval, including information on organized crime. At Dorval Bronfman offered information so frequently that one Mountie characterized him as a pain in the neck. On at least one occasion Bronfman exceeded the role of an informer and became a participant. The RCMP needed a hiding place for the car of an agent going undercover and Bronfman provided his garage.

Through his role as informer, Bronfman had links with the Security Service and CIB's drug squad, but he had no connection with a small and semi-autonomous section within CIB called the National Crime Intelligence Unit (NCIU), which dealt exclusively with organized crime. At the time Bronfman was supplying information to the Force, the NCIU was collecting information on Willie Obront for the Quebec Crime Probe. For somebody with his access, Bronfman would have made a good informer for NCIU, especially since informers on the Mafia are hard to get, but NCIU never took advantage of the opportunity. When on April 26, 1969, the police raided Pal's Café, a noted Mafia hangout, and uncovered a cache of checks linking Obront to the underworld, they launched a major investigation into Obront and made 21 additional seizures at Pal's. The police were convinced they had stumbled onto a whole new arm of the Mafia, and thought Obront was the first link in the chain connecting the underworld with the world of respectable business. When the raid produced evidence of financial transactions between Obront and Bronfman, they concluded that Bronfman was either a dupe or willing accomplice in Obront's money-laundering operation. For a time they even believed Bronfman was financing the underworld.

"Don, Don, come in and see this," said Chief Superintendent

Laurent Forest. "You won't believe this." Forest at the time—June, 1972—was the RCMP's top Security Service officer in the province of Quebec. Don was Staff Sergeant Don McCleery, who followed Forest into his office and peered over his shoulder as the officer pulled open the middle drawer of his desk. After a few minutes the two men were chuckling. The highly confidential report remained in the drawer but McCleery was able to read it. It was an NCIU document citing Robin's Delicatessen was a Mafia command post with a secret meeting room upstairs for underworld figures. Downstairs was a clandestine but elegant nightclub, which Frank Sinatra once visited. The report portrayed Bronfman as an integral member of the underworld. As well, he owned a fleet of fast cars for the Mafia and his airplanes were used for quick movement from the country. By the time they finished reading the document, both Forest and McCleery were roaring with laughter. McCleery could not believe the Mafia would be so stupid as to have a meeting place almost across the street from the RCMP's Quebec headquarters and above a restaurant frequented by Mounties. He had already visited the lavish "nightclub" downstairs and it was a small basement room with cement walls and a set of dust-covered drums.

McCleery's close friend, Sergeant Gilles Brunet, had introduced McCleery to Bronfman. Brunet's wife had worked as a waitress at the restaurant before Bronfman owned it and as Brunet whiled away the hours waiting for his wife to get off work, he drifted into a friendship with Bronfman. Brunet brought along McCleery who, just separated, was also at loose ends in the evening. Both Mounties were highly prized members of the Security Service and had no connection with the CIB side of the RCMP. Nevertheless, they had checked out Bronfman's record with CIB—as they did with all new acquaintances—and were told he was clean.

However, the two NCOs' friendship with Bronfman began to worry the Force when it learned that he would testify before the Quebec Crime Probe about his relationship with Obront. There was never any question about the integrity of McCleery and Brunet since they did not know Obront and had no connection with him. Nor was there ever any thought that the two would be corrupted; they were bright and highly trusted veterans who were privy to some of the country's top security secrets. As intelligence agents and not criminal investigators, McCleery and Brunet would have been of no value to Obront even if they had known him. What worried the Force was that their friendship with Bronfman would emerge at the Crime Probe and the friend-of-a-friend relationship would tarnish the RCMP image. So McCleery and Brunet were advised by Forest to cool the friendship and in the case of McCleery, who was like a son to Forest, he was urged to do so—at least until the heat was of. But they were never given an order and since they had confronted Bronfman with the rumors and were satisfied with his explanation, they continued their friendship with him. McCleery warned Bronfman that he would personally turn him in if there ever proved to be any substance to the allegations.

Bronfman was not the only Mountie friend who became *persona non grata* immediately prior to the Crime Probe. So did Sam Maislin, a Montreal businessman and an honorary member of the officers' mess and a special guest at RCMP banquets. He routinely provided Mounties with tickets to Montreal Canadiens hockey games and wrestling matches. Maislin had a large fleet of trucks and his vehicles and equipment were used in undercover operations. When Mounties did clandestine work, they often posed as workmen and drove trucks emblazoned with Maislin signs. The cover was perfect because Maislin owned an authentic and well-known trucking company. The only benefit he seemed to receive from the RCMP was free parking in the Force's garage, which was valuable for hockey games since the Montreal Forum was almost next door. He had known the notorious Vic Cotroni for years and it apparently never bothered the Force until the Crime Probe started its investigation. Overnight Maislin turned from friend to enemy; his membership in the officers' mess was revoked and Mounties were forbidden to use his trucks.

One night in January, 1973, Bronfman was introduced to two United States Air Force officers while they and eight Mounties were dining in his restaurant. After a while Bronfman realized they were intelligence agents. "It became obvious to me they were in the same line of business as Don and Gilles because they didn't know them that well," says Bronfman. "They weren't some lost friends who had come to town. It clearly was a business relationship but there certainly wasn't any business discussed in any way when I was around."

Bronfman and the two Americans quickly became friends and exchanged telephone numbers and planned future get-togethers. Three months later when the Americans returned to Montreal for a weekend they looked up Bronfman despite a warning from an RCMP officer to stay clear of him. The ranking American, a senior officer himself, told the Mountie that his allegation was a simple matter of guilt by association.

"Look, I think there's something you ought to know," Bronfman told the two Americans at their next meeting. "It's not really my place to tell you about it, but you might as well get it straight right now. Some of these idiots in the RCMP are under the impression that I'm some underworld character. I'm just warning you. If you don't want to see or be seen with me I'll understand and forget about it."

"To hell with that," replied the senior American. "We know all about it."

Bronfman exploded when he heard about the warning Americans had received from the RCMP. He did not mind being investigated since he never claimed to be beyond the law or have any special status. But the Force had now spread its private and unsubstantiated suspicions to outsiders and that constituted slander. He vowed to sue the RCMP. When word of Bronfman's threatened lawsuit reached the Force it sought legal advice from the Department of Justice and was told Bronfman had a good case and should be appeased. Outwardly the Force attempted to soothe his feelings. Secretly Chief Superintendent J. P. Drapeau, the top CIB officer in Quebec, ordered a full-scale investigation designed to find dirt on Bronfman. The RCMP believed the best way to defeat a slander charge in court was to prove it was right, and the Force used its investigatory tools in an attempt to do so. Drapeau, an ambitious and rising star, examined Bronfman's file and then summoned his junior officers and criticized them for so far having produced "just rumors." Drapeau found that Bronfman's file contained no hard information supporting the derogatory verbal reports that had been circulating within NCIU. He ordered Inspector J. A. N. Belanger, the officer in charge of NCIU, to wire-tap his phones and shadow him as he moved about the city.

It would be another year before Canada's Protection of Privacy Act would force the RCMP to obtain a judge's approval to wire-tap.

At this point the RCMP still had the right to eavesdrop and wire tap at will, which is exactly what it did to Bronfman. The NCIU surveillance crew did not match the professionalism of the Watcher Service; and it was not long before Bronfman realized he was being followed. He first noticed the surveillance while driving along Côte de Liesse to Dorval Airport; an unmarked car that was otherwise identifiable as a police car by its plain-Jane appearance was behind him and another one was in front. He followed the car in front of him to the discomfort of the driver who started turning into side streets in the hope of ridding himself of Bronfman. The Mountie did not know the area well and committed the unpardonable sin of turning into a dead-end street with his subject behind him. He parked his car and pretended he was going to make a business call, only to discover the building he was approaching was abandoned. The Mountie knew he had been caught. Bronfman waved and drove off.

Several months later on a Wednesday afternoon in October, 1973, Bronfman was driving a green Torino along Decarie Expressway in Montreal en route to a downtown business appointment when he again encountered two NCIU surveillance vehicles. "I saw these police cars, one before me and one behind me, talking into microphones. I said: 'Here we go again. Why not give them a run for their money?'" Bronfman took off but slowed down when the two police cars refused to keep pace. He then started playing cat amd mouse, first passing the lead car and then slowing down so both cars would pass him. Each time they exchanged positions he waved and grinned just to let them know he knew. The two cars left the expressway. But Bronfman was not finished. He followed them off the highway and cut in front of one car at the first red light. Bronfman soon forgot the incident but it had serious repercussions for McCleery and Brunet. On this occasion the NCIU was following not Bronfman but Obront who, unknown to Bronfman, was up ahead in his chauffeured blue Cadillac.

The three Mounties in the two surveillance cars at the time dismissed Bronfman's tomfoolery and never bothered to report it. But three weeks later they resurrected the incident and wrote a five-page report, concluding that Obront had ordered Bronfman to burn the surveillance. In trying to reconstruct the incident three weeks after the fact, the three Mounties made glaring errors. The times and speeds of the cars did not match. In one report they claimed Obront sped up to 85 miles an hour, while a follow-up report said the incident lasted 10 minutes and covered five miles, which would make the speed 30 miles an hour. Also, the surveillance covered a section of road that did not exist. And the report alleged that Bronfman cut them off in a way that was impossible, but the hand-drawn map accompanying the report made the roadway narrow so it appeared possible. Besides, the green Torino Bronfman was driving belonged to Securex and no private security agency would ever upset a police investigation unless it wanted to lose its license. The RCMP never complained to the Quebec licensing authorities over the alleged incident.

Mike Dare was the RCMP's new Director-General of the Security Service when he visited the Quebec headquarters in Montreal in July, 1973, and had the McCleery-Brunet matter thrust into his lap. He was given the Bronfman file along with a recommendation that McCleery and Brunet be transferred for disobeying Forest's "order" to disassociate with Bronfman. Dare decreed that transfers were too lenient. He dispatched a memo to Commissioner Len Higgitt: "...frankly, I am puzzled as to why these cases have not been pursued as a matter of normal disciplinary action," Dare wrote. What he was saying between the lines was that McCleery and Brunet should be dismissed. The reason Forest never instituted disciplinary procedures was because he had never ordered his two NCOs to break off the relationship. But Dare did not know that and neither did Commissioner Higgitt, and Forest, now fearful for his own position, failed to tell his superior officers. Higgitt readily agreed with Dare and scribbled a note in the corner of the memo saying: "I agree. I would like this followed up along the lines suggested with a complete investigation after which further action can be considered."

A full headquarters investigation was launched under the direction of Assistant Commissioner Joseph Gorman. The Gorman report evidently was favorable to McCleery and Brunet but the Force kept its findings secret and later had Acting Solicitor General Bryce Mackasey invoke the Federal Court Act to maintain the secrecy. After Gorman submitted his report Dare reluctantly backed down and accepted the original recommendation for a transfer.

Just as it seemed McCleery and Brunet would keep their jobs, the NCIU entered the affair one more time. There was rivalry between the NCIU and the Security Service because the NCIU regarded itself as an intelligence-gathering organization too, only with organized crime as the target. What irked the NCIU was that its competence had been challenged and McCleery and Brunet were slipping from their grasp. The NCIU chose to submit to headquarters in Ottawa the report on the Bronfman surveillance incident that had been shrugged off earlier by the Mounties on the scene. That document had a telling effect, for it made Bronfman appear a sinister figure aiding Obront and impeding the RCMP. The NCIU also forwarded a transcript of a wire-tapped telephone conversation in which Brunet called Commissioner Higgitt "the most vindictive, slimiest son-of-a-bitch in the world." That remark was later used to "prove" Brunet disloyal to the Force. The RCMP's legal officer concluded that "the seeds of corruption are being sown in the Force through these two members." And Dare personally came to the view that McCleery and Brunet, despite Gorman's report, were "unsuitable for duties in the Force." Meanwhile McCleery and Brunet, oblivious to the behind-the-scenes maneuvering, had no idea their careers were in danger. It never occurred to them that the Force would ever dismiss them, and for good reason. They were among the Security Service's best investigators and the Force knew it.

When dismissal proceedings were launched against Gilles Brunet, many of the Force's toughest and most hardened officers displayed tinges of guilt and emotion. It simply was not right. Brunet was a stand out and even as an NCO was seen by some as a future RCMP Commissioner. He possessed the perfect combination of brilliance, drive, wit, family background, and good luck. His statuesque frame and broad shoulders fitted the Mountie mold. He was almost born a member of the RCMP: his father, J. J. Brunet, retired Deputy Commissioner, became the first head of the Security and Intelligence Directorate when it was established in 1956.

Gilles Brunet joined the Force in 1955 and saw duty as a constable in northern Alberta. He purchased his discharge to get married in 1957 but re-enlisted later and was put on the Parliament Hill patrol in Ottawa. After that he entered the Security Service in Ottawa and distinguished himself on the Russian Desk by developing cases that at first looked insignificant but became important. As a junior Mountie, he found that his cases were often the subject of regular briefings before the federal cabinet. He conducted the investigation in 1966 that led to the conviction of Bower Edward Featherstone for passing secrets to the Soviets (already described in Chapter 3). Featherstone was the first spy to be convicted nearly two decades after the Gouzenko trials, and represented one of the major espionage discoveries in RCMP history. Brunet was only a constable at the time when a sergeant normally handled such a case. (He was promoted to corporal at the end of the investigation).

The Security Service in 1967 enrolled Brunet in a Russian-language course, in which he scored in the top percent. And in 1972 he received word that he was to be posted to Beirut as RCMP liaison officer. The posting was canceled when he was to be commissioned within the year. The RCMP's 1972 internal assessment report said:

> Sgt. Brunet is well above average and clearly shows that he is capable of assuming heavier responsibilities. He is a very aggressive and resourceful investigator and has developed to a remarkable degree the ability to recognize the significant thereby getting to the crux of a problem and permitting him to cope easily with unexpected developments. In addition to being fully bilingual, he is fluent in Russian, which is a valuable asset in his present position. This is a solid member who is making a most valuable contribution to B Section.

One year later Dare concluded that Brunet was "unsuitable for duties in the Force."

If the Security Service had a legendary character it was Don McCleery. McCleery, a Mountie since 1953, was loud, argumentative, aggressive, and unstoppable. Despite his brashness, he was well liked. He attracted attention quickly by conducting one-man surveillances when the Force maintained it could not be done. "What do you mean I can't do it?" he protested. In the evening he crouched beside an open window of a Communist Party meeting and took notes. He had already identified 300 Communists in Montreal. When the meeting broke up he followed home one of the people he did not recognize, and showed up in the office the next morning with details of the meeting plus the identity of a new target. With a little luck the target would drive another unidentified subject home and McCleery would learn two new identities. Later he received a commendation for investigating the Gerda Munsinger case.

McCleery particularly distinguished himself during the FLQ Crisis in 1970 when his work led to the location of the apartment where James Cross was being held. McCleery was not supposed to be involved in the hunt, but he felt the credibility of the Force was at stake and started a private search in off-hours that eventually broke the case. McCleery will not discuss the FLQ Crisis because "somebody will think I'm trying to blow my own horn." The RCMP never acknowledged his role. "It suits me okay," says McCleery. "I don't give a shit. The guys over here know I was involved. I let the results speak. I don't give a shit about what the Force says. I'd love to go out to Regina and see what they have in their archives and see who gets the credit—the Commissioner or Deputy Commissioner, or somebody in Ottawa who knows nothing. Screw 'em."

The RCMP's internal assessment report said one year before his dismissal:

> S/Sgt. McCleery displays nervous energy and drive to a degree that can only be described as remarkable. He leads by example—his men respond to the heavy demands on them because he demands even more of himself. A man of action, he dislikes paperwork and administrative responsibilities, but he is second to none for resourcefulness and dogged determination when working alone or in charge of small picked groups.

Only months before his dismissal McCleery received the Long Sevice Medal with the inscription: "long service and good conduct."

Chief Superintendent Forest had tears in his eyes when he paraded McCleery and Brunet in his office and read out headquarters' recommendation for dismissal. They were two of his best men and, also, Forest personally knew they were innocent, but he had long passed the point where he could admit it.

McCleery and Brunet had four days to appeal but RCMP procedure prohibited them from seeing the evidence against them or facing their accusers. They hired lawyer Art Campeau but Commissioner Higgitt personally ruled that lawyers were forbidden. Their hastily written appeals were ineffective because they knew not what they were fighting against. They knew nothing about the concocted surveillance report and thus were unable to destroy its credibility. Their letters of appeal were forwarded to the same legal officer who had recommended their dismissal and who used the opportunity of their appeal to write a memo to the Commissioner picking holes in their arguments. It violated all the principles of natural justice: the prosecutor got the last word—without the defense knowing what it was. McCleery and Brunet never did get the opportunity to respond to the last-minute rebuttals, or even to learn of them. Higgitt acted as judge. He alone made the decision. As he read through Brunet's letter of appeal, he penciled uncomplimentary notes into the margin. Two weeks later a two-line telegram arrived in Montreal informing the two men that they were dismissed, effective immediately, and were to be relieved of their badges, ID cards and revolvers.

In January, 1974, a month after the dismissal, all available hands in the Security Service's Quebec headquarters in Montreal were called to the fourth floor for a special meeting. About 100 people showed up—everybody except those on holiday and out of the office on assignment. It was not a regular meeting or a chitchat session; it was called for one reason only: to ostracize McCleery and Brunet. A commissioned officer stood up and gave a speech warning everybody to avoid the pair or at least handle any dealings with them with great care. After a few questions the people were sent back to work. Any doubts RCMP management may have had were probably erased when McCleery and Brunet joined Bronfman and three other former Mounties as partners in Securex.

McCleery and Brunet appealed to Solicitor General Warren Allmand who, when first approached by Art Campeau's law partner, Brian Mulroney, expressed optimism that the pair would be taken back into the RCMP. A little later Allmand promised Campeau that he would recommend reinstatement to the Force. At that point McCleery and Brunet believed their battle was won because the Solicitor General had control over the RCMP—or so they thought. Weeks later Allmand said he was not recommending reinstatement and denied he had ever made such a commitment, even though Campeau later testified under oath that he had.

Finally McCleery and Brunet themselves met Allmand on the morning of February 9, 1976, at his constituency office in West

Montreal and throughout their hour-long meeting the Solicitor General insisted he was powerless to intervene because no provision in the law empowered him to do so.

"Who's running the Force?" asked McCleery. "You've got to draw the line somewhere between interference and ensuring proper control."

"Well, you know," replied Allmand, "I've got to watch my ass. They can screw me too."

Then Allmand explained how he had lied to his Mountie chauffeur about his whereabouts so the RCMP would not know he was meeting them. Allmand told his escort he should meet him at a hospital when in fact he was quietly meeting McCleery and Brunet. The man in charge of the Mounties was playing hide-and-seek so the Force would not know whom he was seeing. It was not very encouraging.

On August 13, 1974, Warren Allmand was out of town and Postmaster General Bryce Mackasey was Acting Solicitor General when he was handed a three-page legal-size affadavit along with five sealed envelopes and an assortment of documents. The affadavit said: "I, Bryce Stuart Mackasey, Minister of the Crown, of the City of Ottawa, in the Province of Ontario, MAKE OATH AND SAY AS FOLLOWS..." and went on to explain how Mackasey had scrutinized all the documents and came "to the conclusion that their production would be contrary to the public interest." Mackasey signed it but acknowledged later that he did so only because he had been advised to do so. He never read the documents that he had sworn he did.

What Mackasey's signature did was withhold RCMP documents from Federal Court, where McCleery and Brunet were suing the Force for wrongful dismissal. The RCMP did not want the documents relating to their dismissal to become public and, through Bryce Mackasey, invoked national security. It was the first time Section 41 of the Federal Court Act had ever been employed. Had Mackasey bothered to read the documents, he might have concluded that some of them were withdrawn to save embarrassment rather than to protect the country's secrets. One of the forbidden documents was the original NCIU report of a mystery nightclub, secret meeting room, and fast cars. The report would have been discredited in open court because it could not withstand scrutiny. Another excluded document was the Gorman report, which did not recommend dismissal of McCleery and Brunet.

The two ex-Mounties did not go to court to seek reinstatement as such. They merely wanted a hearing so that their side of the story could be heard. They believed that once all the evidence was out the RCMP would have no choice but to reinstate them. As expected, the RCMP fought their action and petitioned the court to dismiss their appeal on grounds that the Federal Court had no right to hear the case because the authority of the Commissioner of the RCMP was all-encompassing and not subject to review. The Force argued that the Commissioner could wake up one morning and decide to fire every Mountie with red hair without being challenged. The RCMP claim was rejected unanimously by the panel of three judges and it finally seemed that the Force would be held accountable. It was the first time an internal RCMP decision had ever been challenged outside the Force and accepted for a hearing. It was at that moment the RCMP called on Bryce Mackasey to put those documents out of the court's reach.

McCleery and Brunet were in a no-win situation, especially since only the documents favoring the RCMP remained before the court. Since their case was before the Appeal Division of the Federal Court (as opposed to the Trial Division), the documents had to be accepted at face value. Only if they won the Federal Court action and were given the right to a hearing could McCleery and Brunet start challenging those reports. And even if they won, the rumors, innuendoes, and just plain lies contained in the documents would blacken their names in every newspaper in the country. The process would be very difficult to reverse because it would be months before the false allegations could be refuted. They would be cleared in legal terms but never in reputation. The memory of scandal would linger like a bad odor.

The courtroom in Ottawa was packed with reporters waiting to pounce on the selected documents that the RCMP were prepared to release. The only way McCleery and Brunet could stop the headlines was to withdraw their case before it got under way. Then the documents would never be made public. As veteran Mounties, both of them had acquired a pathological fear of publicity, given the secret nature of their work. Moreover, they feared publicity would drive clients away from Securex. So as court opened on September 25, 1974, they withdrew their appeal.

The decision to do so soon hung around their necks like an albatross and they came to regret it bitterly. "Everywhere I go," says McCleery, "members ask me: 'Why did you drop the appeal? You had something going. Why did you quit?' They think we had something to hide."

"In retrospect," says Brunet, "we should have gone ahead with that appeal without hesitation. I don't know if you can imagine how much soul-searching went into that decision. I guess it was lack of experience and lack of exposure to the press, this inordinate fear of having your name in the paper. The arguments we present today are not that convincing, but at the time they were convincing to us. It was the biggest mistake we made."

Whenever a high RCMP official is asked about McCleery and Brunet he invariably asks the question: "If they had such a good case, why did they withdraw their appeal?" A grin breaks across his face and the subject is closed.

The freedom from false condemnation that they won by withdrawing their case was short-lived. No sooner had they abandoned their case than they were wrongly implicated in the bizarre July 24 bombing of the Mount Royal home of supermarket executive Melvyn Dobrin by RCMP Constable Robert Samson. Securex was the prime suspect after the RCMP passed on information to the Montreal police—who were responsible for the case—that Samson was under McCleery and Brunet's command in the Force and that McCleery and Brunet were connected with the underworld.

"Their theory was that we attempted to sell security to the Steinberg stores," says Brunet. "You're talking about a hell of a lot of stores. They had this theory of a multimillion dollar contract whereas in fact we had nothing to do with Steinberg's. They thought we were putting pressure on Steinberg's to accept us—a typical underworld tactic. They sell their services to legitimate businesses at inflated prices—or it might even be a legitimate service at a competitive price, as long as they get the business. Of course Samson had worked for us in the RCMP and we were using Samson—so they thought.

"Securex's name was used repeatedly, not only in the newspapers, but at the Fire Commissioner's Inquiry. I have a transcript of

Dobrin's testimony and you wouldn't believe how they badgered this poor son of a bitch, trying to get him to say that Securex had been putting pressure on him. This was at the time when they [the police] were floundering and were attempting to tie Securex into it. They kept asking: 'Have you been approached by Securex?' 'Never heard of them.' Then they'd go back to it later on. At that time this was their only theory."

Brunet's phone was tapped, a fact he learned later when he received the notice required under the Protection of Privacy Act, which had become law a few months earlier. The only way of killing the rumors was to uncover the truth and that meant Securex would have to conduct an investigation. Such an investigation was risky because they would have to use Willie Obront's knowledge of the underworld to discover the real culprits and that might bolster the claim that a link existed between Obront and Brunet and McCleery. Bronfman called Obront, who eagerly provided the background since he, too, was being wrongly dragged into the affair and wanted to proclaim his innocence. (The reason the police were interested in him was that Samson dated the daughter of Obront's chauffeur, Leo Robidoux.) Obront told Bronfman that Samson had become friends with a Quebec underworld figure he met in Morocco and subsequently had done free-lance work for him. When Steinberg's had had labor problems the previous winter, the underworld figure had supplied goons. The bill proved too high for Steinberg's, who refused to pay, and the underworld figure applied pressure and hired Samson, still a Mountie, to scare Dobrin into paying by placing a bomb at his house.

"We went out and did the investigation," says Brunet. "It took us a day. We convened the city police investigators and told them just what the facts were and where to get the true story. The Fire Commissioner's Inquiry ended two days later. We had to solve the case to get the police off our backs." Brunet says he later learned from a source in the Montreal police that it was the RCMP who peddled the Securex theory.

The June 3, 1975, edition of the Toronto *Globe and Mail* carried a triple-decker headline that nearly stretched across the top of the front page: "60 BRIBED WORKERS HANDLE DRUGS AT MONTREAL AIRPORT, POLICE SAY, HASHISH 'COMING IN BY THE TON.'" Sergeant

John Leduc of the RCMP Drug Squad was quoted as saying an internal report indicated the existence of a huge drug ring at Dorval: "The airport is more corrupt than the harbour ever was," he said. "...Hashish is coming here by the ton. Montreal must be a major supplier for the Canadian market."

It just so happened that Securex's two major passenger-screening contracts were at Dorval. Suspicion immediately fell on the company because of the earlier Mafia allegations against Bronfman.[1] Once the drug story was released in the newspapers, Securex's name was cited and the rest was predictable. Two days later Pat Nowlan, the Conservative Member of Parliament for Annapolis Valley, rose in the House of Commons and asked why an Immigration Department contract had been awarded to Securex when it was "against the recommendation of the RCMP." Nowlan said outside the Commons he had been tipped off by a source. Exactly one week later the Immigration Department sent Securex a letter terminating the contract. The terms of the agreement stipulated 30 days' notice for cancellation. Securex received nine days. No official reason was given for terminating their services. The following month Allmand told the Commons that only "three or four" were found to be involved in the drug ring. The statement cleared the air but it came 26 days after Securex lost the Immigration contract.

What Allmand did not mention in the Commons was the role the company played in helping the RCMP investigate the Dorval smuggling operation. Securex helped the RCMP apprehend one of the smugglers. "One of our guards was approached by some hood who wanted to import drugs through cargo," says McCleery. "He immediately reported it to us and we immediately contacted the RCMP. We said: 'Okay, they're your boys'—by this time two of our fellows are involved, both reporting to the RCMP. We did everything we could to accommodate the RCMP Drug Squad. We were paying our guards $4.50 an hour, supporting the RCMP in good faith, and everything was splendid. I never asked what the case was about because that would be unprofessional. Then this story about a big

---

[1]. Bronfman has a personal abhorrence of the illicit drug trade, even for soft drugs such as marijuana and hashish, which is why he earlier made Obront swear he had no involvement in drugs.

drug ring at Dorval hits the newspapers. Securex is mentioned and the speculation is that it's us again. We asked Allmand for a denial but he says: 'We can't comment while it's under investigation.'[2] That's tantamount to saying we're guilty.

"All we know is that we were doing an excellent job and they [Immigration] were satisfied. We learned from a contact in the department that a phone call came down from Ottawa to get rid of us and that they were supposed to tell us it was policy from time to time to change the contractors. The guy was even a little embarrassed to tell us. Change in contractor. The fellow who had the contract for supplying the food and lodging to these people was there before us and is still there."

A campaign began, advising prospective Securex customers not to do business with the no-good Mafia outfit. Even existing clients were advised to take their business elsewhere. In the fall of 1976 while I was interviewing McCleery and Brunet at the Securex office, Brunet was called to the next room by a telephone call. He returned, despondent, a few minutes later, saying it was a client who had been warned by the Quebec Provincial Police to break with Securex. The phone call had been tape-recorded and Brunet played back the tape. It was this kind of damage they had sought to avoid by withdrawing their case from Federal Court. But the damage was being inflicted in any case, and with the innuendoes from the Samson bombing and the Dorval drug case their reputations had been maligned nonetheless. Only now they had forfeited their right to a hearing. McCleery and Brunet curse the day they dropped their court case.

The curtain fell in 1977 when Securex's license was revoked over a violation of Quebec's licensing law. A number of clients had strikes and Securex, needing new employees fast, hired agents whose working-permit applications were being proceessed by the authorities, a not unusual procedure because the Quebec Detective or

---

[2.] It was Catch-22. Says Brunet: "That same morning I called Inspector Jacques Brière who was in charge of the Drug Squad and who knew our people were collaborating with his people in this drug case. He wasn't aware of the newspaper articles and said he would look into it. It was early in the morning and he said he would call back. He didn't call back, so at 4:30 I called back. He said he had checked it out and discussed it with his superiors and although Securex was not involved it was not up to the RCMP to make a denial, that it was up to the Solicitor General. By that time the Solicitor General had already refused to make a denial, claiming it was the RCMP's responsibility."

Security Agencies Act itself was contradictory regarding the procedure of issuing permits. One section of the act stated that no personnel shall work for a security agency "unless he holds an agent's permit issued by the Attorney-General." Another section of the same act said: "No person can obtain an agent's permit unless he is in the employ of an agency holding a permit." So it was impossible to hire new employees without committing a technical breach of the law. The normal procedure allowed an individual applying for a license to work while his application was being processed, which was exactly the procedure Securex followed, and for this its license was revoked. Securex could have appealed the cancellation but did not. It had had enough. The RCMP was winning so the partners surrendered and quietly disbanded the company. McCleery and Brunet found work with another security agency in Montreal.

Eight days after McCleery and Brunet were dismissed from the RCMP in December, 1973, Inspector Belanger of NCIU assigned Sergeant Joe Primeau to write a report on Securex. Primeau, a 22-year-veteran of the RCMP and the senior Mountie on the Dorval "Special Squad," an elite group of policemen from three police forces, submitted his findings six weeks later. But the 800-word document told Belanger precisely what he did not want to hear, namely that Securex was a good, honest, and reliable firm and that Bronfman was "polite, honest and extremely cooperative" and passed information to the RCMP. "On numerous occasions they have assisted us in drug cases (finding drugs in the baggage of passenger and detaining everything pending our arrival)," said the Primeau report. "Also they have often reported to us the identity of known travelling criminals, specially on members of the Cotroni organization. All members of Securex are a vast improvement over previous employees of past security agencies such as Pinkerton, Citadelle and Sentinelle."

The report said Securex was informing on the underworld. It was heresy as far as the RCMP was concerned and the report was shelved. But Brunet, through contacts in the Force, learned that a report had been written and was favorable to Securex. The RCMP was furious over the disclosure and started blaming Primeau, who was dumbfounded and told the Force so in an official statement. The

RCMP investigated the so-called leak—it was actually not a leak since Brunet never saw the report or learned any of the details—but did not contact Securex. If the Force had, it would have learned that Brunet was willing to take a lie detector test in order to absolve Primeau.

The Force picked on an unlikely individual to blame for the incident. Primeau was a hard-working, dedicated, and loyal Mountie who from 1968 to 1970 was responsible for Prime Minister Trudeau's security whenever he came to Quebec. Never in nearly 23 years had there been a leak of information Primeau was handling. He knew Trudeau's travel plans weeks in advance and later held highly sensitive information on criminal matters at Dorval. "We were working on everything," says Primeau. "There was classified information from three departments [Montreal police, Quebec police, and the RCMP] and nothing ever came out. And yet on a minor affair like this they're telling me I talked. Come on! If I had talked I would have talked about something important."

Primeau was well traveled in the RCMP. Since he was a bachelor and could be moved cheaply, he had been transferred 33 times in 22 years, an average of one move every eight months. Now he was back in his home of Montreal and thought he deserved to remain there for the final few years of his service. But shortly after the "leak" was discovered he was told he was being transferred to Quebec City where the number of men under his command would jump from two to 12. Ironically, he was to become the sergeant in charge of the General Investigation Section and have direct access to the run of RCMP files—a funny position for someone who could not be trusted with confidential information. Primeau informed the Force he would rather not have the promotion. The officer who ordered the transfer, J. P. Drapeau (who, shortly after ordering the wire-tapping and surveillance of Bronfman, was made the Assistant Commissioner in charge of Quebec and later went to Ottawa as Deputy Commissioner, one rank below Commissioner), replied that Primeau had no choice. He was being transferred whether he liked it or not.

Primeau pleaded with Drapeau to cancel the transfer. He cited compassionate as well as financial reasons. After years of bachelorhood Primeau was planning to marry a Dorval Air Canada employee who could not get transferred to Quebec City for lack of openings and she would be forfeiting a good salary and 12 years' seniority. He was also needed by his father and mother, who were too old and too sick to look after themselves. Primeau lived with them.

Drapeau was unmoved after two separate appeals and would not grant even a postponement. "May I remind you," replied Drapeau in a letter, "that the effective date of your transfer remains set for November 25th, 1974, in the event you may wish to appeal to higher authorities, since I intend to fill that post without any further delay." The only avenue left open was an appeal directly to Commissioner Maurice Nadon, who by this time had succeeded Higgitt. "I feel like a person who has been framed..." wrote Primeau. "Can't anyone else see that the whole affair is too flimsy to be real, that it is too simple, that it is so blatantly evident that it can't be true?"

Primeau was on his honeymoon when Commissioner Nadon's rejection arrived. He was suspended two days before Christmas for refusing the transfer—the 34th in his career. A few weeks later he was dismissed outright for "reprehensible conduct contrary to the rules and regulations."

Once out of the Force, Primeau described how McCleery and Brunet were blacklisted by the RCMP. At first orders went out to all members to avoid them when possible. Then it was stepped up and members were told to avoid any talks except when strictly on business. Finally they were ordered not to talk to them at all unless they approached the RCMP in order to volunteer information. While at Dorval, Primeau did everything possible to avoid McCleery and Brunet. At times it was even comical. Whenever he spotted McCleery or Brunet, he would go to the washroom or duck down another corridor—anything to prevent an encounter.

The vindictiveness of the Force was impressed upon Primeau when even he was placed on an RCMP blacklist in 1976, shortly after he was accepted as a member of the RCMP Veterans' Association. "As president, it is my pleasure to welcome you in the name of all members," wrote Roland D'Astous of the association in a letter of acceptance, September 29, 1976. A month later Primeau received a letter from the RCMP itself saying: "You are not permitted to enter our building to attend meetings of the [Veterans'] Association." Since all meetings are held at RCMP headquarters, Primeau was effectively barred from participating.

"I still have some good friends in the RCMP but I try to keep away from them," says Primeau. "I'm not aware of being on a blacklist the way McCleery and Brunet are, but I'm definitely trying to stay away from my friends because I don't want to cause them undue hardship."

17

The May Mutiny

ON MAY 1, 1974, about 300 Mounties from both the Security Service and CIB crowded into a small hall in Burnaby on the outskirts of Vancouver, B.C. They came ostensibly to learn about their rights and improve their working conditions. The real purpose was to gather support for an "association." No Mountie dared breathe the word "union," but they really wanted to know whether individuals were militant enough to contemplate collective action. Through their history the Mounties had quashed union activity, but this Wednesday night there was no doubt the strike-busters themselves were frustrated over low pay, poor working conditions, and the absence of basic human rights, and were laying out their labor grievances.

The next night more than 600 Toronto-area Mounties—nearly two-thirds the division—gathered at the Metro Toronto Police Association building on Yorkland Boulevard and unabashedly aired their complaints for more than two hours. Reporters standing outside the closed room heard cheering and applauding as speakers like Syd Brown, then President of the Metro Toronto Police Association, urged them to follow the city police and form a union. A vote was taken and 605 out of the 620 voters chose to pursue further the prospect of forming an association.

The vote itself violated the law. In 1918 the Borden government, fearful of the labor unrest that led to the Winnipeg General Strike, which saw the entire city police force dismissed for sympathizing with the strikers, passed an order-in-council prohibiting any form of collective action on the part of the Mounties.

"No member...shall become a member of or in any wise associated with any trade union organization, or any society or association connected or affiliated therewith...and any contravention of this regulation shall be cause for instant dismissal."

As late as 1960 the Department of Justice had assured RCMP management that the order-in-council was still valid.

Eight days after the Toronto meeting, about 2,500 Mounties poured into the Ottawa Civic Centre to further air their complaints. Mounties from Montreal and Toronto arrived in busloads and carloads. It was the biggest RCMP meeting in history. When the speeches from the podium ended, individual Mounties on the floor stood up in front of their commanding officers and made impassioned speeches. Each speaker condemned the 1918 order-in-council. A vote urging its repeal carried 1,102 to 34.

Not quite two weeks later, about 500 Mounties gathered at the Montreal Police Brotherhood Hall and conducted a similar overwhelming vote. This time a concerned Solicitor General Warren Allmand, who had been misled by the RCMP about the level of discontent and who only three weeks earlier had claimed that RCMP morale was "quite high," showed up for a first-hand glimpse at RCMP *esprit de corps*. He left promising to push for lifting the oppressive order-in-council and securing a decent pay raise.

The May, 1974, rebellion was spontaneous and unorchestrated. Since associations were forbidden, no leaders existed to manipulate or inflame events. The events of that month were a liberating exercise for Mounties. After 101 years they finally told their bosses they were joining the modern world and were no longer tolerating inferior pay and long hours with no overtime. They also wanted to loosen the shackles of the paramilitary system. The world had mellowed while the RCMP remained frozen by tradition. Even the military structure of the Armed Forces had become more humane and flexible than the system of the RCMP.

The senior officers, used to a system where orders were given and obeyed, were horrified at the spectacle and, being unschooled in the practice of labor conciliation, did not know how to react. It was one of the few times that the rank and file from the Security Service and the Criminal Investigation Branch joined hands. The impetus had started in the Security Service under former Director-General John Starnes, who trained his men to challenge accepted practices. The Force's top managers had faced all kinds of challenges from criminals, spies, and even the government but never from their own members, whom they had always taken for granted. For several days the upper echelon froze as the top officers — particularly Commissioner Maurice Nadon and his powerful deputy, Pete Bazowski — struggled to maintain the upper hand.

Ironically, the RCMP was a slave to its image. Because of the popular legend, nobody viewed Mounties as workers, including Mounties themselves. They saw themselves somewhat like priests with a mission to carry out, a kind of secular Jesuit order. In the old days leisure, family, wealth, and privacy had been sacrificed for the good of the Force. But by the mid-1960s self-denial began to wear thin. Other groups in Canada were becoming wealthy, particularly other police forces that had formed unions and subsequently surged ahead of the RCMP in pay. By 1974 Canada's finest was only the tenth finest in salary. City police forces in Montreal, Toronto, and Vancouver had unions and received a higher base pay than the RCMP. On top of that they got overtime, which the RCMP did not.[1]

Envy was especially high in Montreal, where Mounties worked side by side with the city police — the highest paid in Canada — and did more work for less money. The jealousy started at Expo 67 when the city police and RCMP worked on teams. The Montreal police refused to start work until 3 PM because in a few hours they would be going on overtime. The Mounties got no overtime and the delay only meant getting home late. The unsubtle Montreal police would flash their paychecks and brag about the "bacon" — overtime — they had made that month. During the FLQ Crisis in 1970 one Mountie worked 16 hours a day for two months without a penny in overtime or a day off in lieu, while a non-Mountie under his command bought himself a new convertible with his overtime bonanza.

[1.] In lieu of overtime, the Force in 1972 granted everybody a $900 annual supplement and later reduced it to $600.

The first public indication of low morale erupted in July, 1972, when Jack Ramsay, a corporal who quit the Force after 14 years, shattered nearly a century of silence with a 15,000-word denunciation in *Maclean's* Magazine that exposed the frustrations of the enlisted man.

"...the RCMP is much more concerned with polishing its image than with pursuing its ideal," Ramsay wrote. "As a result, morale has fallen so low that alcoholism and suicide have become serious problems. And many of the Force's officers only make things worse. Some of them are so inept they can maintain discipline only by fear; they mistreat and pressure the lower ranks who, in turn, often persecute the public. Especially during my last seven years on the Force, I watched fellow members lying, falsifying records and ignoring suspects' rights until I came to dislike putting on the famous scarlet tunic, because it made me feel like a hypocrite."

The Ramsay article is a milestone. It was the first time in history a Mountie or former Mountie publicly condemned the Force. While Ramsay was a renegade to most members, he was a hero to others.

Ramsay touched a nerve and he soon undertook the first significant attempt to unionize the RCMP. He joined with the Public Service Alliance of Canada to push for repeal of the 1918 order-in-council. But at that point Mounties were not ready for a union. Furthermore, RCMP members expressed little enthusiasm for the PSAC, which was regarded as the public servants' union. Mounties regarded themselves as being above ordinary government employees and wanted nothing to do with the organization.

Although the drive by the PSAC failed, union sentiment was gaining ground and word even reached the Ottawa office of Solicitor General Warren Allmand. Individual Mounties phoned Allmand's office with descriptions of senior management's inflexible and insensitive positions and the effect it was having on the men. Journalists picked up rumblings and asked Allmand about it. Even the minister's bureaucrats sensed it and passed on reports. Allmand met with the senior management of the Force each Friday morning and used these occasions to inquire about these reports. He was assured there was nothing to it.

"It's just a few rabble-rousers—a few dissidents," he was told.

They implied these few individuals really were not Mounties. The

RCMP treated these incidents the way the Kremlin reacts to Soviet dissidents: "Every organization has a few anti-social and disloyal members." If caught, they were dealt with arbitrarily and severely.

The strategist behind the RCMP's hard-line stand was Pete Bazowski, the powerful and brilliant yet autocratic Deputy Commissioner. Bazowski essentially ran the Force during the final year of Commissioner Len Higgitt's term when Higgitt was busy touring the country celebrating the RCMP's hundredth anniversary. Higgitt retired at the end of 1973 and Bazowski was the heir-apparent as far as the RCMP was concerned, and the Force ensured that Solicitor General Allmand was aware of that fact. On four occasions Allmand came within an inch of appointing Bazowski Commissioner. Each time he was headed off by his advisors, who were proposing the appointment of unconventional candidates including Superintendent Donald Cobb, who was temporarily seconded to the Deputy Solicitor General's office and who later pleaded guilty to authorizing entry into the offices of the Agence de Presse Libre du Québec without a search warrant and was given a suspended sentence. In the end Allmand and his advisers compromised and agreed on Maurice Nadon, a friendly and likable policeman whose distinction was becoming the first French Canadian Commissioner. Under Nadon things remained much the same. Bazowski was still the power behind the throne.

Bazowski was a paradox. RCMP officers as intellectually capable as he usually questioned the Force's paramilitary system and in the process muddied their careers. The officers who advanced most rapidly were the less cerebrally gifted who paid unswerving loyalty to the system. Bazowski was a strong disciplinarian and espoused the 19th-century values of the Force. And yet intellectually he was outstanding. Those who questioned the system could not match him. He looked boyish—20 years younger than he was—and strangers mistook him for a corporal or a junior officer. He dressed smartly and exhibited the outward signs of progressiveness.

Bazowski in 1972 sensed trouble with the Ramsay affair and realized it had to be defused but was too conservative to correct the underlying causes. His response was to establish in effect a company union and pacify the unrest without disturbing the traditional relationship. He instituted a Division Representative Program in which a representative from each of the 16 divisions came to Ottawa once a year to meet with RCMP management concerning staff matters.

Representatives from some of the divisions were duly elected, others were elected from a list approved by the commanding officer, and still others were selected outright by the commanding officer. The division representatives' first complaint at the initial meeting in October, 1972, concerned the unfair and uneven manner in which they were selected. When they returned to their divisions they were forbidden to disclose the subjects discussed at the meeting except to say they had presented their demands. Agitation soon grew for a transcriptlike account of the meeting so that Mounties back in the divisions could learn which questions were raised and what answers were given. The issue itself became a minor *cause célèbre* and the Force finally agreed to publish an official account.

A year later, in October, 1973, when the division representatives were meeting for the second time, the answers had still not been published.

"How are we going to have a meeting in 1973 when you haven't answered anything we asked in 1972?" Mounties asked.

The debate typified the status of the division representatives. They had not yet tackled a substantive issue. They could not get a transcript. The long-awaited document, about 120 pages thick, was finally issued in early 1974. If its failure to be published in 1973 produced dissatisfaction, its long-delayed appearance in 1974 prompted even greater dismay. The book was a piece of dogma produced at a time when members were harboring doubts and looking to their superiors for a few compromises. Instead, they received a book full of unyielding clichés. The most reasonable questions received stock answers. Even the moderates were insulted.

Each division representative received one book and was told to maintain possession of it at all times, which meant that few members could see it since some divisions had up to 2,000 members. A number of representatives refused to accept delivery of the book because its contents were so demeaning and the restrictions on its distribution so confining. The book engendered negative reaction and seemed to be fostering increased militancy, so it was soon withdrawn.

Little had changed since 1894 when substantive provisions were incorporated into the Mounted Police Act. The system was established by Commissioner L. W. Herchmer whose fanaticism for discipline was so great that some considered him mentally deranged.[2] He was later dismissed by Prime Minister Wilfrid Laurier; however, his legacy of discipline remained.

By 1974 a full-time staff in Ottawa was required to deal with infractions of the thousands of regulations that had been added to the Herchmer Code. The Commissioner could still unilaterally decide to imprison a Mountie for up to a year without giving the Mountie any access to the civil courts.[3] When charged in service court, the Mountie lacked the right to face his accuser, to hear the charges against him, or to be represented by legal counsel even though he had to prove himself innocent. Meanwhile the RCMP had a lawyer to press the case against him. Mounties could be ordered to give statements even though it violated their fundamental right to remain silent. If they refused, they were punished for disobeying orders.

"Many aspects of the Force have changed over the course of its history, but the disciplinary system established during the first twenty years has for the most part remained unchallenged and unchanged," concluded a 1976 Royal Commission into the RCMP's discipline and grievance procedures.[4]

The May 1, 1974, meeting in Burnaby finally forced the RCMP to admit to Allmand that at least some unrest existed within the Force.

"Most of them were there just out of curiosity," they told Allmand the next day. "They don't support this kind of nonsense."

That evening two-thirds of the Toronto members showed up for a mass meeting amid some bitter denunciations of Bazowski. Commissioner Nadon and his three deputies met Allmand the next

[2.] Herchmer dismissed his men for petty reasons even when he was short of manpower. His 1897 annual report says: "It has been found necessary to dismiss 18 men during the year, nearly all for drunkenness. With the few men now at my disposal it is more than ever necessary that all shall be reliable and steady, and while many of those dismissed were smart looking intelligent men, and good soldiers, as constabulary they were useless."

[3.] This provision has never been used but still stands.

[4.] The events of May, 1974, prompted the government on June 6, 1974, to appoint a five-member Royal Commission chaired by Ottawa Judge René Marin to look into the "public complaints, internal discipline and grievance procedure within the Royal Canadian Mounted Police." The commission issued a perceptive 208-page report in 1976 calling for the restructuring of the disciplinary and grievance system.

morning in his West Block office. The four Mounties were visibly shaken and irritated. Bazowski accused Allmand of interfering in internal RCMP affairs because two of his personal aides attended the meeting. When Allmand objected, Bazowski said he had a transcript of the meeting. He never produced a transcript but it appeared that the Force had monitored the meeting since he had not secured a transcript from the organizers.

In the midst of these mass meetings the hapless division representatives met in Ottawa for the third time. But this time the atmosphere had changed. No longer was the foremost claim a demand for the previous year's transcript. The uprising had given the division representatives bargaining power. This time the Force was on the defensive and after three days of meetings scheduled another meeting two weeks later.

The division representatives reassembled in Ottawa at the end of May and at the end of the meeting were advised that they would be receiving the largest general pay increase in RCMP history. Even more significantly, the Force abandoned its entrenched opposition to overtime pay. In addition, the division representatives were given increased power and could act as advocates for individual Mounties with grievances. They were to be put on promotion and pay review boards.

The open agitation for collective action lasted exactly one month, having started in Burnaby on May 1 and ending with the new package on May 31. The union idea was dead, killed by the sudden generosity of the RCMP and the government.

The May Mutiny had a chilling effect on the government itself because the mass meetings coincided with the start of the 1974 federal election campaign. The government was slightly nervous over the prospect of a national police strike in which the public would inevitably take the side of the Mounties. The government had already incurred the wrath of the public with its plan to change the insignia of the RCMP. During the minority Parliament of 1972-74, the NDP secured financial demands from the Liberal administration. The government had grown used to opening the public purse to maintain parliamentary stability and opened it one last time to maintain peace with the RCMP.

The next three years passed with good pay raises and soon Mount-ies were, if anything, being overpaid. For the first time the RCMP mounted a recruiting drive stressing the good pay of a career in the Force. With this new-found affluence individual Mounties forgot many of their nonmonetary grievances, such as their lack of rights before the RCMP service court, since for most Mounties those issues were theoretical while the money was real.

The 1918 order-in-council was quietly rescinded shortly after May, 1974. The following year a handful of Mounties in Ottawa actually formed an association. But they sold only a few dozen memberships, their activities more closely resembling an under-ground movement. The organization suspended all activity in 1977 when the RCMP fell under criticism for having engaged in illegal activity. The association did not want to challenge the Force when it was under public attack.

18

Operation Ham

ON THE EVENING of January 8, 1973, four members of the RCMP waited impatiently at headquarters in Montreal. Three of them belonged to E Special, the ultra-secret subsection of the Security Service that many members of the Security Service did not know existed. The fourth person was a civilian computer expert from headquarters in Ottawa. Each Mountie stripped himself of identifying possessions—driver's license, credit cards, and the like. In case they got arrested that night the Montreal police were to have no clues as to their identities, for the quartet was undertaking one of the most sensitive Security Service operations ever: Operation Ham, the clandestine entry into the offices of a private company holding the computerized membership lists of the Parti Québécois. Their intent was to remove the PQ computer tapes shortly after midnight when the building was empty, copy them in another location, and return them before the night was out. E Special specialized in surreptitious operations and had performed many of them, but never such a sophisticated or ambitious or politically delicate project as this. The CIA had earlier been consulted and concluded it could not be done.

The seeds were planted the previous spring when Inspector Joseph Ferraris of G Section (Counterterrorism in Quebec) had a talk with Assistant Commissioner Howard Draper, one of the top Security Service officers in Canada. Three things bothered Ferraris. First, the Security Service had been tipped off by the Privy Council Office that the Parti Québécois received up to $350,000 from foreign sources. But Ferraris did not know which countries might be supplying these alleged funds and, in fact, did not know for sure if the report was true. At least six foreign countries operated in the Montreal area with activities aimed at agitating nationalism in Quebec. Second, the RCMP believed radical Quebec elements were infiltrating the PQ with the possible aim of taking it over. But without the PQ's membership data the Security Service was unable to investigate this suspicion adequately. The biggest immediate worry was number three. Federal civil servants with access to classified information were leaking material into PQ hands.[1] The federal government wanted the Force to get to the bottom of it. If the Security Service obtained the PQ membership list it could check the names of PQ members against the civil servants working for the federal government to start off an investigation. Since neither Ferraris nor Draper committed anything to paper, it is not known how far they carried their discussion.

The wheels began turning in August, 1972, when Corporal J. M. Goguen, one of Ferraris' men, identified Les Messageries Dynamiques on Jeanne Mance Street in the north end of Montreal as the company storing the PQ's computerized membership list. The company had a Burroughs B500 computer and the PQ rented computer time during specified nonbusiness hours. The computer was on the upper floor of the firm's two-story red brick building.[2] The main floor was used as a warehouse. A stairway from the front entrance led directly to the plain offices upstairs. Headquarters later recommended the recruiting of an informer within the company.

At some point during the next two months E Special was brought into the operation because on October 12 it issued a telex saying: "Developing a source [informer] within this company is considered too risky in view of the nature of this investigation and the possible political issues that could mate.ialize." E Special was much too secret to have anything to do with outside informers. So the idea of

---

[1]. The third concern happened to be true. The information was being passed along the so-called "Parizeau network" run by Jacques Parizeau, later Minister of Finance in the PQ government of Réné Levesque.

[2]. The company has since moved and the building is occupied by Frank's Rental and Catering Service.

developing an informer already on the inside was dropped and there was no practical alternative but to enter the premises surreptitiously and copy the information.

The Ham team consisted of the E Special crew plus three others whose expertise and close RCMP ties made them ideal for the job. Ken Burnett, a civilian member of the Force at headquarters in Ottawa, was picked because of his expertise in coordinating the RCMP's $40 million computer linking police forces across the country. His technical knowledge was vital. R. E. Meyer, Burnett's colleague at headquarters, was of particular value since he once worked for Burroughs, the computer manufacturer, and was familiar with the product. The only non-RCMP employee was a former Mountie Jim Emberg, who worked as a salesman for R. L. Crain Limited and sold business forms to the targeted company. Emberg was initially used as a door opener since he could arrange an open visit at the premises without raising suspicion.

Accompanying Emberg on the visit was computer expert Burnett, who used the alias Burns and claimed to be representing a trucking company interested in doing business with Les Messageries Dynamiques. In case Mr. "Burns" was challenged, the manager of a local trucking company agreed to back up the story without knowing any details. The cover was not needed and Emberg and Burnett successfully learned that the computer was located at the rear of the building on the second floor. Their visit enabled them to make a rough sketch of the premises. It was after that meeting that Emberg was "indoctrinated" and brought into full confidence.

From there events moved quickly. Emberg hired a friend who worked for MICR Systems Ltd. in Westmount Square to transcribe tapes on short notice during the middle of the night for $100.[3] The free-lance copier knew no details and had no inkling it was an RCMP job.

Surveillance was placed on the building for about three and a half months. First, routine surveillance was conducted from an observation post inside Crown-Meakins, Inc., a paint brush company with a back office looking out at the target. Crown-Meakins rented the

---

[3.] The price was a bargain. Emberg checked with IBM's 24-hour-a-day copying service and its rate was $700 an hour. The copying time was estimated at one and a half hours.

office to the RCMP for a small sum, thinking it was being used in an investigation of a pornography ring. The surveillance crew had a key and could come and go at odd hours. As a precaution RCMP vehicles were never parked in the vicinity.

From the observation post two Mounties week after week recorded every coming and going in order to establish a pattern. They wanted to know when the first person arrived in the morning and when the last left at night and on which nights people worked late. A log was kept and everybody was checked in and out. The observation post knew the building was vacant when everybody on the list was checked out and also because the last invididual locked the door on the way out. Then the observation post phoned the company just to make sure it was empty. Such detailed scrutiny allowed E Special to conclude that the building was vulnerable to "attack" during certain nonbusiness hours and know how many hours' safety margin it had.

The observation post disclosed some interesting details. Cleaning on the second floor was done by a Montreal city policeman moonlighting as a janitor. The temptation existed to recruit him because he had unencumbered access and the mere fact he was moonlighting suggested he either needed or wanted extra money. Although his involvement would have simplified things immensely and save costly and time-consuming planning, it was rejected. E Special never dealt with other police forces.

The observation post also picked up the fact that at a certain time in the evening an on-duty Montreal police constable—with no apparent connection to the janitor—drove up to the building in his squad car and deposited something through the mail slot inside the front door. The policeman worked night shift and operated a delivery service on the side. He arrived at the same hour, but not every night. Operation Ham had to circumvent his visits.

The first "external survey" was taken on November 16. There was no entry that night but technical specialists approached the building with a view to studying such details as locks, the alarm system, and lighting. Whenever Security Service men entered such property, even if only to look at the outside, full-scale surveillance was put onto the premises. The observation post was backed up by a Watcher Service team of five cars patrolling the area five blocks deep and reporting any suspicious activity such as an approaching police car or a pedestrian walking in that general direction. If an emergency arose the Watcher Service radioed the observation post, which in turn radioed the "survey" team to vacate the premises in a hurry.

The first exterior survey proved successful in acquiring information on the front-door lock and alarm system. But it could not be determined whether the alarm was hooked into the system of an outside security agency. The alarm apparatus on the front door was sophisticated and it was decided nothing further could be done without additional research.

The alarm system had been installed by Montreal Alarm, Inc., and five days later owner Albert Pinet was interviewed on the pretext that the RCMP was investigating a pornography ring and that Les Messageries Dynamiques was a suspect. Mr. Pinet was more than cooperative. He described how the alarm was connected to a telephone answering service that would contact city police. The alarm had a delay that gave the person entering 30 seconds to shut off the control box beneath the stairway. Otherwise the alarm sounded. Furthermore, Pinet turned over the key to the control box which enabled the Security Service to neutralize the alarm. It was a big break. E Special did not need to cut a duplicate since it had an original.

Armed with the key and knowledge of how the alarm system worked, Ham Command prepared for the first "interior survey" at around midnight on November 23, two days after the interview with Pinet. An internal survey was not the same as a dry run. It merely meant the Ham Command team entered the premises to in effect "case the joint." However, the premises were unexpectedly occupied that night and entry had to be postponed a week. In the meantime the Force returned to Pinet for more information.

Entry was gained on the night of November 30. At 11:30 PM, when the target was confirmed vacant, the two RCMP corporals noted that the alarm was not working and banged on the windows and returned to their cars just in case it could be triggered. An hour later they returned and entered, turning off the alarm even though it was not working. However, they could not gain access to the second floor where the computer was stored because the glass door had a lock they could not jimmy. They noted the brand and number for later research and left at 1:15 AM.

The first dry run, in which a blank computer tape was used, was scheduled for the night of December 3, but two things upset the plan. First a snowstorm snarled traffic, thus threatening transfer of the simulated computer tape. Then the police cruiser making its delivery did not show up at the usual time. The decision was made to go ahead anyway and the team was about to enter the premises when the observation post signaled an emergency. The police cruiser was on the way. The crew had just enough time to disperse. The snowstorm must have slowed up the Montreal police officer because that night his delivery was an hour late.

The plan to enter the premises was aborted but it was decided to conduct a partial dry run since the computer employee had been hired and was waiting for the dummy tape at Westmount Square. It would be a good test for the transportation times under the worst circumstances. The whole operation took an hour and a half, which bettered the time limit despite the weather.

The other half of the dry run, which consisted of entering the premises and getting the tape, was set for December 7. The Ham team had not yet penetrated the locked glass door on the second floor. A lock specialist from Ottawa accompanied the team. However, the premises were occupied and the operation had to be canceled again. It was the first time the building was occupied on a Thursday night. A complete moratorium was called while surveillance attempted to determine a more accurate pattern of activity. After five days the observation post concluded that despite the assistance of the Watcher Service "we have been unable to establish any definite pattern. We could continue the surveillance for several months and still be no further ahead."

Another internal survey was scheduled for December 13-14. In the meantime final approval for the plan was received from Director-General John Starnes, the chief of the Security Service. But entry had to be postponed another time because the building was again occupied. Ham Command at this point made one last effort and rescheduled the internal survey for the following Monday, December 17.

"If our Monday night survey does not materialize we will have to seriously consider another approach to this file investigation," Ham Command told Ottawa in a telex.

That Monday night the dry run that started in a snowstorm two weeks earlier was finally completed. With the assistance of the lock expert from Ottawa the master cylinder of the lock on the front door was removed completely and replaced by another lock. In case the owner came by his key would not fit the door and he could not enter during the operation. He would be forced to leave and thereby give the Ham team time to vacate the premises. But, just in case the Ham team was interrupted, it kept handy a 18-inch metal bar with which to club any intruder. Despite all the sophisticated briefing and preparation, one rule stands out over all others: if you become compromised, don't get caught. The metal club accompanied E Special on every clandestine operation.

On this outing the lock on the second floor posed no problem. Using information from the previous internal survey, the lock expert came prepared with the right blank key and in about 20 minutes filed it down by hand. Once the team was inside there was a tense moment when the observation post issued an alert that a Montreal police cruiser was approaching and it was not the regular policeman making a delivery. Activity inside froze for several moments while the metal bar was readied for possible emergency use. The police constable stopped in front of the building, got out of his car, and shook the front door. It was secure. He did not know the lock he tested was a replacement and that men were hiding inside. He left and the operation continued. The incident went unexplained.

A shelf full of computer tapes had been spotted and the Burroughs code for the Parti Québécois was identified. The only thing not done was to locate the tapes themselves on the storage shelf. The crew left and the front lock was replaced. The operation was successful and the dry runs were over. The next entry would be the real thing. More surveillance determined the safest time was shortly after midnight on January 9, 1973.

As planned, the Ham team changed the front door master cylinder and entered the premises at 12:20 AM. Soon after that a snag developed. The plastic containers holding the computer tapes on the second floor were identified only by numbers, leaving the team to wonder which numbers belonged to the Parti Québécois. Despite the planning this relatively simple point had been overlooked. The team members spread through the second-floor offices in search of some code key to identify the tapes. The mini-crisis ended five minutes later when a computer printout identifying the correct tapes was spotted on the desk in a small office next to the computer. The four tapes were taken and replaced by four blank replicas. Before the team left, a battery-powered listening device was planted in the computer area in case an employee entered the building while the real tapes were gone. That way the observation post could determine whether the tape disappearance was detected.

The car carrying the four crew members drove into the city of Westmount on the edge of downtown Montreal but, according to plan, stopped short of Westmount Square where the computer operator and his equipment were waiting. At Victoria Hall on Sherbrooke Street, Burnett, who was carrying the tapes, got into another car driven by Emberg and was taken to Westmount Square. Meanwhile the original car carrying the other team members drove into downtown Montreal and parked next to a telephone booth in front of the Avenue Snack Bar on St. Catherine's Street. The maneuver was a precaution in case they were followed. The pay phone was the communication link between Westmount Square and the waiting car.

Because the operation was so politically sensitive the Force at the last minute assigned to the case an officer and staff sergeant not attached to E Special who were parked at the corner of Wood and de Maisonneuve in downtown Montreal. The two cars communicated by radio. It is the only known instance where a nonmember of E Special, even though a commissioned officer, was brought in to supervise an E Special operation. It soon proved to be a mistake.

The only real snag occurred at Westmount Square during the copying process. One and a half hours had been allocated for copying and it was supposed to be routine. But the pay phone in front of the Avenue Snack Bar soon rang with a message that unexpected difficulties had developed and more time was needed. The tapes would not transcribe because of problems with the code. There were four computer specialists in Westmount Square—Burnett, Emberg, the co-opted computer operator, plus a sergeant from Ottawa—and none could handle the code. A phone call was made to Chicago where another computer expert was awakened at 2:30 AM for instructions.

Meanwhile the commissioned officer at the corner of Wood and de Maisonneuve was unaccustomed to the tension and grew more nervous with each minute that exceeded the 90-minute copying allotment. Finally he called the project off. E Special refused to comply. He was told the project was not finished and that if he wanted the tapes back he could go to Westmount Square and get them himself. Such defiance was cause for dismissal in the RCMP and only E Special could get away with it. The copying took three hours. When it was finished the commissioned officer ordered the men to forget the exchange at Victoria Hall and speed back and violate all red lights.

"You're crazy," was the reply. "If we get caught we have no identification. We have no driver's license and we're caught with the goods in our hands."

"Okay, okay," admitted the inspector. "I forgot that. But try to do it as quickly as possible."

The return proceeded exactly as planned, with the change-over at Victoria Hall, and without incident. The computer tapes were returned to their proper storage place, the eavesdropping device retrieved, the original front-door lock replaced, and the building vacated at 5:15 AM. The 90-minute delay notwithstanding, the operation was a perfect success. The duplicated tapes were sent to Ottawa for print-out processing. Assistant Commissioner Draper sent a telex:

> Re: Ham, I wish to express my appreciation for the efforts put forth by the personnel who were instrumental in bringing this delicate operation to a successful conclusion. I realize that considerable research and study were necessary in setting up the operation, in order to make it as swift, efficient and secure as possible."

Once processed, the print-out material measured approximately 16 inches by 12 inches. When all the sheets were piled on top of each other they were six feet high. They were crammed with valuable information categorized four ways: alphabetically, by occupation, a financial count, and a list of public servants.

Operation Ham epitomized the strengths and weaknesses of the Security Service. The operation was planned meticulously and executed almost flawlessly. The entry crew, the Watcher Service, and the locksmiths performed beautifully. In other words, the technical aspects were outstanding. However, the Security Service did not know what to do with the information once it had possession. The Force lacked expertise to make assessments. The print-out material, which filled three large cardboard boxes, was stored and seldom looked at. With time the material became increasingly viewed as useless and on July 18, 1975—a Friday afternoon—the Ham material was burned in an RCMP incinerator. Despite its technical superiority the operation was a flop.

As the planning for Operation Ham gained momentum, E Special was approached to do another clandestine operation: Operation Bricole. Again, the object was to obtain intelligence through a break-and-enter job. The target was a three-story brick building at 3459 St. Hubert that served as headquarters principally for two left-leaning action groups of prime interest to the Security Service: the Agence de Presse Libre du Québec (APLQ), a politico-journalist organization that worked at the community level, and the Mouvement Pour la Défense des Prisoniers Politiques du Québec (MDPPQ), a more hardened group of FLQ sympathizers that lent assistance to the jailed "political prisoners." It also housed the Co-op Déménagement 1er Mai, which was of lesser concern. The request for an operation against these groups came from G Section, the newly created anti-terrorist section that concentrated on separatist organizations in Quebec. E Special responded with one simple question: Were other police forces involved? The answer was yes—E Special refused to touch the case.

It was not the first time E Special refused to take a case against the APLQ. It had been asked to install eavesdropping devices in the St. Hubert Street premises on two previous occasions and refused both times. Surveillance had been conducted and revealed an unpredictable pattern of activity that made the operation too risky. Too many people used the building and too many individuals had keys. Also, their habits were irregular. The project was studied a second time with a view toward installing a bug from the outside, thereby avoiding the need to enter. One side of the building shared a common wall with a rooming house in which E Special considered renting a room and installing the listening device.[4] However, a stairway on the otherside of the wall blocked off a lot of the sound in most places except the top floor. Besides, E Special had reservations about the value of the operation even if good audio was possible. So the project was turned down again.

In those days G Section was in no mood to accept E Special's cautious approach. It introduced a new *provocateur* element into the Security Service and was then at the height of its belligerence. It had stolen dynamite earlier in the year and prior to that had issued a faked FLQ communiqué denouncing Pierre Vallières for renouncing terrorism on the assumption it would disrupt FLQ ranks. It had virtually kidnapped a number of FLQ sympathizers and through threats pressured them into acting as informers. Not too many months earlier a barn at Anne de la Rochelle could not be bugged for a meeting of terrorists so G Section chose to burn it rather than let the meeting proceed unmonitored. If E Special would not enter the APLQ premises, G Section would do it itself.

G Section was linked to other police forces through CATS, the Combined Anti-Terrorist Squad, a commando-like unit formed originally to fight the wave of bombings that plagued Quebec in the 1960s. Three police forces—the RCMP, Montreal, and Quebec— were members. Over the years the organization had expanded and grown increasingly aggressive. It is difficult to say which was more bellicose, CATS or G Section. Since G Section formed part of CATS, it did not really matter. The bottom line was that the APLQ break-in was devised by hotheads who happened to be amateurs as well.

The operation featured none of the long-range and minute planning of Operation Ham. Surveillance was provided by the Montreal police. On October 5, 1972, only a few weeks after the proposal was first discussed, the surveillance team reported that the premises would be vacant the following evening—a Friday night—because people usually in the building would be gone for the weekend. CATS met the following day and decided to swing into action that night.

---

4. Such an installation still requires an entry into the premises to ensure the installer did not poke a hole through the wall. However, this is not considered an entry in the accepted definition since it would last only a minute or two and would not require the planning of an inside operation.

Last-minute details were quickly arranged and at 4:15 PM Friday, only hours before the operation was to begin, Sergeant Henri Pelletier entered the office of Inspector Don Cobb with an outline and a request for approval. Cobb sought approval from higher authorities, but Inspector J. H. Vermette, the officer in charge of G Section, had already left for the weekend on a moose-hunting trip. Chief Superintendent Laurent Forest, head of the Security Service in the province of Quebec, was also gone—accompanying Vermette on the moose expedition. Cobb attempted to raise John Starnes, the top Security Service official in Canada, but Starnes was in Halifax and out of reach until Tuesday morning. Everything was ready to go, the other two police forces were waiting for RCMP approval, and Cobb felt pressured. When he asked why there was no warrant, Pelletier simply said: "Montreal [police] didn't get one." Cobb did not press the matter further and gave his okay. The decision would return to haunt him and freeze a blossoming career.

At 1 AM four teams descended upon the vicinity of 3459 St. Hubert. Group number four consisted of four men and was the emergency team monitoring police calls in the area. Group three constituted two men on foot at a nearby bus stop looking out for pedestrians walking through the area. Their duty was to divert passers-by with innocuous conversation long enough for the surveillance team to warn the men inside. Group two was the surveillance team itself, stationed inside a truck parked in front of the building. It had radio contact with the five men inside who constituted group one—the shock group.

The shock group had no trouble entering the premises since the Montreal police had done it at least twice previously. Wearing gloves and clutching pocket flashlights the five men carried canvas hockey bags to accommodate the booty of documents. Stealing the documents was truly amateur and something E Special would have never done. E Special had a high-speed duplicator that could copy 6,000 pages in 35 minutes.

By 2 AM half a ton of paper had been loaded into the truck outside and driven to Montreal police headquarters on Hochelaga Street. Not too many hours later policemen from that same building were dispatched to investigate the theft.

The APLQ knew instantly it had been a police operation, for who else could take files and leave untouched $125 in cash and several expensive IBM typewriters? The only unresolved question was *which* police force, for few in their most paranoic moments ever believed it was a conspiracy of all three police forces. The APLQ called a press conference and accused the police, but in those days the established media did not take such allegations seriously. The APLQ sent letters to all three police forces, the Solicitor General of Canada, and the Justice Minister of Quebec, and none of them took the query any more seriously than the news media. Nevertheless, a time bomb was planted that would eventually explode.

Meanwhile at Montreal police headquarters an unanticipated problem arose: what to do with the 1,000 pounds of paper. The documents were more voluminous than anticipated and the police abandoned the original plan of hiding them in their headquarters because of their sheer bulk. As a temporary measure they were moved to the basement of RCMP Sergeant Claude Brodeur's home, which was put under 24-hour guard for the next several weeks while members of the three police forces sifted through the documents and microfilmed selected material. At one point RCMP Constable Robert Samson, a member of the shock group which actually entered the APLQ premises, snapped a picture of his colleagues scrutinizing the material but Samson later testified the negatives disappeared mysteriously. Worthless material—mostly publications—was burned. The remainder—two hockey bags full—plus microfilm copies, was transported to RCMP headquarters in Ottawa in a truck rented by Samson under the name of Robert Lemieux, the FLQ lawyer. The material was transferred out of Quebec because the police feared Quebec law might have allowed legal searches.

Like Operation Ham, Operation Bricole produced in the end very little advantage for the authorities. The information was effectively useless. Its origin was so obvious the Force refused to distribute it through normal channels and instead relegated it to a locked filing cabinet. The financial data produced evidence of unemployment insurance fraud on the part of APLQ staff but the police did not dare lay charges. To do so would have required submitting the evidence in open court and exposing the police role in the break-in.

The MDPPQ died shortly thereafter but it had been in serious difficulty and may have died anyway. The detrimental effect on the

APLQ lasted only a few months when it could not operate for lack of records; then it rebounded and became even stronger and the raid may have contributed to this new-found dynamism. The easygoing APLQ grew more militant and more extremist in political posture. Within a few years it joined the Canadian Communist League, Marxist-Leninist. The raid helped push a mild socialist community-oriented group into a hard-core collection of revolutionaries. So Operation Bricole was a triple disaster: the police exposed themselves, failed to obtain usable intelligence, and helped consolidate the position of an extremist organization such as the CCLML.

The APLQ moved to Beaudry Street and into a building it purchased soon after the raid. G Section once again requested a bugging installation. This time E Special agreed. Through contacts in the credit union where the APLQ secured mortgage money, E Special learned the location of the new APLQ office before the sale was closed and made arrangements with the seller to enter the premises to plant bugs. The entry was entirely legal since it was done with the permission of the owner. When APLQ took possession it moved into a bugged building.

It was not the calculated and repeated activities of E Special that landed the Security Service in political trouble. E Special had never been caught in clandestine entry. The elements responsible for alerting the public to this entrenched dimension of the Security Service were the amateur operators in G Section.

19

The Rise
of E Special

BEFORE CHRONICLING THE rise of illegal activity, I should explain
that members of the Security Service have their own interpretation
of that term. From dozens of interviews, both with Mounties who
have performed illegal acts and with civilians who have watched
them, I am convinced that they do not see their acts as illegal. Such
methods are accepted as the basic tools to protect Canada's security.
Security Service members do not philosophize about the deed; it is a
practical matter. When challenged, most members fall back on the
old paramilitary excuse that the actions are approved by their superior
officers and therefore are not illegal.

Despite the Mounties' inability to articulate an intellectual justification, a rationalization of sorts does exist. They believe their acts are
morally right and view impeding legal statutes only as technical
barriers, not ethical ones. A Mountie has a more committed sense of
duty than most Canadians and holds long-standing grievances that
the country's lawmakers do not know what the RCMP is doing, and
pass laws restricting the Force and assisting the enemy. They believe
that lawmakers, although they want to preserve order, are so mis-
informed and consumed by politics that the results of their legislation
do not meet their objectives. And so there is a gap and the Security
Service has a duty to plug it. If a Mountie held up a corner grocery
store he would commit an illegal act because he breached the law
both technically and morally. The country's lawmakers never

intended the RCMP to hold up grocery stores but they intend the Force to halt subversion and espionage.

Furthermore, I am convinced from interviews with senior Mounties and government officials that lawmakers in positions of administrative and executive authority almost without exception at least suspected law-breaking by the Security Service but deliberately failed to explore it and, in fact, avoided opportunities to learn of it. Generally, the ministers responsible for the RCMP also avoided sensitive security issues whenever possible, even to the point of sometimes making themselves unavailable. The problem was most acute during the minority governments of the 1960s when administrations were in constant danger of falling. No minister wanted responsibility for bringing down the government and sought to avoid controversy, since security decisions by their nature were political dynamite and the minister preferred not to know.

Whether they admit it or not, most ministers support illegal activity as long as it is directed against fringe elements, such as subversive individuals and foreign espionage agents. But cabinet ministers, especially the Solicitor General and Justice Minister, are sworn to uphold the law and cannot afford to say so. The politician is not alone in his hypocrisy. Most Canadians want the police to exceed the law if it disrupts motorcycle gangs and exposes the Mafia. From time to time motorcycle gangs complain about police brutality and are ignored. Their complaints are heeded only when the abuses grow so obvious that they can no longer be disregarded and then an official commission holds an inquiry and condemns the police. The public then condemns the police, not because they committed abuses but because they committed abuses so incompetently they were caught. Society wants its biases while believing it has none. And so do cabinet ministers.

Soviet nationals in Canada are harassed in a myriad of ways: sex traps, blackmail, minor frame-ups, constant recruitment approaches, and even police harassment on the highways. The Soviets complain to the Department of External Affairs, which does nothing except possibly caution the Security Service to back down. The incidents are too small to prick the Canadian conscience. But if the Security Service used rougher tactics, such as those the Russians have used against Westerners in Moscow, and they were revealed publicly, Canadians might be forced to react with outrage.

Despite the Government's double standard, the relationship was mutually advantageous because the Security Service generally did not want to say much more about cases than the government wanted to hear. It did not withhold such information but it did not divulge it either. The Security Service believed one did not tell the king certain things for his own good and that the king understood this. The Force also believed that ministers come and go but the RCMP always remains. Mail opening was an example. During World War Two mail was opened legally and routinely to investigate subversion and espionage and also to censor information of possible value to the enemy. When the emergency powers of the War Measures Act expired in 1945, so did the authority to open mail and from that point on it became illegal. In the 1950s the RCMP petitioned the government for legislation to intercept postal communications and succeeded in gaining the support of Justice Minister Stuart Garson. However, when Garson asked Prime Minister Louis St. Laurent he was almost thrown out of the Prime Minister's office. Postal interception ceased and at that point Operation Cathedral—the code name for clandestine mail openings—became a dead file for as long as St. Laurent was Prime Minister. But it did not stop the Security Service from resuming the practice after St. Laurent was gone.

At no time did the Security Service make a formal decision to condone illegal activity. It was embraced through a series of gradations over a number of years. Illegal acts had always been committed but an endorsement of systematic illegality by the Security Service began in the early 1950s with organized disruption campaigns against the Communist Party of Canada. It was a straightforward program aimed at crushing the party. Since the cold war was near its height the issue was viewed not in legal-versus-illegal terms but as good versus bad. The Communist Party was gravely wounded and the cold war faded.[1] Without ever realizing it the RCMP had adopted illegal activity as a fundamental investigative technique. If the Force was unable to recruit an informer within the targeted group, it resorted to breaking and entering its premises for a clandestine look through the files. It happened so slowly and out of such seeming

---

[1.] The RCMP attacks were not responsible for the decline of the Communist Party of Canada, although they undoubtedly contributed.

necessity that nobody stopped to consider it. Occasionally a Mountie refused to go along and he was considered an oddball and shunted aside. His values and loyalty were questioned and he was transferred out of the Security Service.

For the most part illegal activity was accepted with enthusiasm since it was exciting, was good for one's career, and contributed to the fight against communism. The Force recruited 18-year-old babies out of high school and taught them morals in a closed and peculiar environment. At first they were given minor roles, which were increased with their experience and status. Given the circumstances —the perceived threat, the dedication, the conviction of rightness, the RCMP's propensity to obey orders, the closed environment, the lack of sophistication, the excitement, and the desire for advancement within the Force—it is not surprising that a group of honest and decent individuals *en masse* accepted illegal activity so casually.

Specialization arrived in the 1960s. The Security Service became more sophisticated in technique and attempted more exotic operations. But more important, the electronic era of eavesdropping had arrived and bugging became commonplace. Eavesdropping in those days was not forbidden by law and the Force needed no prior authorization to make an installation. But planting bugs required access to the targeted premises and that usually involved an entry operation that definitely was illegal.

The eavesdropping revolution introduced the need for specialists. Planting bugs required electronic experts to select and handle the devices as well as artisans who could drill holes in the wall and quickly and expertly cover them up. Locksmiths were also needed. The RCMP responded informally at first as individuals seemed to create niches of expertise in little groups across the country. Toronto, Montreal, Vancouver, and other centers had their own people who could perform the needed specialized functions. Soon an informal group at headquarters in Ottawa began offering guidance to these groups scattered among the divisions. Rather than allow the system to evolve further, headquarters—still informally—began recruiting certain individuals by encouraging them to develop expertise in specified technical areas and offering them training. The groups in each division became more defined and, with each project, better and more experienced. Eventually they started drawing up actual plans and sending them to headquarters for comment and approval.

In the late 1960s the first murmurs of discontent were being heard. The number of illegal acts was rising all the time relative to the number of conspirators. So the risks grew greater but were being shouldered by certain individuals who became increasingly reluctant to accept the hazards of discovery. The task was unnerving and the tension took its toll. A sergeant in the Ottawa Division became a bundle of nerves and had to be transferred. Mounties were wary of the legal consequences in the event of capture. They had always been assured that their families would be looked after. The assurance was hollow, but in the old days it was accepted because Mounties were taught to believe in their superior officers. But in the late 1960s a newer breed of younger and more skeptical Mounties started demanding guarantees. They had few illusions and realized that if caught they would be disowned and sent to prison, suffering legal and social shame and also acquiring a criminal record. Once out of prison they would hardly be permitted to rejoin the Force. Their lives would be ruined while the Force merrily carried on. The young Mounties were smarter and acutely aware of a basic principle in the intelligence world: the individual is expendable; the organization must always be protected. The anti-Communist doctrines of the 1950s had faded slightly and the new targets were not so evil anymore, and the issues not so clearly defined. In the rebellious 1960s some young members had the odd doubt about their role. However, their objections for the most part concerned not morality but their own safety.

The Security Service management had its own worries and doubts. Hundreds of illegal acts had been committed over the years and no one had been caught. The record was remarkable. However, the officers, many of whose careers had been enhanced by illegal acts, realized that the RCMP had been lucky and that disaster would inevitably strike and bring embarrassment and disgrace to the cherished reputation of the RCMP. What would the Force tell the Solicitor General? At one time a compromised Mountie would play the role of fall guy and silently go to prison. The officers were worried about the newer Mounties who would not make such a sacrifice and would talk loud and long on their way to jail. So Security Service management had a vested interest in revising the clandestine program in order to better protect the safety of its members.

Ironically, it was the Criminal Investigation Branch of the RCMP that brought the issue to a head. CIB had also come to rely on illegal acts as a basic investigative tool. Sub-inspector Donald Wilson, the Assistant Adjutant, was giving a seminar on "basic police personnel management training" to CIB Mounties on June 19, 1970, when the issue arose and dominated the meeting. The policemen complained that the question had been raised before and no answer had been given. One policeman went as far to say that he would drop his work forthwith if protection was not provided. Sub-inspector Wilson, like previous officers, could not give a reply or calm their fears. However, he did write a memo to the Director of Organization and Personnel, thereby starting a chain of events that resulted two months later in a statement from Commissioner Len Higgitt promising protection for Mounties involved in illegal acts that had the Force's explicit or implicit approval.

Commissioner Higgitt's statement was issued in August, 1970, and acknowledged the Force had transgressed the law in the past, was doing so in the present and would continue to do so in the future.

> More recently it has come to my attention that some members involved in delicate operations are concerned with the protection they and their families will receive in the event that an operation goes sour and they become subject to civil or criminal processes as a result. It is not difficult to imagine a situation wherein one or more members find themselves compromised and for reasons of security, no explanation of the operation could be disclosed.[2]

Higgitt's statement outlined the protection members could expect. Mounties caught performing approved illegal acts would be protected from legal prosecution to the greatest extent possible. If prosecution could not be avoided, the Force would hire a lawyer and pay any fine. If imprisoned, the individual would continue to draw his salary and be re-employed upon release from jail. If a Mountie was caught breaking the law independently and on his own initiative, the RCMP

[2.] See Appendix B for Higgitt's complete statements.

still had a "moral responsibility" to protect him unless the action was deemed unreasonable. Furthermore, Higgitt's policy added, Mounties may refuse to break the law without fear of discipline but the individual may be transferred to other duties.

Although CIB started this formal review of policy it also applied to the Security Service, for which Director General John Starnes was most grateful. While Higgitt's statement was in the process of being formulated, Starnes on July 14, 1970, wrote a secret memorandum to the Deputy Commissioner in charge of administration endorsing the proposal:

> I might add that in the past this problem of "protection" has been raised on a number of occasions by members in attendance at our courses; however, due to inadequate guidelines, it has not been completely resolved.
>
> We are most appreciative of the attention that this matter has received and I am sure that the views expressed will alleviate a good deal of the concern which our members have expressed in the past.

Starnes was right: the new policy largely did satisfy the concerns of Mounties. The enlisted men never really quarreled with the concept of illegal acts and in fact relied on them and endorsed them as heartily as RCMP management did. All they ever wanted was immunity from legal retribution and this came relatively close to satisfying that concern.

But senior management had one other concern about illegal activity that was not covered in Higgitt's statement, and it related to the reporting system. The officers felt illegal acts were being carried out with too little management scrutiny; this encouraged sloppiness, which was bound to result in an exposure. So the Security Service introduced guidelines and review mechanisms that centralized the control and put it into the hands of headquarters even more than before. Operations could not be undertaken without making formal application to headquarters. The originating division had to submit a proposal listing the purpose and method of the operation with all the details, including the safety precautions. The new procedures accorded formal status and bureaucratic legitimacy to the collection of individuals who handled clandestine acts. They were made into a unique unit called E Special.

E Special was formed under the tightest secrecy. It was not made a section unto itself for, among other things, that would have required its own letter and merely advertised its existence on any bureaucratic flow chart. People would have wondered what this mysterious section did and soon word would have leaked out. Besides, each of the E Special units across the country had only a handful of people and the size did not justify designation as a Section. E Special needed the cover of another section and yet have autonomy from it.

J Section was the most logical home for this new unit, since it had responsibility for bugging, a not unrelated activity, and by far the greatest number of illegal acts were done to allow J Section to plant bugs. The second most logical cover was B Section, the counter-espionage section, since it was so large it could absorb the new unit without a ripple. Also, this section requested the majority of illegal acts—whether planting bugs, photographing files, or just conducting a general search. Both J and B sections were passed over. The Force opted instead to house the new unit in sedate E Section, a minor and technically oriented section whose main responsibility was to trans-form tape recordings of wire-tapped and bugged conversations into transcripts. There was to be no connection between E Section and this new unit, hence it was called E Special.

E Special has taken the need-to-know concept to an extreme. Only E Special staff are permitted to enter its offices. The curtains are lined with lead to stop laser or other beams from picking up conver-sations. Some even have alarms on the door and the filing cabinets are encased in heavy-duty safes. All files are identified only by a code name and are labeled Top Secret, the highest level of secrecy in the government classification system. That means they enjoy the same secret status as Canada's military plans in case of war. Not even the Security Service investigator on whose behalf a project is done has access to the files. The files never leave the E Special complex except when scrutinized by a superior officer with direct-line responsibility, in which event a member of E Special delivers them by hand, waits for the officer to read them, then returns them to the compound.

Since E Special was given responsibility for surreptitious operations, it exercised complete operational control and could not be counter-manded at the divisional level. If an investigator from B (Counter-espionage), D (Countersubversion), or G (Quebec Anti-terrorism, now defunct) submitted a request and it was approved by E Special, the operation was taken out of his hands. E Special did the rest. If the purpose of the operation was to plan a bug, the bug-planter from J Section entered the premises without worrying about anything except accomplishing his designated task in the most professional manner possible. He arrived on the scene knowing that the locked door would be opened and he would not be interrupted by unexpected visitors. He knew in advance precisely where to place the listening devices because E Special had already secured sketches. The quality of his work had to satisfy E Special; if it did not, he was required to redo the job until it did.

In keeping with the RCMP's tradition for excellence in technical operations, E Special never failed and consequently Security Service investigators in many divisions lined up for its services. The bugging crew in J Section reached its peak effectiveness in the first three years of the 1970s since it got highly sophisticated, albeit slightly used, equipment from the CIA. (This was before relations between the two organizations turned chilly and the flow of hardware was cut off.) I Section—the Watcher Service—was also an invaluable resource. In fact these three technical resources—clandestine operations, eavesdropping, and physical surveillance—were probably too effective for the over-all good of the Security Service. Investigators started to count on them as the mainstay in their investigations rather than the support services they were designed to be, and tended to forget the basics, such as recruiting informers and interviewing acquaintances of the target. The Security Service had yet to learn that the most expensive technical aids cannot replace an investigator's shoe leather or a well-placed informer. A notable exception was the British Columbia division, which continued to recruit informers just as actively as it had before. Quebec, the most reliant on hardware, was consequently left unprepared and virtually helpless to deal with the FLQ Crisis of 1970, although that failure partly belongs to headquarters too.[3]

3. Even bugs have technical limitations, as an incident during the October Crisis of 1970

The events of fall, 1970, were a nightmare for the Force. Two people had been kidnapped and the FLQ was setting forth its conditions for their release. The scene in the government's East Block situation room told the story. On one side of the table sat a row of harassed Mounties; on the other side were impatient cabinet ministers and senior government officials. The government wanted dramatic solutions and the RCMP had nothing dramatic to offer. In fact, the RCMP could offer nothing at all.

At the very time the Security Service needed a paramilitary approach, the organization collapsed into chaos. With Director-General John Starnes in bed with pneumonia for the first month of the crisis, nobody else seemed to take charge. Each telephone tip produced a burst of activity and another false alarm. The Security Service was reacting rather than acting.

There were several reasons for the Force's collapse during the FLQ crisis, the most important being the failure to recruit informers. Penetrators had been recruited in the past but failed to infiltrate FLQ ranks when the Security Service refused to sanction the petty acts of terrorism the FLQ demanded as demonstrations of commitment. The Security Service, which routinely broke the law itself, could not reconcile such actions even to achieve infiltration.

There were other reasons for the Force's poor performance. Much of the Security Service's bad information originated from the Quebec and Montreal police forces. Lacking its own information network, the Security Service used the intelligence of its sister forces when the crisis erupted, accepting this information in good faith. There was no time to check for reliability. Meanwhile the Montreal police wanted to settle old scores and used the War Measures Act to imprison Quebeckers who had no connection with the FLQ. The situation was aggravated by the fact that the WASPish RCMP was not at home in Quebec. Information was gathered (partly) by Anglophones

---

illustrates. A decision was made to bug the apartment in which James Cross was being held shortly after the location was identified. The tenants in the apartment above were given $300 plus expenses to move out for a week while a listening device was planted in the floor. Conversations were duly picked up and for several days the Force thought it was getting a good product. As it turned out the conversation was coming from the apartment next door. Although the bug contributed nothing, the device was later mounted on a plaque and given to the British High Commission as the device that bugged the kidnappers.

in Montreal and analyzed (almost exclusively) by Anglophones in Ottawa. It was not the way to probe French-Canadian nationalism in Quebec.

Cabinet ministers were livid when they later learned that the two FLQ kidnapping cells had not been in communication and that the operation was not a conspiracy. It was RCMP information and analysis that moved the government into invoking the War Measures Act unnecessarily. Prime Minister Trudeau and his staff were outraged. They had no idea the Security Service's intelligence was that bad. It was later determined that the regional desk system in the Prime Minister's Office had better information.

The government and the Security Service blamed each other for the failure. The government accused the Security Service of failing to collect adequate intelligence on the FLQ and then withholding from the government what information it had until the crisis erupted. The Force vehemently protested the claim, saying the government would have known had it bothered to read the reports the Force had been sending. Both sides were partially correct. The Force had here and there submitted snippets of information that were vague and badly composed. The one attempt to pull it together was an ill-written and puzzling 29-page report that raised more questions than it answered. It left the government confused and not knowing what to do with it, so it was shelved. As it turned out, much of the report's information was wrong but it did include fragments of solid intelligence that allowed the Force to say the government had been warned of a major and dramatic FLQ initiative.

The FLQ Crisis had hardly ended when Prime Minister Trudeau established clear lines of authority within the government to handle future domestic threats. Until that time the Solicitor General had been responsible for the RCMP, but responsibility over internal security had never been clearly delineated between the Prime Minister and the Solicitor General. Trudeau wrote a formal letter giving this responsibility to the Solicitor General. To provide assistance in those new duties a group known as SPARG (Security Planning and Research Group) and headed by Colonel Robin Bourne was created to initiate a systematic assessment of the intelligence the Security Service was supplying.[4]

[4.] Not surprisingly, Bourne's group was greeted initially with hostility by the Force. It also

The government started applying pressure to the Force even prior to the enactment of these measures. The government insisted on knowing what went wrong and what was being done to correct the situation. RCMP management was already angry, resentful, and somewhat embarrassed. When the post-mortems began, the Force was also intimidated. Just as the RCMP overreacted during the crisis, similarly it overreacted in the searching aftermath of the crisis. As a remedy the Force established G Section to deal exclusively with Quebec militancy. The overreaction came, not in forming G Section, but in determining the manner in which it was to operate.

The RCMP is not given to subtlety and the government's pressure on senior management was passed directly on the enlisted men. The officers started demanding results and wanting them immediately. To emphasize that fact, the Security Service changed its priorities for the first time since Gouzenko and gave subversion precedence over espionage. It was a radical reversal since the counterespionage section had been the elite and tended to attract the best and most ambitious Mounties.

The anti-terrorist program for G Section got formally under way in February, 1971, when a top-secret memo from headquarters set out the policy of "disruptive tactics." The memo was approved personally by Director-General Starnes, who signed it on February 12. The rationale was that the recruiting of informers would take a long time but results were needed immediately and the best short-term strategy against the FLQ was "disruptive tactics." This memo was followed on June 11, 1971, by another policy memo on techniques for recruiting informers and signed by then-Sub-inspector Joseph Ferraris, who was in charge of G Section in Ottawa. It combined disruption and recruitment:

became the object of a political attack in the House of Commons by the Conservatives who, led by Member of Parliament Erik Nielsen (Yukon), charged the government with tampering with the internal operations of the RCMP. Actually, the reverse was closer to the truth. SPARG quickly became a lobbying force for RCMP interests in the Solicitor General's office. The police side of the RCMP soon realized the value of SPARG to the Security Service and requested a similar group to look after CIB interests. In response the government widened SPARG's mandate to include police matters and changed the name to the Police, Security Planning and Analysis Branch. Bourne had the rank of Assistant Deputy Minister and a staff of about 20, including secretaries. Bourne submitted his resignation about 10 days before the May, 1979, federal election, which saw the Conservatives defeat the Liberals. He was replaced by Michael Shoemaker, a lawyer and career civil servant with no background in security.

A. Selective Interview of Activists: This method was used during Expo 67 and did meet with some success. If no agents develop out of this, we have noted that it has in some cases neutralized the individual.

B. Disruptive Tactics: Making use of sophisticated and well-researched plans built around existing situation such as power struggles, love affairs, fraudulent use of funds, information in drug use, etc. to cause dissension and splintering of the separatist-terrorist groups.

C. C.O.D.: Approach known separatist-terrorist and offer a lump sum payment in return for good information leading to the arrest and or neutralizing of terrorist groups. They would be run similar to criminal groups on a short term basis, with cash paid on delivery for good information. They would be aware that if they were caught committing a criminal act they would expect no help from us.

The new G Section got the pick of personnel. The dominating officer was Donald Cobb, a rising inspector whose youthful arrogance suited the task assigned him by headquarters. Cobb was endowed with two traits lacking in many Mounties: he was articulate and philosophical. These characteristics enabled him to defend the Force's new aggressive policy aimed at radical separatists. Cobb was also a dissident because he feared nobody and questioned everything, including orders from superior officers, and he got away with it because his superiors were intimidated by his intellect.

With the government looking over the Security Service's shoulder, Cobb's new job contained risks, political and otherwise, and the Force may have felt Cobb should be the sacrificial lamb. It may also have felt that if Cobb was so smart, let him handle the mess. Cobb did not collapse. Instead, he was summonsed to Ottawa in December, 1972, for a two-year term as Executive Assistant to the Deputy Solicitor General, Roger Tasse, and his presence made such an impression that a small but determined group in the Solicitor General's office in 1973 lobbied for his appointment as successor to retiring Commissioner Len Higgitt.

Cobb had long been challenging established procedures within the RCMP and used his position in the Deputy Solicitor General's office to arm both the Solicitor General and the Deputy Solicitor General with penetrating questions for their weekly meeting with the four top RCMP officers. The Force soon figured out what was happening and withdrew Cobb before his two years expired and parachuted him into another suicidal posting: security for the upcoming Montreal Olympics. However, the Olympics went smoothly and Cobb flourished again.

Back at G Section from 1970 to 1972, Cobb in a sense was the executive and Sergeant Don McCleery the operations man who led the anti-FLQ troops in the trenches. McCleery never did anything in half-measures; he possessed an amazing amount of energy and determination and was a hot-shot hero—one of the few—of the October Crisis. Most of his career was spent in counterespionage. It was felt that with his enthusiasm the attack against the Quebec political underground would be prosecuted aggressively and thoroughly.

"I didn't want anybody who was just concerned with working eight to four," McCleery later testified.

Cobb was in charge of subsection G-1 (Administration); McCleery took command of an elite group of about 50 known as G-2 and was responsible for the investigation of known FLQ sympathizers. Another subsection, G-3, the largest and more sedate, monitored the Quebec scene generally.

G Section was given special status. The Security Service had always practiced rigid centralism. Hardly an investigation could be started without Ottawa's approval. Certainly no bug could be placed. Headquarters had to know everything. G Section proved to be an exception; it was given unprecedented local autonomy. The Force concluded that an all-out assault on radical separatism required more local initiative and less headquarters scrutiny. The top officers also knew that unpleasantness was to follow and they did not want to know the details, much less take the responsibility.

There was another important factor. The RCMP was facing growing Francophone nationalism within its own ranks. The Force had always been English-dominated, and pressure, from both inside and outside, was applied to boost French Canadian representation within the Force generally and specifically within the officer corps. The government was applying pressure because the Force was deficient in the bilingualism targets. As well, Francophone Mounties in Quebec kept insisting that Quebec was unique among the divisions and that headquarters did not understand it and should leave it alone so that it could do its job. Faced with all these pressures, the Force threw up its hands and surrendered. If G Section could infiltrate the FLQ, raise the bilingual component to federal standards, and generally get the government off its back, the Force was prepared to go along and give Quebec greater independence. But in the end headquarters did not so much cede authority as much as G Section took it.

It did not take long before G Section's independence ran into conflict with established procedures, most often over the practice of recruiting informers. The Force had a meticulous and proven technique for enlisting human sources. Headquarters never intended to throw out the rules when ceding greater autonomy to G Section. But G Section decided on its own not only whom to recruit as informers and when, but violated all the professional criteria. Despite requests from L Section in headquarters, G Section did not inform Ottawa about its activities, reporting only the successes and usually only because money was needed to pay the informer since without a report money was not provided. Its recruitment techniques can be described only as thuggery that happened to be both crude and ineffective. FLQ sympathizers were virtually kidnapped and taken to motel rooms for long stretches and bullied. Some informers were obtained but they lacked motivation and commitment and soon were lost.

Word of G Section's hooliganism reached headquarters often enough, but it constituted essentially the type of agitation that the panic-stricken officers at headquarters had ordered, with possibly an added dash of overzealousness. The only individuals who were genuinely offended were the purists in L Section, who worried about its fruitlessness and lack of professionalism. Even if the senior officers in Ottawa had not set the stage for G Section's gangsterism, they were in no position to point fingers because they, too, were implicated in dirty tricks of their own making. For at the same time an incident was developing in Vancouver that was as crude and vulgar as any of G Section's escapades.

Dirty Tricks
in Vancouver

THREE MEN LOOKING like bush workers arrived at the Vancouver International Airport in early October, 1971. Their clothing was ragged; a razor had not touched their faces for about a week. Two of them possessed physiques suggesting they could look after themselves in a fight. They were not the kind of men who would normally be met at the airport, but two well-groomed men in business suits were on hand to greet them and take them away. At the parking lot the three travelers climbed into the back of an unmarked windowless van, which drove over the Oak Street bridge and in the direction of the city center.

All five men were noncommissioned officers in the Security Service. The three travelers arrived from Ottawa; two were corporals and one a sergeant. Their role as unemployed lumberjacks was a cover. The two well-dressed men were a sergeant and a corporal stationed in Vancouver. What brought them together in such a conspiratorial way was a dirty prank the Force planned to unleash on a radical left-wing Vancouver group called the Partisan Party.

The van moved directly to the underground parking garage behind a plush new high-rise office building at 1177 West Broadway in uptown Vancouver. The building was the new British Columbia headquarters for the Security Service. It had been occupied only a few weeks and was already showing its advantages over the old complex at Jericho Beach on the edge of the University of British

Columbia campus since the three Ottawa Mounties could be moved from the truck to the inside without being seen. A private elevator from the underground parking garage took them directly to the Security Service complex on the upper floors.

Inside the carpeted offices the plan unfolded. The three roughnecks were to physically assault the Partisan Party members at night and steal their files, which they would be carrying home for safekeeping. Two of the Mounties would attack the Partisans while the third ran off with the file box. Their instructions were to rough them up without quite killing them. The idea was to knock them unconscious or break a limb—in any case to do enough damage to put them into the hospital.

Ironically, the Security Service was adopting a policy of violence just as the Partisan Party was rejecting it. The party was an outgrowth of the radical student movement at Simon Fraser University. The university leaders had moved off campus in March, 1970, and formed a grand alliance composed of radical political groups, black activists, militant feminists, American war deserters, and draft dodgers under the name of the Vancouver Liberation Front. The VLF was sympathetic to violent revolution and formed a target-shooting club and started collecting guns. The War Measures Act seven months later cured that romantic notion and VLF members realized they could not fight the state on military terms. The VLF collapsed and after months of discussion the Partisan Party was formed in April, 1971, and adopted an anti-violence posture. The Partisans' program concentrated on community-oriented work with the long-term goal of winning the support of the masses. The few remaining members sympathetic to violence were purged and went underground. From then on the party stressed adherence to the law and even took the unprecedented step of banning dope-smoking for fear the police might use that as a pretext for conducting raids or engaging in other forms of harassment.

For its office the Partisan Party used second-story space in a green barnlike warehouse at 399 West Third Avenue in Vancouver's manufacturing district. The space was large—easily big enough to put out its newspaper—and rent was only $66 a month because there was no heat. Around the corner less than a block away, some party members lived in a communal house. Each night they locked up the office and carried home the most sensitive material in a box of files and index cards. However, this daily file-transferring routine would not last much longer because the party was moving its headquarters to the Strathcona district next to Chinatown as part of its policy of integrating into the community. The new office would have two live-in residents and the files would always remain on the premises. The attack on the Partisan Party would have to occur before the move if this weak link in security was to be exploited.

The three Ottawa roughnecks arrived in Vancouver one week before the move. During the briefing in the Security Service's offices, only about eight blocks away, they were told to launch the attack at night. Two of them were to hide around the corner waiting for the Partisans to move into the darkness between lampposts. At the appropriate moment they would jump the Partisans from behind; one would grab the files and run while the other stayed and fought. The third Mountie would rush from across the street to help administer the beating. The task would not be finished until all the Partisans—there were usually three or so—lay helpless on the street. A rented car that could not be traced would pick up the fighters and whisk them away. There would be no witnesses because the area was always deserted at night. One side of the street had an open field while the other side had commercial establishments closed at that hour. A back-up surveillance team would keep watch to ensure that the Vancouver police or other passers-by were not in the vicinity.

If disaster struck and they were somehow caught and arrested, the three Mounties would give no hint that they were with the RCMP or that the Force was in any way associated with the incident. It was precisely to avoid being recognized in the event of capture that they had been brought from Ottawa. They had false names and carried no identification. Their cover story was they were Easterners coming to British Columbia for logging work and had stopped over in Vancouver for a week of fun before heading north to job-hunt and they got involved in an ordinary street fight. If necessary the RCMP would back up the claim by refusing to acknowledge the individuals and dissociating the organization from the incident. But once the individuals were booked the RCMP would use a liaison with the Vancouver police to get them off. Ironically, if the operation went smoothly the Security Service was counting on the Vancouver police to take the blame.

The operation was strictly a disruptive tactic designed to scare the Partisans. It possessed no intelligence objective at all since the Partisan Party, although only six months old, was already thoroughly penetrated electronically and otherwise. The office was bugged and all conversations within the premises were being monitored. (It was through the eavesdropping device in the office that the three Mounties knew precisely when the Partisans would be leaving the building with the files to go home for the evening.) Also, the telephone lines were tapped so that the Security Service heard both ends of each phone conversation. Every scrap of information in those sensitive files the Partisans guarded so assiduously was known, including all the party's secrets. The Security Service knew about the party's every action within 24 hours, whether it involved calling together a strategy session, writing a letter, or adding another subscriber to the newspaper subscription list. Inside the party were two informers.

Two months earlier, David MacKinnon, a revolutionary from the Halifax Marxist-Leninist group New Morning, arrived in Vancouver seeking a liaison between his group and the Partisan Party. He met with members of the Central Committee both collectively and individually.

The David MacKinnon story remains a source of debate within the Marxist-Leninist community in Canada. One thing is certain. He collected information on various radical groups for the RCMP and was rewarded at least $3000 over a period of months; these groups included his own organization, New Morning, as well as the Partisan Party and the Toronto Marxist-Leninist group Red Morning. In addition, he sought aggressively—too aggressively—to establish a liaison with the FLQ. What is not certain was his ultimate loyalty. Was he a double agent for New Morning or a triple agent for the RCMP?

MacKinnon was sitting in a Halifax restaurant in May, 1971, when a sergeant in the Security Service came over and sat down at his table and introduced himself as Randy Izsak. Izsak talked about youth alienation—MacKinnon was 20 at the time—and the newly created Opportunities for Youth program because New Morning had applied for a grant. During the conversation MacKinnon said he hoped the application would be successful so that people would not be forced into doing crazy things. Of course, Izsak was familiar with

MacKinnon and selected him as a potentially exploitable target for recruitment as an informer. Although the father of an infant daughter, MacKinnon was a nervous type and not always emotionally mature. Izsak raised the subject of the RCMP's earlier raid on MacKinnon's home when a small amount of marijuana was found. Izsak said he could probably help out if he liked. The offer was gently laughed off but the seeds had been planted.

On another occasion MacKinnon was leaving his apartment in Dartmouth and was met again by Izsak, who had been sitting in his car waiting for MacKinnon to emerge alone. They went to a motel and MacKinnon told him he was scared about where the talk of bombs and guns was leading. Izsak said he had talked to the judge about the dope bust; all he wanted from him was background information about his fellow revolutionaries and general information on what was happening. Izsak naturally did not disclose his purpose for wanting such details, but it would provide him with material to use as a basis for pressuring others into an informer's role as well as providing valuable intelligence on the organization. MacKinnon was offered a salary of $400 a month plus traveling expenses, which could be considerable since he would be encouraged to travel extensively and meet other left-wing groups.

MacKinnon agreed, although his true reaction is a question mark. He reported the offer to New Morning's Central Committee, which agreed to let him act as a double agent, pretending to work for the RCMP while taking its money to help finance New Morning. The organization took the naïve view that the information he provided could not hurt.

In June MacKinnon traveled to Toronto to visit Red Morning and told the group that New Morning had a double agent within its ranks but did not say that he was that agent. It was an amateurish abuse of the need-to-know principle since there may have been, and probably was, a Security Service informer inside Red Morning. In August he went to Vancouver and made contact with the Partisans, packing in his luggage a sawed-off shotgun.[1] He also told the Partisans that New

---

[1]. MacKinnon, on returning from Vancouver, decided to stop over in Ottawa to visit his daughter and former mate. His luggage ended up in Montreal where the shotgun was discovered. He refused to pick up the luggage for fear of being charged.

Morning was operating a double agent, but again did not reveal that he was the one. After each of these encounters he met Izsak and other Security Service handlers and provided briefings about his travels.

MacKinnon seemed to enjoy his jet-set role and perceived himself as a *macho* individual. He liked to boast and one of his claims was an involvement with a recent fire-bombing of a federal building in Halifax, attributed to a mysterious organization known as the Eastern Front. He eventually could not keep secret the fact that he was the double agent in the New Morning group. Upon learning this, the Partisans particularly were outraged since the party had opened itself to MacKinnon and discussed secret matters. The Partisans felt they had been compromised by a loose-lipped egotist.

MacKinnon visited Montreal in October for a second meeting with lawyer Robert Lemieux for the purpose of establishing a link with the FLQ but was thrown out of Lemieux's office. The Partisan Party had notified Lemieux beforehand of MacKinnon's involvement with the Security Service. For all practical purposes, MacKinnon was exposed and excommunicated from revolutionary activity in Canada, as was New Morning.

In November, 1971, New Morning issued a formal "statement of self-criticism":

> David MacKinnon, member of Central Staff, New Morning Collective, has recently been exposed as a *conscious paid agent*[2] of the Solicitor General department's Special Security Force. For an unknown period of time he has been operating as a double agent, collecting data at the highest level on the revolutionary left, and on his bosses, he has documented both (*sic*) to play both (*sic*) sides against the middle. Because of this and the huge problems it has created for us, and because of a general and consistent trend in MacKinnon's practice that this is counter-productive to New Morning, he is hereby *expelled* from Central Staff and from New Morning Collective.
>
> MacKinnon has been a dominant figure in New Morning, but his leadership has in fact been adventurist mis-leadership. He has consistently pushed the organization towards the stand of left adventurism, through manipulation and domineering. He is highly individualistic, egotistical and short sighted, and though he has been struggled with at great length around these

[2.] Italics throughout the statement belong to New Morning.

problems, they have only increased to crisis proportions. MacKinnon has and will always play the politics of *Provocateur*, and this is not only dangerous but intolerable.

Although the importance of these criticisms of him has been realized in the past, MacKinnon has been tolerated, partially out of respect for his contribution, partially out of fear of his rampage, and although the one-time dependence of the organization on his dominance has diminished, the danger of his role as agent provocateur has grown. That it has been allowed to reach its present state is cause for an intense criticism and evaluation of the rest of Central Staff who are guilty of liberalism and naivete in the extreme.

The statement ended:

> Dave MacKinnon now has no connection with New Morning. New Morning emphasizes that Dave MacKinnon is a pig and should be treated as one.

MacKinnon in the meantime protested that he had been sincere and loyal, and took his case to the public although established newspapers refused to report the story. However, MacKinnon appeared on CBOT, CBC's local television station in Ottawa, and told his story and denounced the RCMP and the Solicitor General's department.

The following April, five months after the expulsion, New Morning issued another statement saying MacKinnon was not a pig after all.

> ... we feel that MacKinnon should no longer be kept in isolation so he will be returning to the collective very soon. Initially when he returns he will go through a period of re-orientation and his role within the collective will be defined, but that role will not be of primary leadership at least for some time because he has been away for so long.
>
> We don't feel that we were correct in setting MacKinnon up as a double. In other words we don't feel we were capable of carrying out that difficult task. At this time there are very few organizations which could successfully carry it out. However we don't think that there is anything wrong with infiltrating the pigs if you are capable of doing it.

The New Morning statement acknowledged that MacKinnon's

double agent role provided New Morning with "very little concrete stuff" about the Security Service. In other words, New Morning admitted the flow of information had gone only one way and that the RCMP was the victor in this battle of agents. What appears to have happened was that the Security Service was able to exploit MacKinnon's character instabilities and his need for ego gratification. As is the case with many informers, MacKinnon did not realize how valuable he was to the RCMP.

In fact, MacKinnon's greatest contribution to the Security Service was not his information but his value later as a source of disruption. The MacKinnon fiasco scotched plans for a pan-Canadian network of radical groups, and the Partisan Party and Red Morning severed relations with New Morning. A spate of accusations erupted that sowed disunity throughout the country and precluded an alliance in the immediate future.

While the Partisan Party sorted out the damage caused by Mac-Kinnon's informing, another insider was dutifully recording the party's inner workings for the benefit of the Security Service. One of the Partisan's Central Staff members was a square-faced and muscular individual named Richard Benning. If he looked like a Mountie it was because he was. In reality he was Constable Rick Bennett and his inroads into the Partisan Party went considerably deeper than MacKinnon's. Whereas MacKinnon was an informer, Bennett, a 200-pound, six-foot-two Mountie attached to the Security Service in Montreal, was a penetrator in the classic sense. As Richard Benning he carried a legend as an orphan who came to radical politics through driving cab in Montreal.

The Partisan Party had been in existence for only four months and was highly active for only one month when Bennett arrived on the scene. According to his manufactured legend his father, a career military man, was posted to Europe, where both parents had died of food poisoning when he was 13. He lived in Switzerland at a hotel owned by friends of the family for the next four years before returning to his native Montreal. He then drove taxi in Montreal for J. L. Tremblay on Lagauchietière under the SOS sign and became a loose participant in the Mouvement de Libération du Taxi. After that he worked for Maislin Transport, Ltd., in the warehouse.

Bennett was with the Partisans for nine months and most of that time had access to the organization's intimate secrets, including the party's sensitive files and index cards that were carried home every night. After several months a number of character traits emerged that set him apart from genuine revolutionaries. He was willing to do the menial chores that other members could not be bothered doing. Like everybody else, he was fluent in his grasp of terminology but he never engaged in ongoing political debate. He talked details but never discussed general philosophy. Most members harangued for hours about the fine nuances of how many leftists can dance on the head of a pin, and avoided the drudge work.

After a while it became apparent that he had no social background in the leftist political movement. Everyone got involved with the Partisans through some social or political connection with various peripheral groups, and everyone had philosophical comrades located at various spots around the country. Bennett dropped in from the blue. He isolated himself by opposing the party's line against illegal activities. During demonstrations he attempted to rouse others into kicking in windows and engaging in trivial illegal activity but never serious illegal acts. He was always anxious to meet other radical groups and argued within the party for more liaison. When the Partisans decided to send a representative to the Conference of Anti-Poverty Associations in Montreal in September, 1971, Bennett lobbied for the assignment on the basis that he was the only bilingual member. Later he sought rather strenuously to go to San Francisco to meet Black Panthers because he possessed a car.

Suspicion eventually fell on Bennett and he was asked for information on his background, which constitutes the first step in a loyalty investigation. The party discovered that there was no J. L. Tremblay Company in Montreal and that no Richard Benning was ever listed as possessing a taxi license. An initial check with Maislin's also bore no record of employment.[3] Bennett's old address in Montreal also proved phony. Not only was there no such street number, but there was no such block. Also, Bennett described the general neighborhood inaccurately when asked to depict it. He told the party he learned his

---

[3.] When Bennett was confronted with the fact that Maislin's had no employment record he told them to try again. The party did and on second effort was given fictitious information that Richard Benning had worked there and was dismissed for unsatisfactory work.

karate knowledge at Ecole de Karate on Metropolitan Boulevard in Montreal which again proved fictitious since such an institution did not exist. A check among other Partisans revealed that he once said his parents were killed in a car accident, not food poisoning, his original story.

A Partisan traveled to Montreal to investigate his background and two days after his return, Bennett was confronted with these discrepancies, and vanished. Proof that he was a Mountie turned up some time later when one of the Saturday newspaper magazines used an old photograph of him escorting FLQ kidnap victim James Cross from an airplane in London. The magazine was running an anniversary feature on the kidnapping affair and just happened to select a picture with Bennett in it. During the FLQ crisis Bennett was in the middle of the action as assistant to the then Sergeant Don McCleery.

During his nine months' penetration of the Partisan Party Bennett managed to maintain his cover for more than half the length of the organization's life.[4] After Bennett returned to his normal Security Service duties he was transferred from Montreal to headquarters in Ottawa and promoted to corporal.

Bennett was at the peak of his effectiveness when the three Ottawa Mounties arrived in Vancouver for their disruption operation, the sole purpose of which was to intimidate the party since the Security Service already had complete intelligence on the organization.

Last-minute administrative details were being arranged when a complication arose. Among the Partisans transporting the documents home every night was a woman who happened to be visibly pregnant. Orders came down not to hit her. A debate broke out within the senior ranks of the Security Service: should the operation be canceled over this development? Identifying the pregnant woman would be difficult because it would be dark, and also because the men had long hair too. The attack coming from the rear would make it even harder. Memos moved between Ottawa and Vancouver. The debate carried on and the days slipped by. Headquarters requested more details as

---

[4.] The Vancouver police also tried to penetrate the Partisan Party with a constable fresh out of training school. The constable hung around for several months but never was accepted in the party. Whereas Bennett was erudite and slippery, the Vancouver policeman had no facility in political issues and was eventually kicked out as a tagger-on. He now drives a patrol car in Vancouver.

it agonized over the decision. Finally the project was canceled at the end of the week and the three strongmen went back to Ottawa.

The Partisan Party, which absorbed much of the Security Service's energy, proved as ill fated as the aborted attack. A year later it was dissolved and amalgamated into the Canadian Communist Party (Marxist-Leninist).

Public Disclosure

THE SECURITY SERVICE was lucky the APLQ break-in had not been exposed at the outset. The operation was professionally inexcusable. The Force escaped public scrutiny only because the target lacked credibility and because the established news media in Montreal failed to pursue or even carry the story. Moreover, the RCMP was still a holy cow. Even after Watergate in the United States Canadians held to the RCMP legend and refused to believe the Mounties could do the same things. The myth might have remained intact except for the APLQ fiasco. The APLQ burglary was a ticking time bomb and in March, 1976, three and a half years after the event, it exploded.

The first trouble emerged with the arrest of Constable Robert Samson following the July 26, 1974 bombing attempt on the Mount Royal home of Steinberg's supermarket chain executive Melvyn Dobrin. The bomb exploded prematurely, while still in Samson's hand, shredding the fingertips on his left hand and lacerating his neck and chest and permanently damaging his left ear and eye. Samson, whose RCMP assignment was to follow the activities of the APLQ, stayed away from work claiming he was injured while working on his car. The Security Service visited the hospital and then tipped off Montreal police that Samson might be the bomber, fully realizing he might talk. He was not protected by Commissioner Higgitt's policy of giving legal and financial support to Mounties

278

caught performing illegal acts since the bombing attempt had nothing to do with his RCMP duties: Samson had been free-lancing on his spare time for a Mafia type from Sherbrooke.

At his trial Samson claimed in closed session he had "done worse things for the RCMP than plant bombs." He was referring to the APLQ burglary. Samson was one of the officers in the shock-troop group who entered the premises and stuffed documents into hockey bags and loaded them into the truck outside. Samson, as feared, was not going to prison quietly. His sentence for the bomb-planting was seven years.[1]

When Samson's statement was made public it created momentary excitement in the news media but again the established press did not pursue the story. It was written off as a few overzealous policemen exceeding their mandate. A few days later the matter was dropped.

Eight months later the Vancouver *Sun* published a copyrighted story outlining the conspiratorial origins of the APLQ break-in—that Samson was acting under direction from higher authorities—and that headquarters in Ottawa knew about it shortly afterward. It was the first public evidence of a Watergate in Canada since RCMP management had been for the first time implicated in methodical illegal activity. Canadian Press refused to carry the story. A question was planted in the House of Commons and not one reporter in the Parliamentary Press Gallery reported it.

Commissioner Maurice Nadon was surprised at Samson's confession and ordered an investigation. Nadon was an honest and well-meaning policeman who had never spent a day of his 36-year career in the Security Service and knew nothing of the APLQ break-in. The Commissioner knew that most policemen stretch and even break the law, but was bewildered at the report that three police forces had combined to carry out the raid. This indicated formal planning, organization, and liaison. CIB's illegal activities had been on a less grandiose scale. Had Nadon, like some of his predecessors, spent time in the Security Service and become indoctrinated in the

---

[1.] Samson in March, 1978, received a one-year sentence, which was added to his seven-year sentence, for a $135,000 fraud conspiracy. Samson pleaded guilty to using four checks signed by his lawyer, to get money from a bank when there was no margin of credit to cover the checks. Altogether he spent slightly less than three years in prison and was paroled on December 22, 1978.

practice of illegal acts, he would not have been disturbed and might have attempted to stonewall Quebec legal authorities, who were investigating.[2] Nadon received a report within days and later passed it to the Quebec Solicitor General, who decided that Don Cobb and his two counterparts from the Quebec and Montreal police forces would face a *pre-enquette* (preliminary hearing) on whether charges should be laid.[3]

In Quebec Sessions Court on May 26, 1977, all three pleaded guilty to the reduced charge of failing to obtain a search warrant. Judge Roger Vachon gave them conditional discharges, which freed them from the taint of a criminal record and allowed them to resume work for their respective police organizations.

The national news media picked up the story only after the three officers pleaded guilty. The fact that three officers, not just lower-ranking members, were involved meant the break-in was not the work of a few overzealous policemen after all. The Quebec government appointed a Commission of Inquiry headed by Quebec City lawyer Jean Keable to investigate the affair, and dug out new information, which the news media used. The Keable Commission pursued its search aggressively and demanded access to confidential Security Service information that the RCMP and, for constitutional reasons, the federal government did not want released. Ottawa later successfully challenged in court the commission's mandate and reduced its effectiveness.

Ironically, the first substantial scrutiny in the House of Commons centered, not on the RCMP's misdeeds, but on statements made by Prime Minister Trudeau at a press conference about the RCMP.

"It seems to me an attempt is being made to cast some measure of ministerial responsibility on the Royal Canadian Mounted Police,"

[2.] The manner in which Commissioner Nadon ordered the internal investigation can be questioned. The individual who recounted many of the events was none other than Don Cobb, the officer who had approved the operation and had been promoted to chief superintendent and made responsible for the Security Service in Quebec. Furthermore, the officer responsible for the internal investigation was Superintendent J. A. (Al) Nowlan, who had been in charge of E Special, hardly an untainted figure when it involved investigating clandestine acts. However, it is possible that Commissioner Nadon did not know about E Special at the time. As for Cobb, despite his conflict of interest, he wrote a forthright account in which he readily acknowledged his responsibility and urged the Force also to come clean.

[3.] The other two officers were Assistant Chief Inspector Paul Beaudry of the Montreal police and Inspector Jean Coutellier of the Quebec Provincial Police.

stormed Conservative House Leader Walter Baker.

Right-wing Tory Member of Parliament Erik Nielsen[4] accused Prime Minister Trudeau of leaving "the inference that the RCMP is somehow guilty of a cover-up vis-à-vis passing on information to the government."

The debate revolved almost exclusively around the issue of ministerial responsibility and whether the Solicitor General knew about the illegal raid instead of on the APLQ break-in itself. The politicians were largely afraid to question or attack the RCMP.[5]

Solicitor General Francis Fox delivered a carefully crafted 3,000-word statement on June 17, 1977, saying the government seriously considered establishing a royal commission at the time of Samson's outburst in March, 1976.

"The government received, however, repeated and unequivocal assurances from the RCMP that the APLQ incident was exceptional and isolated and that the directives of the RCMP to its members clearly require that all of their actions take place within the law," Fox told the Commons.

Before making the statement Fox on his own behalf asked the same question his predecessor, Warren Allmand, had asked, and received the same reply: there were no other cases of illegal activity. APLQ was one of a kind. The assurance was false both in spirit and in letter. Mounties were not told, as claimed, to abide by the law. Quite the opposite. The 1970 memo of Nadon's predecessor, Len Higgitt, made it clear that the Force supported illegal activity as a policy. E Special was created for one purpose and that was to perform clandestine activity. Commissioner Nadon claimed he knew nothing about this element.

After Fox's statement his office received dozens of letters and phone calls from people claiming the APLQ incident was not "exceptional and isolated" because they knew of others. Fox's initial reaction was that people were just paranoid, that everyone in the

[4.] Both Baker and Nielsen became Cabinet Ministers when Joe Clark defeated Pierre Trudeau in May, 1979.

[5.] And for an overwhelming reason. Public reaction, from opinion surveys to letters to the editor, suggested that Canadians supported the RCMP despite illegal acts. During the parliamentary debate the Opposition parties received criticism from constituents while the government got letters of congratulations for defending the RCMP. It was this unquestioning public support for the RCMP that caused Opposition parties to mute their criticism.

country seemed to think he was the victim of an illegal act. Some of the responses clearly came from cranks concocting massive police conspiracies, but others came from credible and normal individuals. The most disturbing responses came from Mounties who claimed they knew of other illegal acts because they had participated in them. These Mounties knew the Solicitor General was not getting the truth and felt they had a duty to come forward.

One of these Mounties happened to be former Staff Sergeant Don McCleery, who days after Fox's statement was meeting two senior officials in the Solicitor General's office concerning his dismissal from the Force. McCleery, seeking a hearing to have his name cleared, used the occasion to warn them of RCMP stonewalling.

"Look, don't be mislead," he cautioned.

McCleery, a straightforward individual, even at his own expense, told the two officials of the barn-burning and the theft of dynamite that occurred near Montreal in May 1972. McCleery thereby implicated himself because he had been involved in both incidents, but such was his honesty.

The former staff sergeant was complaining not because the activities were illegal but because the Force was withholding information from the minister and this offended his sense of democracy.

"The KGB doesn't play by your rules, so we shouldn't either," says McCleery. "You've got to play by their rules or else they've got one hell of an advantage. But you still have to be answerable to somebody and it's got to be to a civilian authority. Then if a guy complains about a miscarriage of justice he can at least go to the minister, an elected official, who can intervene on his behalf and get the answer. At least the guy can do something about it. The police will never do anything about it."

Fox took McCleery's testimony plus the evidence from other respondents and confronted the Force. Nadon's own quick inquiry about the new evidence revealed that there was substance to a number of the allegations, and two months before his retirement the abashed Commissioner recommended the establishment of a royal commission of inquiry. Fox on July 6, 1977, told the Commons that "considering these new developments" a royal commission had been established "for determining the scope and frequency of inquiry practices and other activities which are not permitted or provided for in the law ..." The commission had three members, Mr. Justice David McDonald, the chairman, of the Alberta Supreme Court; Don Rickerd, President of the Donner Foundation; and Guy Gilbert, a Montreal lawyer.

The McDonald Commission was more than three months old when Fox rose in the Commons during the Throne Speech debate on October 28 to reveal that the Security Service had clandestinely taken the Parti Québécois' computer tapes and copied them. Fox disclosed the case because Quebec's Keable Commission was planning to make it public. Fox outside the Commons exhorted reporters "not to be overly hasty in passing judgement in this case." Less than two weeks later CBC Television reporter Brian Stewart uncovered two new widespread and entrenched sets of illegal activity: Operation Cathedral, the RCMP's mail-opening practices dating back as far as World War Two when performed legally under the War Measures Act, and Operation 300, the code name used to identify material gathered through illegal means.

Early in 1978 Fox made more disclosures. In 1971 the Security Service, under the direction of Don Cobb, had produced a fake FLQ communiqué urging separatists to violence and censuring Pierre Vallières for renouncing violence. Its purpose had been to start a debate that could cause dissension within FLQ ranks. Also, Fox announced, the Security Service during the same years had attempted to recruit as informers four FLQ sympathizers through the use of force and pressure. These disclosures, he said, "cleared the slate."

Fox soon regretted that statement. Two days later in testimony before the McDonald Commission Cobb acknowledged that an APLQ-style break-in, which he did not identify, had occurred outside Quebec. And soon the list of FLQ sympathizers subjected to crude recruitment attempts grew from four to nine. Fox reversed himself a few days later and said more illegalities would likely emerge. He added that the Security Service had been doing illegal things for 20-30 years.

The controversy and atmosphere of new disclosures had an overwhelming impact on the Security Service. The organization disliked publicity and, with brief exceptions, had historically avoided it. This low-profile stature provided comfortable anonymity. Many Canadians did not know there was a Security Service. When the spotlight was turned on, the Security Service reacted with stage fright. Operations froze. Controversial operations were avoided at all costs. Even routine operations proceeded cautiously. Resources were diverted from its major task of investigating espionage and subversion to liaising with the government and two commissions of inquiry and also investigating leaks to the media, which hitherto had been virtually nonexistent. The atmosphere was filled with apprehension, from both Mounties investigating and those being investigated. The Security Service was neither happy nor productive.

Robert Henry Simmonds was enjoying the normal career of an RCMP officer. He grew up on a farm in northern Saskatchewan but left because life on the land had little appeal. He served with the Fleet Air Arm of the Royal Navy in the dying years of World War Two and grew attached to flying. After the war he checked with the RCMP because he heard pilots were needed. He lacked sufficient flying experience to qualify as a Mountie pilot but was talked into joining the Force anyway. He nearly quit several times during his first two years but eventually grew to like police work, especially detachment work on the prairies where he spent most of his time as a constable and NCO. The one extraordinary event in his career was a trip to England in 1953 as a member of the RCMP mounted contingent for the coronation of Queen Elizabeth.

Simmonds was commissioned with 19 years' service, which is average or slightly under, and became the second in command for the RCMP detachment of Burnaby, one of the largest detachments in Canada. Two years later he sent Mounties to the top of Burnaby Mountain to evict and arrest 114 students occupying the administration building at Simon Fraser University. After an administrative stint in Victoria he was transferred to Vancouver in 1973 and promoted to superintendent. His advancement as a commissioned officer was average at best, and at that point it looked as if he would retire in British Columbia at the superintendent level or possibly one level above. But in June, 1975, members of the Mount Currie Indians Band blocked a road between Pemberton and Lillooet Lake about 90 miles north of Vancouver and that incident had remarkable consequences for Superintendent Simmond's career.

The blockade was a month old and prospects for a compromise

were exhausted when the RCMP was summonsed by the British Columbia government to open the road. The case started when the Federal Fisheries Department seized fishing nets from two Mount Currie Indians for catching spring salmon in Lillooet Lake during a closure. The seizure was symbolic of larger grievances and the Indians retaliated by closing the road with a barricade consisting of a large log, some smaller stumps, and, incongruously, a Ping-Pong table.

Over the weeks two sets of confrontations developed: between the Indians and the provincial government, which had jurisdiction over the road; and another between the Indians and the local whites, who were two miles apart but not talking to each other. Ill will festered on both sides and violence seemed imminent. Twice, drunken whites confronted the blockade, once with a convoy of six vehicles and again by abducting an Indian woman with a shotgun and using her as a hostage to pass through. Nor were the Indians particularly passive. Their ranks included members of the militant American Indian Movement.

When Simmonds arrived on the scene July 17, exactly a month after the blockade was erected, relations were at a flashpoint. The night before, an Indian who was fishing illegally was killed falling over a cliff and into the Fraser River while being pursued by a fisheries officer. Indians viewed it as a white man's murder.

Violence would have erupted had Simmonds forced down the blockade that night. Instead, he went to the Indian hall to persuade the band to withdraw voluntarily. An Indian sat on the step of the front door and refused to let Simmonds into the hall.

"I'm going in," Simmonds barked. "You get off that step or I'll throw you off."

The man moved. Inside a group of Indians beating drums paraded around Simmonds' chair for an hour. At midnight they finally talked. Simmonds had entered at eight.

Simmonds showed that he could be compassionate as well as tough and took an interest in the Indians' welfare that went beyond his role as a policeman. The meeting had opened a dialogue and eventually the Indians agreed to consider withdrawing the blockade. The next day the band voted to maintain the barrier, but by 8 P.M. feelings had cooled so dramatically that the stand-by contingent of

50 Mounties was able to arrest the 53 native demonstrators without disturbing the peace. The agitated Indians of 24 hours earlier passively allowed themselves to be arrested and serenely beat their drums during the hour-long arresting procedure. Every time a drummer was arrested the drum was passed to an unarrested protestor.

When he returned to Vancouver Simmonds wrote a philosophical report outlining Indian problems and urging the government to make a better effort at understanding natives. For a Mountie to look at causes rather than symptoms was unusual and it came to the attention of various government officials, including Solicitor General Warren Allmand, who was sympathetic to Indians. From there on Simmonds' career skyrocketed. His rise may be the fastest in RCMP history. Within months he was promoted to Chief Superintendent and put in charge of the Lower Mainland district in British Columbia. He remained there less than a year. In 1976 he was leapfrogged over the rank of Assistant Commissioner—an unprecedented move—and sent to Ottawa as one of four Deputy Commissioners reporting directly to Commissioner Nadon. He was put in charge of administration, the most senior of the four deputy posts. In a sense he was the commanding officer of all the divisions without ever having been in charge of a division. Simmonds protested that he had no administrative experience except for two years in personnel at Victoria.

"Get yourself some experience in administration," replied Allmand. "When we go to pick a commissioner I want several alternatives."

Simmonds was named Commissioner the following year.

Nobody knew what to expect when Simmonds assumed the top position on September 1, 1977. The Force was under public attack—at least from the Force's point of view—and changes in policy and personnel were imminent. Yet Simmonds had been in Ottawa so briefly he had no track record on which to base predictions about his actions. Many Mounties hardly knew his name. First impressions were favourable. Simmonds was thoughtful and obviously intelligent; he was articulate—probably the most articulate commissioner ever—exactly at a time when there was need for an able spokesman to defend the Force. He was also fresh out of operations at the division level and had not been at headquarters long enough to fall into a bureaucratic rut.

But for the Security Service, disappointment soon set in. Simmonds was intelligent all right, but not progressive in some of the fundamental areas of concern to the Security Service. In fact, he was considerably less liberal than Commissioner Nadon, his predecessor. Whereas Nadon had an accommodating management style, Simmonds, as one NCO put it, worked "right out of the 1947 manual." He believed that members of the Security Service had gotten out of line because the organization was too loose and that the answer was to reinstitute discipline. Even some commissioned officers in the Security Service were disillusioned. Simmonds was a strong leader and a man of opinion and did not follow Nadon's practice of keeping clear of Security Service affairs. Consequently the old specter of policemen running the Security Service returned to haunt the organization.

The extent of Commissioner Simmonds' dabbling in the Security Service became evident with his first major personnel shake-up. Career-long Security Service officers were shuffled into CIB positions and career-long CIB officers were moved into the Security Service. The most worrisome single move involved making Assistant Commissioner Bert Giroux the Deputy Director of the Security Service and thereby the organization's chief operations officer. He had never spent a day in the Security Service. The message was clear: the Security Service was returning to the old days when it was an arm of the Criminal Investigation Branch. Three decades of increasing autonomy and effectiveness for the Security Service were being rolled back.

Morale, which was already low from the public disclosures, dropped further. With Simmonds taking an active role in the Security Service, the shuffle meant that the top three officers overseeing the Security Service had no security experience. The top man was Simmonds as Commissioner, then Director-General Michael Dare, the soldier, and now Dare's deputy, Assistant Commissioner Bert Giroux. All three were militarily oriented and disciplinarians. The latest turn of events impaired the Security Service's effectiveness more than the raging climate of scandal.

One of the unmistakable lessons from the Gouzenko case, and many cases since, is that Canada needs protection from espionage and subversion and that these duties should be performed by individuals selected and trained for that task. Most of the problems associated with combining the Security Service with the national police force have been outlined in earlier chapters. One problem not mentioned is probably the most dangerous of all: the risk of penetration from hostile organizations. The Security Service is a sitting target for penetration since it is part of a larger organization that accepts applications for employment. Any Soviet sympathizer or agent with a cover deep enough to deceive the security screening procedures (which are fallible and not exhaustive) can apply to become a Mountie merely by visiting the nearest RCMP detachment office and filling out a form. This weakness in the system can be avoided only if the organization seeks out the individual rather than the other way around. It cannot be corrected under the RCMP because the force is a hungry machine that devours nearly 1,000 recruits each year. The appetite cannot be satisfied any other way. (Besides, Canadians wishing to join the national police force should have the opportunity to seek such employment)

One cannot help comparing the RCMP to the Soviet Union. Russia convinces itself that its economic system works despite shortages and black markets—and a significantly lower standard of living. Anybody caught exchanging currency in the black market is punished severely because black markets illustrate a shortcoming in the system. Consequently coercion is required to maintain the system.

The RCMP requires coercion too. The structure governing the Security Service is so ill suited that obedience and discipline are used to cover up the deficiency. Those who question the order of things are viewed as disloyal and treated harshly. The officers who rise to the top are not necessarily the ablest but the best defenders of the organization. The RCMP has been denying the obvious for decades.

To maintain perspective, it must be noted that the Security Service has improved remarkably in 35 years and will continue to do so, just as the Soviet economy had made strides since World War Two, and will continue to grow. However, the Security Service's effectiveness is restrained and will continue to be held back as long as it is stifled by a structure designed to accomplish another task.

Appendix A

Unofficial List of Foreign Diplomats in Canada Expelled or Withdrawn for Questionable Activities

1956—**Gennadi Popov,** Second Secretary at the Soviet Embassy, was expelled for "activities incompatible with his continued presence in Canada"—trying to get military secrets, namely the plans of the CF-105. James Staples, then 30, a civilian clerk with the RCAF, was fired.

1958—**Stanislas Michno,** a Polish Embassy official, was expelled for attempting to get secret military information. His Canadian contact was cooperating with the RCMP.

1959—**Viktor A. Kuznetsov,** Assistant Military Attaché in the Soviet Embassy, was expelled. The expulsion was done quietly and the event itself, let alone the reasons for it, has never been revealed.

1960—**Miloslav Cech,** Second Secretary at the Czech Embassy, was effectively expelled. Although never specifically declared *persona non grata* he was away on leave and was asked not to return for engaging in unacceptable conduct with the Czech community in Canada.

1961—**Lt.-Col. Anotoly Loginov,** Assistant Military Attaché, was expelled for trying to buy information from a Canadian civil servant who helped the RCMP lay a trap. He was caught in the act of accepting secret documents.

1964—**Vasily Tarasov,** correspondent for *Izvestia,* was expelled for attempting to bribe a civil servant he had cultivated for nearly a year. Again, the RCMP laid a trap and caught Tarasov with classified papers in his hand. He did not have diplomatic immunity but the government did not prosecute.

1965—**A. E. Bytchkov,** Soviet Commercial Attaché, and **V. N. Poluchkin,** an embassy clerk, were expelled for reportedly paying "thousands of dollars" for secret defense and industrial information from two Canadians. One of the Canadians was later identified as Victor Spencer, a sickly man who was not much of a spy and later the object of a Royal Commission investigation. The other Canadian, a naturalized citizen, who was given the task of compromising female government employees, has never been charged or publicly identified.

1967—Two Soviet Embassy officials were expelled in a case that resulted in the conviction of Bower Featherstone, a government mapmaker who passed on classified naval maps. Soviet attaché **Evgeni Kourianov,** returned to the Soviet Union in 1966 following the arrest of Featherstone. Featherstone was sentenced to 30 months in jail for violating the Official Secrets Act but served only 10. To date this is the only successful conviction under the Official Secrets Act since the Gouzenko trials.

— A member of the Czech Embassy was expelled for attempting to obtain military information. The expulsion was not made public.

1968—**Lt.-Col. Vasily Didenko,** the junior of four Military Attachés at the Soviet Embassy, was expelled in retaliation for the expulsion of Lt.-Col. Jack Watson from the Canadian Embassy in Moscow. Watson, an Air Attaché, was the subject of a staged incident on a train across Siberia in which Soviet authorities broke into his compartment and roughed up his wife.

— **Phillipe Rossillon** was never formally expelled because, although a representative of the French government, he never belonged to the French Embassy in Canada. However, as an official in the office of Premier Couvé de Murville in charge of expanding the use of the

French language around the world, he acted as a disruptive influence in Canada. Behind the scenes Rossillon helped precipitate Charles de Gaulle's "Vive le Québec libre" statement in Montreal in the summer of 1967. Later that year he was attempting to inflame nationalistic feelings among Acadians in New Brunswick. In 1968, while contacting the French-speaking community in Manitoba, he was called "a more or less secret agent" by Prime Minister Trudeau and his time in Canada was up.

1970—**Janos Hegedus,** First Secretary (Economic and Commercial Affairs) in the Hungarian Embassy, was expelled quietly in January for trying to establish a spy network in Canada. The Hungarians retaliated first by harassing Stanley Noble, Canadian Attaché (Immigration) in Budapest, by having police cars crowd his car and then by expelling him. Consequently Canada made public the Hungarian expulsion the following month.

— Also in January, a member of the Soviet Embassy on leave was informed he could not return. He had attempted to gain access to classified Canadian information.

— **Mikhail Murnikov,** of the Soviet Embassy, was withdrawn voluntarily after the Canadian government raised protests about his activities in the Estonian community in Canada. Murnikov was causing suspicion and fear among local Estonians, who in turn complained to the Canadian government.

1971—A member of the Hungarian Embassy on leave failed to get his visa renewed. He had been involved in the Hungarian community in Canada in a way that was unacceptable.

1972—A Soviet diplomat failed to return from leave after External Affairs informed the Soviet Embassy that the individual's activity in the ethnic community in Canada was not compatible with his diplomatic status.

1974—**Konstantin Yervandovich Guevandov,** a reporter for *Pravda* who was returning from a holiday in Russia, had his re-entry application rejected. From 1971 to 1973 he purchased assessments on events in Canada from a Canadian journalist and allegedly persuaded him to act on behalf of Soviet interests when reporting on events.

1975—**Alexander Gavrilovich Kovalev,** a GRU officer posing as Assistant Air Attaché, was told in January not to return from leave in the Soviet Union. He was interested in UHF communications research, and in 1973 initiated a liaison with a postgraduate student at the University of Ottawa and held clandestine meets and "tasked" him to obtain classified information.

— **Kuo Ching-An,** Press Attaché at the Chinese Embassy, was expelled in May for funding Marxist political groups in Canada. At about the same time another Chinese national was expelled for acting as a courier of intelligence from the United States to Canada for transmission to Peking.

1976—There was an incident involving the Cubans. A Cuban on the verge of leaving was told pointedly to make sure he left.

— **Major Vladimir Mikhaylovich Vassiliev,** Soviet Assistant Air Attaché, was expelled in December for activities "incompatible with his diplomatic status." He tried to obtain information from a Civil Aviation medical advisor in the Department of National Health and Welfare. Since he was not away on leave at the time, this represented an outright expulsion. It was the start of a new get-tough approach on the part of External Affairs.

1977—Four Cubans were expelled from Ottawa and Montreal in January for activities involving terrorism in a third country. Among other things, they recruited, trained, and tasked an American mercenary.

— **Lev Grigoryevich Khvostantsev,** an exchange scientist, was expelled in February for trying to buy nonclassified documents from another exchanged scientist at the National Research Council who reported it. The Khvostantsev case is a departure since he was a legitimate scientist and his activities jeopardized the exchange program.

— **Lt.-Cmdr. Valeria Smirnov,** 36, a known GRU officer listed as a Soviet Assistant Naval Attaché, was accused in July of activities close to "industrial sabotage"—seeking and buying industrial information from a Bell Northern Research scientist in Ottawa. Smirnov was on home leave at the time and was not expelled outright. He was ordered to cease the activities but could return. The Soviets chose not to send him back.

— **Abu Al-Khail,** Minister Plenipotentiary at the Iraqi Embassy, was requested to leave in August. Publicity was given because the Iraqis retaliated.

1978—Thirteen members of the Soviet Embassy were expelled in February—11 were asked to leave and two on leave were prohibited from returning to Canada—for attempting to recruit a Mountie. The 11 expelled outright were **Igor Vartanian, Vladimir L. Souvorov, Oleg D. Reztsov, Vera A. Reztsov, Nikolai M. Talanov, Anatoly A. Mikhalin, Vadim A. Borishpolets, Vladimir I. Oshkaderov, Yevgeniy K. Koblov, Gennadi V. Ivashavitch, Petr R. Lillenurm.** The two barred from returning were **Voldemar P. Veber** (left July, 1977) and **Andrei V. Krysin** (left December, 1977).

— **Abdul Latif M. Al-Niaimi,** Second Secretary at the Iraqi Embassy, was expelled in May for buying information on the Kurdish community in Canada and for having agents disrupt Canadian Kurdish organizations. Iraq retaliated by expelling W. A. McKenzie, 40, First Secretary and Chargé d'Affaires at the Canadian Embassy in Baghdad, and, again, Canada made this case public for that reason.

1979—**Alexander Aleksandrovich Palladin** (see Chapter 4), a KGB officer undercover as a journalist for the Soviet news agency *Novosti*, was refused a brief visit to Canada in February. He cultivated two Special Assistants to a Liberal Cabinet minister during his four-year term in Ottawa, which ended in 1978.

— **Ho Xuan Dich,** sedate looking Second Secretary of the Vietnamese Embassy, was expelled in March for threatening "to retaliate against relatives still in Vietnam of Vietnamese residents in Canada," in order to "influence the ideology and loyalties" of such Vietnamese landed immigrants. He was also accused of stage-managing public demonstrations against China by Vietnamese residents of Canada.

Appendix B

ALL C.O.s, C.I.B. OFFICERS AND S.I.B. OFFICERS

Re: **RCMP Protection for Members Engaged in Sensitive or Secret Operations**

For some time the R.C.M. Police has been engaged in sensitive and/or secret operations both in the field of Security and Intelligence and in the C.I.B. operational spheres. Our——have become involved along with our regular operational personnel. Though it has not been the subject of general conversation, and should not be, it may have been considered necessary in the past, and may continue to be necessary in the future, to transgress the common, civil or criminal law of the Country in order to work effectively or to achieve the desired end results in a given case.

2. More recently it has come to my attention that some members involved in delicate operations are concerned with the protection they and their families will receive in the event that an operation goes sour and they become subject to civil or criminal processes as a result. It is not difficult to imagine a situation wherein one or more members find themselves compromised and for reasons of security, no explanation of the operation could be disclosed.

3. In order to reassure personnel with respect to their respective positions and that of their families, this whole question has been studied by our "C" Directorate, "I" Directorate and "A" Directorate. The following guidelines have been established and have received my approval.

294

4. Three potential situations have been considered:
    (1) Where the operation has received express approval or has been directed by the member's senior NCO or a Commissioned Officer; or
    (2) Where the operation has received the tacit approval of the member's senior NCO or a Commissioned Officer; or
    (3) Where the member operates independently, on his own initiative, without either direction or express or tacit approval.

5. In the first and second situations where the member acts within the scope of the direction or the expressly approved plan, he will be protected to the greatest extent possible from criminal, quasi-criminal or civil responsibility. In the event complete protection cannot be afforded, a solicitor will be appointed to protect the member's interests. The Force will accept responsibility to pay any fine or reward levied against our member. In the event of incarceration for a period of time, the member will be paid as usual and on release will be employed again by the Force. This all presumes of course, that the member and his conduct has otherwise been acceptable to the Force.

6. With respect to the third situation, action taken by the Force would be dependant [*sic*] upon the application of CSO 1208. There would not be the same moral responsibility to continue to pay a member or to retain the member in the Force. In the event that the independent action was deemed unreasonable, the member could be subject to dismissal per Regulation 177 for acting outside the scope of his authority.

7. It will be appreciated that I have simply attempted to lay down broad general guidelines. It stands to reason that each and every case coming to my attention would be judged on its merits and final decision made after thorough and careful examination of the facts.

8. It must always be born [*sic*] in mind, of course, that where a member is directed to perform a duty which may require him to contravene the law for any purpose or where the means required to achieve a specific end can reasonably be foreseen as illegal, a member is within his rights to refuse to do any unlawful act. Such a refusal may be given with impunity. Though no disciplinary action would be taken, a transfer may be directed in such a situation.

9. Information contained herein should be disseminated on a "need to know" basis to the members of your command. In the meantime various courses, whether C.P.C., senior investigators or S.I.B., will be instructed as to a member's position in the circumstances envisaged above.

W. L. Higgitt,
Commissioner.

Index

Royal North-West Mounted Police, 57-
60, 71
Security Service, *see* Security Service
Veterans' Association, 227
Royal Commission (Kellock-Tascherau) into
Gouzenko disclosures, 65, 82-83, 114, 116
Royal Commission (Marin) into Discipline
and Grievance Procedures, 235
Royal Commission (McDonald) into RCMP
wrongdoing, 41-42, 156, 282-83
Royal Commission (MacKenzie) into Secur-
ity, 42, 119, 194-95, 197n
Royal Military College, 96
Royal York Hotel, 86
Rumania, 190

Sabotka, Anton, 171-74, 181
Saint John, N.B., 70
St. Laurent, Louis, 75, 78-79, 94, 254
Samson, Robert, 221, 224, 250, 278-79, 281
Scott, Charles E., 66
Seafarers' International Union, 192
Section 98 (of the Criminal Code), 59-61,
65-67
Securex, 209, 214, 218, 221-26
Security Panel, 116-17, 119, 126, 129-31,
134, 137, 147n, 199
Security Planning and Research Group,
262, 263n
Security screening and clearance, 21-22, 71,
110, 112-19, 121-22, 126-28, 144-48,
182-85, 195
Security Service:
A Section, 21-22, 125-27
B Section, 22-24, 34, 38, 99, 187,
259-60
C Section, 24
D Section, 24-27, 38, 260
E Section, 25-26, 259
F Section, 26, 28, 48-49, *see also* Files
G Section, 26-27, 238, 247-49, 251,
260, 263-66
H Section, 27, 187
I Section, *see* Watcher Service
J Section, 28, 259-60, *see also* Bugging
K Section, 28
L Section, 26, 28, 47, 266
E Special, 25-26, 28, 209, 238-51, 259-
60, 280n, 281
Civilians, 27-28, 34-36, 99-100, 108-10,
197-98, 201, 252
Cuban Desk, 4-8, 24
Czech Desk, 23
education and training, 19, 35, 106,
197n, 197-98

formation of, 110, 197
Hungarian Desk, 23-24
Internal Security Branch, 132
liaison with U.K., 14-16, 22, 28, 34, 44,
54-55, 67, 69, 79, 81, 97, 99-101, 106,
110, 119-21, 141, 143-44
liaison with U.S., 4-16, 22, 28, 43-45,
79, 81, 86-88, 110, 143, 145-48, 160,
162, 183, 188, 196, 238, 260
paramilitary system, 106-07, 198-202,
230, 233-35, 252, 261, 287-88
Polish Desk, 23
Russian Desk, 23, 27, 107, 158, 185,
187, 215-16
Satellite Desk, 23-24
Security and Intelligence (S & I), Dir-
ectorate of, 109-10, 215
separation from RCMP, 103-10, 195-97,
201
Special Branch, 96-110, 113-15, 117-19,
121-22
versus CIB, 17-20, 103, 105-10, 130,
180-81, 200-01, 231, 287-88
Security subpanel, 119, 128, 199
Sévigny, Pierre, 192
Shalnev, Anatoli, 173
Sherwood, Percy, 58
Shevchenko, Arkady, 85n
Shoemaker, Michael, 263n
Shorteno, Mr. Justice Peter V., 178-80
Shugar, David, 95n
Sieradzki, Miecyzslaw, 50
Simmonds, Robert, 41, 284-87
Simon Fraser University, 268, 284
Skardon, William, 101
Smirnov, Valerie, 156, 292
Smith, A. E., 61-62
Smith, Philip, Durnford Pemberton, 95n
Smith, Stewart, 63
Soboloff, John, 95n
Solicitor General, Ministry of, 193-94, 196,
214, 218, 250, 256, 262, 263n, 264, 272-73,
281-82
Sourwine, J. G., 87
Southam, Hamilton, 15
Souvorov, Vladimir L., 293
Spector, Maurice, 62
Spencer, George Victor, 30-32, 192, 194-95,
290
Stalin, Josef, 62-64
Staples, James, 289
Starnes, Cortlandt, 65, 199
Starnes, Henry, 199
Starnes, John, 15, 19, 196-222, 231, 243, 249,
258, 261, 263